Fashion Merchandising

FASHION MERCHANDISING

Principles and Practice

James Clark

 macmillan education palgrave

First published 2015 by
PALGRAVE

Palgrave in the UK is an imprint of Macmillan Publishers Limited, registered in England, company number 785998, of 4 Crinan Street, London N1 9XW.

Palgrave Macmillan in the US is a division of St Martin's Press LLC, 175 Fifth Avenue, New York, NY 10010.

Palgrave is a global imprint of the above companies and is represented throughout the world.

Palgrave® and Macmillan® are registered trademarks in the United States, the United Kingdom, Europe and other countries.

ISBN 978–1–137–41387–1

This book is printed on paper suitable for recycling and made from fully managed and sustained forest sources. Logging, pulping and manufacturing processes are expected to conform to the environmental regulations of the country of origin.

A catalogue record for this book is available from the British Library.

A catalog record for this book is available from the Library of Congress.

Typeset by MPS Limited, Chennai, India.

Printed and bound in the UK by The Lavenham Press Ltd, Suffolk.

Short Contents

Contents

List of Figures

List of Tables

List of Case Studies, Focus Points and Profiles

Case Studies

Focus Points

Profiles

Preface

The world of buying and merchandising in 1988 was very different to the one that exists today, but it did exist, and was the one that I joined in the April of that year. I learned quickly about the processes and activities of a busy buying office, the first being that it was very loud. The buzz of telephones ringing, fax machines and people blended together into a constant background noise, which seems to have been lost in many of the buying offices of today. Activities were different, too: technology was almost non-existent and there were periods of time when we had nothing to do because we were waiting on some other function to provide information or complete a task.

The most striking of the differences was this waiting. My early role as an allocator meant I had to go and collect sales and stock data print-outs and bring them to the department for review. Our allocation system did not work on a Monday because it took all day to process weekend sales data. Stores had to send stock requests in the post, and we had to queue up to send a fax or telex from the only machines able to do so. If one contrasts that with the retail business world of the 21st century, there is little that has not changed. Online data is readily available at one's desktop, meaning that the concept of waiting to make a decision is rarely experienced. One of the benefits of having waiting-time is that one has the opportunity to think, and even today I find that I make my best decisions when I have had the luxury of being able to wait before committing to a course of action. Today, the inevitable surge of data availability often feels as if one cannot see the core message, but instead focuses on the many micro messages which can often conflict. This 'analysis paralysis' is symptomatic of a loss of focus required to create that perfect product range and earn that life-changing bonus.

Fashion Merchandising: Principles and Practice has been written, therefore, to lay out not just the role and activities of the fashion merchandiser, but also demonstrate why I believe the role to be integral within fashion retailing. The scale of the fashion industry is large, the competition fierce and the opportunities to connect with the consumer huge. With all the noise of social media and new business models, it feels timely to stop and offer the opportunity to think about not just what the fashion merchandiser does, but also why. The approach to its writing has always been to identify the practical process and the principles that guide, to explain why that process is important, but also how it can add value within product management.

Acknowledgements

This book has taken several years to write, and along the way many people have contributed to its gestation. At Palgrave Macmillan, Martin Drewe, Ursula Gavin and Rachel Bridgewater have been supportive, and helped me throughout the journey from the first concept of this book to its final form.

Within the University of the Arts, I would like to acknowledge the support and encouragement of Andrew Hughes, Heather Pickard, Sally Bain, Rachel Cosford, Matteo Montecchi, Liz Gee, Ellie Herrington, Liz Parker, Karinna Nobbs, Louise Johnston, Bill Webb and David French. In particular, I must thank Rosemary Varley individually for supporting and facilitating much of my journey, and without her help, this book would not have been completed.

Within the fashion and retail industries, support has been greatly received from Angus Barclay, Jason Marr, Elizabeth Simpson, Sally Heath at New Look, Ellie Turner at Clear Returns, Katrine Karlsen, Tracy Stone and Fareeda Qureshi at Gant, Kayleigh Jackson and Megan Jones.

Finally, I would like to thank members of my family: Tim, Ann, Lucy, Percy, Mildred, John and Kathleen.

Abbreviations

4P	Marketing mix
B2B	Business to business
B&M	Buying and merchandising
BAA	Buyers administration assistant
BTA	Balance to achieve
C2B	Customer to business
CR	Continuous replenishment
CRM	Customer relationship management
DC	Distribution centre
EBITDA	Earnings before interest, taxes, depreciation, amortisation
EDI	Electronic data interchange
ESS	End of season sale
ETI	Ethical Trade Initiative
EU	European Union
GATT	General Agreement on Tariffs and Trade
GDP	Gross domestic product
IBS	Incentive bonus scheme
ICT	Information and communications technology
JIT	Just in time
KPI	Key performance indicator
L	Large
LFL	Like for like
LFW	London Fashion Week
M	Medium
MCO	Minimum credible offer
MFA	Multi-Fibre Agreement
MIS	Management information systems
MRP	Manufacture resource planning
NGO	Non-governmental organization
OTB	Open to buy
PO	Purchase order
POS	Point of sale
QR	Quick response
S	Small
sku	Stock keeping unit
SOR	Sales or return

SWOT	Strengths, weaknesses, opportunities, threats
USP	Unique selling point
VAT	Value added tax
VM	Visual merchandising
WSSI	Weekly stock, sales and intake
XL	Extra large
XS	Extra small

Introduction

Many people have met emerging professionals who have aspired to becoming a fashion buyer. A lot fewer have met aspiring merchandisers, and even fewer have heard of the role. Of those who have, many confuse it with the visual merchandising or supply chain disciplines. This is not surprising, as many of the role's activities are hidden from view and not easily identifiable within the ranges within stores. A second complicating factor is that the role is not a globally uniform one, and in different places around the world its title and activities differ. In North America, for example, the term *merchandising* is more akin to the UK buying role, while in Asia, it sits more comfortably within the supply chain role.

There have been many excellent resources created for the creative and buyer-led activities within buying and merchandising, but few for merchandising. Of those which do exist, many refer to merchandising activities within the context of a bigger subject such as retail management, or provide a review within a related specialism, most notably fashion buying. The fundamental aim of this book, therefore, is to provide a perception of the role, its relevance and place within fashion management. This is achieved from the perspective of the UK and provides a mix of discussion and application. As such, it will debate various topics and present an argument for a delineation of the merchandiser activities as distinct from those of the buyer, and then move on to a practical demonstration of the role.

One characteristic of fashion retailing industry today is the myriad of business models that exist, all of which differ in some way in their use of the buying and merchandising function. It therefore would be impossible to cover every possible nuance of the role and then comment on its use in differing businesses. In addition, it would be impractical not to have to make assumptions within the text to help make the practical demonstration concise. As full a review of the processes of the merchandiser has been made as possible, but this text cannot be authoritative and is offered to add to the debate and be a springboard for further research and publications. Those in the industry studying in further and higher education, and in particular postgraduates, should find that the text provides a framework around which they can further develop their careers or studies. The exercises that have been created and are available on the companion website will also enable readers to try out their own planning process to see it at work.

To facilitate all of the above, the book is divided into three parts:

1. An introductory discussion, justification and explanation of the fashion merchandiser role.
2. A fictional case study to demonstrate the role in action that follows a 'concept-to-carrier bag' process model.

3. A summary discussion of influences and factors that current fashion merchandisers must consider in the discharge of their duties.

To support the context of the role, Part One also includes a review of the fashion buyer role, and the support roles within a buying and merchandising department. Beyond that, the book concentrates almost exclusively on the fashion merchandiser, and so some chapters, particularly in Part Three, are discussed within the remit of the fashion merchandiser role only.

At its heart, this book presents a view on product management from the perspective of a highly numerate and logical standpoint. As the book unfolds, the reader is encouraged to relate this theoretical standpoint with the world around them, to make their own informed judgement of its relevance within their own individual set of professional or educational circumstances.

Online resources available from www.palgrave.com/companion/clark-fashion-merchandising

Fashion Merchandising: Principles and Practice is supported with online resources for both lecturers and students.

For lecturers – a range of lecture slides are provided that can be used to form the basis of a lecture programme. The slides follow the structure of the chapters for which they are relevant and offer discussion points and in some cases practical walk through examples. The detail of some of these should be reinterpreted as required.

For lecturers and students – a range of exercises are provided to support the case study provided in Part II. The case study has been written to show a process and to present ideas more clearly the decision points have been simplified but where relevant the numbers used exaggerated. The exercises provided concentrate on re-enforcing the mathematical calculations but also offer discussion questions to allow interpretation of data.

Introduction to Part One

Part I will set the scene for the demonstration of the activities of the fashion merchandiser, and has been written to draw attention to the retail context which makes the rationale for the role so compelling.

These first four chapters will dissect the factors that influence a retailer's ability to secure a competitive advantage within a highly lucrative but risk-laden industry. It will draw attention to topics such as industry deregulation, technological advances and supply-chain structures to prompt thought about what makes it imperative for the role to exist. Part I will then go on to summarize the role of buying and merchandising, to pinpoint where the fashion merchandiser adds value to the process of product management. Finally, it will identify a definition of the buying and merchandising function, to in turn, discuss how the buyer and merchandiser role works alongside other areas of a fashion retail business.

The one caveat to the accurate depiction of this role is that there is no single version upon which one can rely. Throughout this book, it should become clear that the very breadth of the fashion retail industry means that roles, processes and activities vary from business to business and sector to sector. At best, this first part will provide a generic review that takes key points and influences and discusses them to build an argument in favour of the addition of a distinct merchandiser role within a fashion retail business. This role that can be described as uniquely placed to bring a modicum of effective order and process to the fast-paced and volatile creativity of buying and merchandising.

1 A Review of the Fashion Industry

INTENDED LEARNING OUTCOMES

1. An appreciation of the size and scale of the fashion retail industry.
2. The influences that have contributed to the industry size and shape of today.
3. The twin impacts of supply and demand developments within the industry.
4. Competitive advantage and its relevance within product management.

INTRODUCTION

The fashion industry by any measure is significant – it is large by value, employment and cultural influence. The tentacles of fashion reach almost every aspect of our day-to-day lives, fulfilling a functional need for clothing, but also enabling personal projections of ourselves to the world. The business case for participating within such a diverse and multifaceted market is compelling, offering many commercial opportunities – different product types, distribution channels, markets, employment and of course wealth. It is also an innovative and ever evolving industry, influenced by the inevitable changes in culture, emergent trends and attitudes which rise and fall, eventually giving way to those that follow.

To get an immediate snapshot of its scale and proportions, if one were to review a single retail destination, in a single city, some impressive statistics would emerge. Within the Westfield Shepherd's Bush mall towards the west of London, 1.5 million square feet (150,000 square metres) of prime retail estate offer a total of 319 fashion and general merchandise stores that compete to attract potential customer spend (Westfield 2012). The stores that can be found within the mall range from large anchor department stores such as Debenhams, House of Fraser, Marks & Spencer through to small-sized, but well-known multiple stores such as All Saints and Top Shop. In addition, premium luxury stores can be found in a distinct section of the mall called The Village. On top of all that, there are also non-fashion businesses such as Boots and Apple trading to complete the mall's offer to its potential consumers.

So what? How does this information add relevance to the subject of this book? Well, by itself, beyond being a set of impressive statistics indicating a large shopping mall, not a great deal. However, using this information it is possible to make a rough estimate of the cumulative number of style/colours that are offered over the course of a year by all of the retailers combined. In the case of Westfield Shepherd's Bush, the figure could be approximately 750,000. That is a huge figure, but of course the mall is not alone in the world. Shoppers will also find stores in Oxford Street, London, the Bullring in Birmingham, Fifth Avenue in New York or the Ambience Mall in Delhi, with the list going on to millions of other locations and distribution channels such as e commerce and catalogues. The sheer potential size and scale of the fashion industry are both awe-inspiring and near incalculable. But one fact rings true: it is a commercial activity, and a very competitive one at that. Success within this industry is not found in whim or fancy – it comes from commercial business acumen as much as any creative or artistic flair.

To help emphasize this point, this chapter briefly reviews the retail industry and comments on its characteristics, whilst recognizing the permanent state of flux which the industry is in. This will be done predominantly from a UK perspective to keep it in line with the definition of the fashion merchandiser role that forms the bulk of this book. The chapter will conclude by discussing the implications of developing an enduring competitive advantage, first, because a retail business needs a compelling reason for consumers to shop with it and second, to simply ensure survival in a wonderful but challenging sector.

A BRIEF INDUSTRY REVIEW

The Latin phrase attributed to Sir Francis Bacon 'scientia potentia est' – or in English, 'knowledge is power' – suggests that with knowledge comes increased ability. The emphasis on knowledge is no less important within the fashion industry, and there are a number of excellent sources with which one can develop that knowledge. Organizations such as Verdict or Mintel can provide up-to-date and relevant market data, whilst industry bodies such as the British Retail Consortium and the British Fashion Council mix market data with industry debate. Above those resources sits the UK Government, which through the Office of National Statistics offers data such as economic indicators with which market research can be contextualized.

Despite this, reviewing the industry and its size and shape is complicated due to the many different factors that comprise it. There are also many perspectives to review the industry from – those of the retailer, the supplier, the government or the consumer. This section will therefore give a short review of a salient mix of variables to open the discussion, and as such is not comprehensive but rather indicative of the industry to lead further discussion within the chapter.

At the national level, The Office of National Statistics reported that in 2012 the retail market of the UK recorded sales in excess of £310b. Within this, textile, clothing and footwear sales value was £43b or 14 per cent of consumer spend (ONS 2013) (see Figure 1.1).

Retail sales values within the textile, clothing and footwear sector had risen in all but one of the preceding five years. The offending year where sales values fell was 2008, during the peak of the banking crisis that still affects retail trade six years later in 2014. Indeed, as late as April 2013, the effects of the recession were still the topic

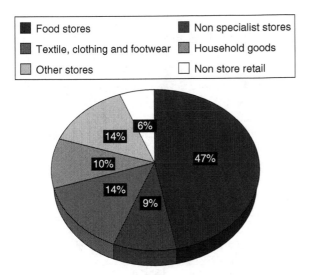

Figure 1.1 *UK retail market share by product category*

Source: ONS (2013)

of conversation for retail analysts. The *Independent* quoted Nick Hood, a business risk analyst at Company Watch, as saying that 'the retail sector has been one of the worst hit since recession first hit the UK in 2008 and the pain goes on and on, made worse by structural changes caused by the relentless growth of online and mobile, or smartphone app shopping' (Thompson 2013).

Despite its size suggesting invincibility, the retail industry is vulnerable to shocks to the system such as the banking crisis, recession, national events such as a royal wedding or even, on a day-to-day basis, the weather. As an example of this last point, in April 2013 *Retail Week*, a trade journal, reported that retail footfall had 'plunged 5.2 per cent in March as the cold snap put shoppers off hitting the high street' (Retail Week 2013). Notwithstanding increasingly regular macro-economic shocks such as those which interrupt market stability, scale within the retail industry has been achieved, not just in the total cash size of sales but also in terms of the numbers of individual businesses and trading locations.

Taking the UK clothing and footwear market in isolation, Mintel estimated that the top ten retailers within this retail segment accounted for over 51 per cent all sales in 2011 (Mintel 2012). The top ten includes brands such as Marks & Spencer, Next, Primark, Asda, TK Maxx and New Look, which is interesting as different types of business model are represented within the list. High-street stalwarts such as M&S and Next are on the list, but so too are supermarkets, off-price retailers and young fashions. Brands such as these offer large product ranges from multiple locations. Marks & Spencer for example, trades from over 700 locations in the UK, whilst the Arcadia group, also in the top ten for market share, has over 2,000 stores. In addition to physical stores, there are of course new emerging distribution channels such as e and m commerce, which year on year increase their own shares of a crowded market. The ONS estimates that £4b of the total retail sales within textiles, clothing and footwear were derived from online trading in 2012 (ONS 2013).

Below these examples of market data lay a plethora of information that can be reviewed and analysed, such as data by product category, price data and unit volumes, all of which would reinforce to the reader that fashion is big business. So big that the British Fashion Council reported in 2010 that the UK fashion industry contributed almost 2 per cent to the gross domestic product (GDP) of the country and employed over 800,000 people (British Fashion Council 2010).

FROM CONSUMPTION TO CONSUMERISM

The result of the growth and reach of the fashion industry within our lives is evidenced by taking a walk down any street in any town in any country. The different trends, creative ideas and product concepts that go into the ranges of clothes, accessories, shoes etc. offered to consumers are broad and diverse. The sheer scope, interpretation and application of fashion today comes from these myriad sources, which are in turn translated into the latest fashions to tempt a chosen consumer type.

The emphasis on getting the right product to the right consumer is well placed. Fashion retailers compete not just with each other, but with other industries vying for the consumer's disposable income. The continued penetration of technology products – most notably in the form of smartphones and tablets – has the effect of diverting consumer spend away from purchasing fashion product. Similarly, other products such as holidays and leisure activities such as sports and eating out continually strive to tempt the consumer to spend with them.

Despite various strong competitive headwinds, recent post-war history has pointed to continued economic growth, rising incomes and consumer expenditure, which have enabled the differing competing industries to thrive alongside each other. With increasing wealth and status come further increases in purchasing power and consumerism; an accepted order of purchasing products in ever increasing amounts beyond the limits of necessity. The development of consumerism is nicely articulated by Douglas and Isherwood, cited by Jeacle: 'shopping has become a daily preoccupation, in Western society at least, and one which is no longer necessarily linked to the satisfaction of any economic need' (Jeacle 2009: 3).

The concept of buying product other than just to fulfil an immediate need is not new. Consumerism is said to have developed from early civilizations, but the development of commerce and international trade from past centuries to today has driven us to aspire to ever greater wealth, status and, as a result, possessions. For the fashion industry, an obvious route to personal self-expression and creativity, the immediate benefits of consumerism have been aggressively pursued in the form of increased product ranges, diffusion brands and, as barriers reduced, international expansionist strategies to widen market reach.

This development and expansion though could be seen as a paradox. If fashion is based on creativity and individual self-expression, the resulting mass-market ranges in generic chain stores that capture maximum sales and profit opportunities have de-emphasized fashion's true unique selling points (USPs) of desirability, individuality and prestige. As fashion has moved towards mass production, and the value in individual products being distinct has diminished, new technologies have been able to negate this. The move towards fast-fashion business models, limited capsule collections and celebrity endorsements have all helped re-create aspiration within fashion. These in turn have created new challenges and, it can be argued, a changed remit for product management and the traditional well-known buying role. Highly targeted ranges require good micro planning to make sure the opportunity identified is maximized to ensure a good return on investment (ROI). Product management today places greater emphasis on such approaches and the focus has moved further towards understanding consumers by responding to them, rather than by forecasting demand and hoping to have got the product offer right (Varley 2001).

The cohesion of these wider and more extensive influences on product lead towards a consistent message that the consumer sees, hears and feels over time. This contributes to the development of distinct business personalities with traits that resonate positively with current and potential consumers. This in turn sets a business aside in the consumers' eyes from the competition, and this branding of business enables it to identify to the world how its particular product or service is distinct through characteristics such as:

- brand image and logos
- signature product heritage
- craftsmanship and perceived value of its products
- brand equity
- ability to stay in a customer's mind.

Consistency between these characteristics encourages consumer loyalty and a relationship that is based on trust and uniform delivery of product, communications, retail environment and service level. A good summary definition of this point is made by De Chernatony and McDonald: 'A successful brand is an identifiable product, service, person or place, augmented in such a way that the buyer or user perceives relevant, unique added values which match their needs most closely. Furthermore its success results from being able to sustain these added values in the face of competition' (De Chernatony and McDonald 2003: 25).

For those charged within a fashion retailer to manage product development, the remit of the function and its success criteria have become wider to encapsulate more than just developing and executing a good product idea. Wider brand management approaches require broader skill sets, and as a result are increasingly open to spectacular failure should brand consistency not be maintained. This widening of success criteria has inevitably placed more emphasis on the relevance of targeted product ranges, creativity and art within product management, and the buyer is central to their successful delivery.

CASE STUDY 1.1: BURBERRY AND THEIR BRAND PERSONALITY

The difficulty for a business to deliver both fashion credibility and maximized profitability cannot be understated. Reliance on occupying a particular market, product type or distribution channel that has consistently delivered acceptable returns can in time lead to a business that is stale and increasingly irrelevant within its market. The maintenance of a brand and its place within an ever changing fashion world depends on its ability to update, refresh or even reinvent itself.

In the late 1990s, Burberry was perceived as a conservative heritage brand that sold trench coats with an in-house check design. Keen to move into the new millennium and to capture a bigger share of the growing trend towards designer labels, the business reinvented itself with a profile that tapped into the emerging culture of the new century. All too soon, though, the early success of the reinvention went wrong. The overemphasis of the Burberry check on baseball caps, accessories and non-apparel products led to the brand's adoption by consumers whom the company was not trying to attract – hooligans and celebrities of dubious character.

The appointment of Rose Marie Bravo as chief executive led to a rethink. Bravo recognized the strength within the heritage, history and Englishness of the brand which had once supplied the likes of the British Army and the upper crust. In 2001, Christopher Bailey was appointed as creative director to lead the brand's fight back to both financial health and fashion credibility. The product was reviewed with its archives scoured to reconnect the brand with its heritage. The prevalence of the in-house check was pared back from overstated to understated to emphasize sophistication and luxury.

This approach was extended to marketing activities, with early campaigns using models who reflected an aristocratic look, further emphasizing the brand's history, and more recently the brand has used new marketing tools to communicate to its customer base. This emphasis on connecting brand credibility to consumer was enhanced with the launch of its retail theatre, broadcasting catwalk collections to Burberry flagship stores where shoppers use an app to purchase the pieces that take their fancy. This linking of product, marketing and retail to present a consistent personality across customer-facing activities is supported by a back-office function that is designed to support the requirements of the front office. Burberry completed a major overhaul of its information technology systems, including retail and warehousing software to improve operational efficiency and refine its distribution network, enabling the demands of quality product and customer expectation of product availability to be aligned more closely.

The defined and updated brand personality has translated into its product, marketing, retail operations and a supportive back office process resulting in spectacular success.

Activity: Review five fashion retailers and assess how well they communicate their brand personality. Look for consistencies between product design, marketing approaches, retail store and online formats and added service values such as personal shopping or free delivery and returns. Which of the brands is the most consistent? Which is the least?

INDUSTRY DEREGULATION

Increased demand, as witnessed in market statistics and the seemingly limitless rise of consumerism is one part of the recent story of the fashion industry. In terms of economics, to maintain a balanced industry, increased demand must be matched by increased supply. The deregulation of many commerce agreements has enabled that balance to remain in place as product supply has been able to keep pace with ever growing demand. There have been consistent efforts by governments worldwide to manipulate trade to ensure this continued economic wellbeing. Since the Second World War, successive governments have nurtured world trade by engaging in a variety of initiatives designed to reduce or eliminate barriers to trade. These have been accomplished at many levels, between countries, groups of countries as a bloc (for example the EU) or through pan-government organizations such as the General Agreement on Tariffs and Trade (GATT) and later the World Trade Organization (WTO) in 1995.

A significant example, relevant to the fashion industry, was the ending of the Multi-Fibre Agreement (MFA). The MFA was agreed in 1974, and established a quota system between countries that limited the export of textiles and clothing from lower-cost developing countries to developed ones. It was originally established to allow a period of adjustment for the developed economies facing rising imports that were feeding growing domestic demand. The effect of the setting of artificial limits on the amount of export trade was estimated to have been costly to the exporting countries affected by the agreement as it depressed their trade opportunities.

The MFA was highly restrictive and expired in 2005. That year saw a surge in exports from China, which responded to the greater flexibility within in the marketplace by increasing its production of textiles and clothing. The BBC reported at the time that concern about the pace of China's increase in exports (items such as t shirts had increased by 164 per cent year on year and pullovers by over 500 per cent) meant that developed countries would again limit trade with her (BBC 2005). Ultimately, through negotiation, an orderly transition to the removal of quotas was established, with the final ones removed in 2009, freeing businesses to fully exploit lower-cost production, economy of scale and supply-chain flexibility.

Deregulation does not have to be limited to international trade and many initiatives have had a domestic focus. Within the UK, there has been a steady march towards the opening up of the domestic market. Initiatives such as the 1964 resale price maintenance legislation removed agreements for retailers to sell products at set prices with their supplier. More recently, the 1994 relaxation of Sunday opening hours, which allowed retailers to trade on a Sunday, has increased trade and contributed to the reduction in retail prices to the consumer.

The impact of this continued and on-going effort to open up domestic and international markets has had several effects within fashion retailing. First, it has enhanced the sourcing process, allowing volumes to rise and cost prices to decrease. This has enabled fashion businesses to increase stock availability, passing on cost reductions in the form of reduced selling prices, further encouraging market growth. Second, flexibility has been built into the supply chain, with sourcing strategies being able to turn on and turn off production in different locations depending on product trend and trading conditions. A third impact is that product-quality levels have risen as a result of the intense competition to supply product to the consumer.

Of course, deregulation is also a double-edged sword. The increase in supply afforded by it has been matched by the demand increases from a consumerist society. Where there is opportunity there is competition and, as the market has increased, so too have the number and type of players within the retail market.

CASE STUDY 1.2: BRA WARS

In September 2005, the EU and China settled a near year-long dispute that had resulted in nearly 80m Chinese-made clothes being held in warehouses and ports and not delivered to retailers and their customers. Describing the negotiations in Beijing as tense, Peter Mandelson and Bo Xilai described the final agreement as a fair and equitable compromise for both sides.

But how had this happened? Why had such a compromise been required at all, when the aim of both the EU and China had been to build stronger ties? The origin of the dispute was in the ending of the MFA and its replacement by a new quota system that enabled greater volumes of trade to occur but did not totally remove the quotas on certain product types until 2009. In principle, it was a move forward and cemented further the growing trading relationship between China and the EU.

Unfortunately, somebody forgot to tell the consumers of fashion that there was still a selective quota in place. An example of this was bras. In 2005, the average woman owned 10 bras and very few consumers could afford the prices of Rigby and Pellar or Myla. Instead they opted for the plentiful supply of cheap products made in countries such as China. This should of course have been of no consequence to the governments of the two countries. The problem though was that the consumers of the EU were obsessed with shopping, buying ever more bras and t shirts and pullovers and every other kind of fashion clothing available to buy. Sensing opportunity to increase sales and profit margins, the retailers diverted much of their buying budgets to China, so much so that within months of the new quota being introduced, orders and deliveries had surpassed the agreed levels, resulting in the excess products being impounded on the EU borders.

To resolve the issue, China agreed not to export any more pullovers, trousers and bras for the remainder of the year and to count around half the blocked items against its 2006 quota. Economically, the seizure of goods was a failure.

It hurt European retailers, dependent on cheap Chinese goods to keep the tills busy, and the consumer who was unable to buy that eleventh bra.

Activity: Research the impact of domestic deregulation such as the lifting of restrictions on Sunday trading. Did total trade rise or not as a result of increased opening hours?

THE CHANGING PLAYERS IN THE RETAIL MARKET

Within all commercial industries there is a long history, built up over time, that has contributed to creating the business world as we know it today. Fashion is no different, and there have been many great success stories. Businesses such as Gucci and Marks & Spencer have long histories of success. The luxury Gucci brand, for example, has been recognized as one of the top global brands and was ranked 38th in the world in 2012 by the branding consultancy Interbrand. Marks & Spencer meanwhile has evolved from a market stall operation into a major force on the UK high street. In 2011, it commanded a clothing UK market share of around 10 per cent (Mintel 2012) and is also a major force in food retailing. New emerging businesses such as asos and Net-a-Porter have captured unique positions within the newer e-retail market, growing significantly within short periods of time. From its start in 2000, asos has built a business that turns over in excess of £300m per year and aims for turnover to reach £1b by 2015 (Asos 2011). Against these examples of fashion businesses that have found success, there are also many that have failed. Names such as Jane Norman and Peacocks in the UK fell into administration in 2012, while brands such as Allders and C&A have long since disappeared from the UK high street.

Within the fashion retail market today, many distinct business models have evolved, all of which offer a different aspect of the shopping experience. Table 1.1 below gives a summary of different models, their USP and retailer examples.

Table 1.1 Differing retail format examples

Business model	USPs	Retailer example
Luxury	Fashion leaders, scarcity of product, status	Chanel
Department stores	Anchor store in location, wide product offer	John Lewis
Multiple chains	Wide distribution and value for money	Top Shop
Independents	Wholesale brands, high service levels	Fifi Wilson
Supermarkets	Simple designs and pricing. Ease of purchase	Tu at Sainsburys
Off price	Discounted prices across all products	TK Maxx
Specialist	Wider choice within limited product type	Accessorise
Niche	Offering an alternative approach – for example, ethical	Timberland
Catalogue	Home shopping not requiring a computer	Boden
Pure play online	Home or mobile shopping 24 hours a day	Asos

In reviewing the Table 1.1 above, one is struck by how much choice the consumer has, as in where and when to spend on fashion product. When this example list is then considered as a snapshot of the retail industry and the deregulated arena in which fashion brands operate, an appreciation of the fundamental risks of doing business is amplified. The competitive risks of fashion can be tangibly felt in the recent histories of brand such as Marks & Spencer, which has met with varying degrees of success in repositioning itself to cope with competitive pressures, and in a non-fashion example WHSmith, which has significantly altered its product ranges to better reflect both consumer trends and its newer and nimbler competitors.

But what are these new competitive pressures that are forcing such change, and what is their potential impact on the process of product management?

- Online trading – 'It's phenomenal what the last few years have done. If you loved fashion 10 years ago and you didn't have easy access to Oxford Street you were presented with a local high street with two to three clothing stores. The same girl living in the same town can now effectively purchase from any brand in any country. It has opened up a whole new world' (Robertson cited in Thomson 2012). The rise and rise of first e- and then m-commerce has been an outstanding feature of the early 21st century, and the move into the market by new and existing business has been marked. Not only has asos found success, but the online stores of legacy businesses such as John Lewis and House of Fraser now count as the biggest single stores within their estates.
- Fast fashion – The flexible sourcing strategies enabled by deregulation and the buoyant demand of recent years mixed with much improved technological capability have meant that retail has been able to respond to the consumer's desire for up-to-date catwalk trends in ever reducing timeframes. The Queen of fast fashion is Zara, part of the Inditex group. The group's success and its unique business model – based on innovation and flexibility and which melds creativity, quality design and rapid turnaround to adjust to changing market demands – has irrevocably changed the concept of stock management within fashion. With a focus on speed to market and regular deliveries of new collections every two weeks, product management is as much about efficiency and supply management as it is about trend and product development.
- Internationalization – In the early 1990s, a few big players – including Marks & Spencer, Next and Littlewoods – offered a relatively straightforward fashion retail choice. Since then, the market has become more crowded (Retail Week 2012). Retail businesses have operated internationally for many years; brands such as Gap have traded overseas for many years and have built up large estates of stores. Historically, the UK high street has welcomed overseas brands, most obviously from the USA and Europe. Forever 21, Zara, Victoria's Secret and Banana Republic are recent examples of entrants into the market. However, with rise of new developing economies, brands such as China's Bosideng – which has 10,000 stores in its home market – are now moving into international markets. Bosideng, for example, opened a store on South Molton Street in London in 2012 and has plans to expand further.

The ever changing face of UK retail has brought us to a changed market, and it is not just the names over the doors which have changed but the business models too. These strategic changes have had the effect of altering the importance of the retailer–customer relationship and created new pressures around which a business needs to develop its product ranges.

SUPPLY-CHAIN DEVELOPMENTS

Central enablers to the demand and supply changes within product management have been supply-chain improvements, and the reduction in technological limitations, swept away by continuous developments within information and communications technology (ICT). It is not that many years since purchase orders were manually written, replenishment systems needed all of a Monday to process sales weekend data, and communications with suppliers were through telephone, fax and telex. The speed with which technology has transformed the retail sector is breathtaking, and it has played its part in the modernization of the retail supply chain.

A supply chain is the network of roles, processes and activities that together create, deliver and sell product. Within a globalized industry such as retail, where a product range may be conceived and sold in one location, but sourced, manufactured, delivered and stored in another, the demands of integration and collaboration between the different roles is of vital importance. This concept is reinforced by the definition of supply-chain management as being 'the management of upstream and downstream relationships with suppliers and customers in order to deliver superior customer value at less cost to the supply chain as a whole' (Christopher 2011: 3).

There are many examples of how retail has put technological development to use in improving product management throughout the chain and maximizing sales and stock management within the ever shortening product lifecycle.

- Data mining – The use of product catalogue data updated with sales and stock history in real time allows any product, store or supplier to be analysed quickly, enabling decision making to be current and accurate.
- Integrated planning – The ability to link various processes together either in one system or by linking different systems together so that they can 'talk to each other'. This is an invaluable benefit of technological improvements as all relevant roles within the fashion supply chain can see what the others are doing, and the effect that each has on business success.
- Standardization and linkage – The ability to link systems together enables standardization of terminology and business processes to improve efficiency in the flow of stock. This linkage need not be limited to being within the retailer. The advent of EDI (electronic data interchange) and then internet trading has meant that retailer and supplier have been able to link systems, processes and terminology.
- Tracking – The total tracking of stock through the development of RFID (radio frequency identification) which uses wireless technology to automatically track and locate a product's journey through the supply chain. Stock management

is greatly enhanced through faster delivery processes, real-time stock location visibility resulting in lower shrinkage (loss of product through misplacing or theft) leading to faster stock availability and customer service. It is particularly beneficial as a value-added tool for the customer experience as customers can use technology to track online or catalogue-ordered items;

- Customer experience – Store technology designed to enhance the multichannel shopping experience is a key theme among major retailers' current innovations. The rollout of transactional and non-transactional websites has been enhanced more recently with moves to merge the two distribution channels with click-and-collect technology, the provision of in-store iPads, augmented-reality developments and the creation of sophisticated, data-rich customer loyalty schemes such as Tesco's Club Card.
- Business reporting – This area has been vastly improved with the development of business reporting systems that allow product and financial data to be shaped into custom reports which can be shared throughout the supply chain. Beyond this, planning and forecasting tools can add a dynamic element to business reporting by taking collected actual data and using it to forecast the likely outcomes of a range of activities against any budgetary requirements that the business may have set.

This short summary of the use of technology within supply chains, serves to give a flavour of a modern retail business's various technological abilities. More importantly, it demonstrates the sheer versatility required of retailers to be able to support the product management process. The vast amount of data available to be collected, researched and analysed, coupled with the flexibility now inbuilt within a supply chain, changes the dynamic of decision making. It is now much wider than it ever has been, requiring a multitude of skills to accurately interpret and recognize the stories that the data is telling the reader. A second impact brought on by the linkage within supply chains today is that control of the process is more professional, with a greater emphasis on collaboration and relationship building between supplier and retailer, and in turn between the retailer and consumer. Finally, consumers have possibly gained the greatest benefit of all – power. The power to review and assess product ranges across a number of retailers. The power to influence the timely flow of stock between distribution channels And, ultimately, the power to judge – they can now see all, both good and bad.

FOCUS POINT 1.1: BUSINESS-TO-BUSINESS ONLINE TRADING

The development of business-to-business (b2b) trading capabilities has transformed the way the various stakeholders in the product management process work together to create product ranges. Fundamental to this is the exploitation of the opportunities afforded by electronic business, or e business.

E business relies on effective ICT to support the coordination of the various activities that together comprise the retail supply chain. E business uses relevant ICT to link the various activities into a seamless, effective and reduced cost process of data management and fast 24-hour communication methods that allow the businesses to benefit from reduced cost bases. The consumer meanwhile benefits from responsive supply chains that get product to them at the appropriate quality, price and timing.

At the heart of e business is the linking of all internal and external systems and processes into a single unified approach by way of the Internet. Early examples of this were the moves to use electronic data interchange (EDI) as an interface to allow two or more computer programs to talk to each other. Within buying and merchandising, linking retailer to supplier meant that purchase orders could be transmitted electronically between them and advance delivery notifications could speed up the delivery process.

With the increasing sophistication of the Internet, businesses have been able to make use of intranet and extranet sites to further develop supply-chain efficiency. Intranets allow the coordination of internal activities – such as buying and merchandising, design and retail operations – to facilitate quicker decision making, visibility of data and improved communications. Extranets meanwhile link the internal activities to the external activities – such as suppliers, manufacturers and logistics – to allow all activities to work in real time together despite being physically separated.

The scope of extranet trading goes well beyond the supply chain. It also brings the most important stakeholder – the customer – into the relationship. The development of e and m commerce, ordering online, customer relationship management (CRM) and online marketing has put ICT at the centre of a modern retail business and has significantly changed the dynamics and lead times involved in planning and delivering a fashion product offer.

Activity: Think about the potential number of activities that are needed to create a product range, and how and at what point in the product management process they all communicate with each other.

SEEKING COMPETITIVE ADVANTAGE

The previous sections of this chapter have presented summary thoughts on the retail industry and the influences that have contributed to its size and shape today. These influences are of course fluid and their strength can grow or decline depending on the unique set of circumstances that face a particular retailer. Their relevance to each differing business model will also vary. The highly competitive city-centre locations such as London, New York or Beijing face very different challenges to those in small country towns. However, no matter what the mix of influences at any given time, they do exist, and being able to thrive while managing them is at the heart of all successful commerce.

One fact above all is starkly apparent. The critical mass of today's industry has emerged over several decades, where growing demand patterns have been matched with improvements in product supply. While the industry may not have been in perfect supply and demand equilibrium as shown by the farcical bra wars, the opportunities afforded by strong market opportunities meant that the focus within product management has moved beyond the philosophy of Joseph Cohen – founder of Tesco – to pile it high and sell it cheap to an era of targeted ranges. In this new trading world, businesses respond to customer demand in the planning of product ranges, but do so with a focus on the efficient supply of the range to ensure maximum benefit is derived from it.

For the consumer, this all translates into choice, and lots of it! In a diverse and competitive industry such as this, there is inevitably a need for a fashion business to focus on achieving an enduring advantage over all of its competitors. Through having a competitive advantage, businesses can become the first choice of consumers and, by being in this position, will gain a significant long-term advantage in the pursuit of customer loyalty, and also relative financial security in complex and uncertain markets.

Porter's Competitive Advantage model (Porter 1985) argues that there are two routes to achieve a competitive advantage within an industry: either a product-differentiation route or a cost-management one. A business that is able to differentiate itself results in the customer seeing a distinct value in and reason for buying its product, and by reviewing differing fashion business models it is easy to see this in practice.

Fast-fashion businesses, for example, were able to differentiate by offering new fashion collections faster and more frequently than the existing players in the marketplace. A second example, asos, harnessed the opportunities of the Internet to differentiate by operating as a pure player through a single distribution channel.

Porter's second route, cost management, implies that a business could aim to be the lowest-cost producer of product within its market segment. Therefore it is perfectly acceptable that the costs for Gucci to produce a shirt should be very different (higher) than the costs of Primark producing a shirt, as the two businesses compete in different segments of the same industry. To gain a cost advantage, Gucci would, however, be more concerned with comparing its cost management with a similar businesses such as Louis Vuitton, while Primark would compare its cost management to a competitor such as Matalan in its market segment.

Whichever route is taken has a significant impact on product within a fashion business. A clear focus on adhering to its strategic-differentiation or cost-reduction route results in a business with unique and balanced fashion ranges that are relevant to the values held by its target customer and business model. The delivery of a product range in line with both fashion trend and business model adds an extra dimension to product management. The differentiation route taken by Zara, for example, requires as much expertise in stock management and financial control as it does trend awareness and product knowledge.

CASE STUDY 1.3: ZARA AND COMPETITIVE ADVANTAGE

The Cube is the central hub of the fast-fashion brand Zara and has, in its design and operation, contributed to the revolution in the design, manufacture and retailing of fashion led by the brand. By defying long-established business practices within the industry, a truly global brand has evolved with a consistent and proven track record of success both in terms of financial and commercial strength.

The contemporary term *fast fashion* describes the effect of reducing the lead times of translating catwalk trends into physical products ranged in stores. Fast-fashion businesses such as Zara can translate trends into product in a matter of weeks as opposed to the months that the process took as recently as the 1990s. This reduction in speed to market has delivered to brands such as Zara a clear competitive advantage over older more established rivals.

The business model that has delivered this advantage is geared around the customer, and the organization has been constructed to reflect this. Recognizing that consumers appreciated design at affordable prices, and that fashion by its nature is fluid and ever changing, Zara created a vertical business model where the design and production processes were kept in-house. This meant that lead times were shortened, enabling product to be available in store before the competition. This business operation, headquartered at The Cube, delivered value additions to the brand and cost reduction.

The shortened lead times enabled Zara to commit to production later than its rivals, meaning that the risk of emerging trends changing in that shorter timeframe were reduced. Ranges that were in line with fashion trends meant greater sales opportunities, allowing bigger production runs and so reduced unit costs. The shorter lead times also enabled Zara to offer a bigger choice in its ranges, and so the ability to offer two to three times more options in any given season, so reinforcing in the minds of consumers the fashion credentials of the brand.

The increased product options available within Zara's range naturally meant that the shelf life of each was reduced and so allocations per store were reduced. The reduced cost of stock holding and a reduced need to mark down excess stocks enabled Zara to benefit from a reduction in costs associated with creating and selling a product range.

The clear competitive advantage enjoyed by Zara required a different approach in its business structure. The Cube – as a central design, manufacture and distribution centre held together by astute use of ICT – created a seamless process that was also able to be reactive to emerging sales trends. Within store, for example, Zara is able to maximize the sales of best sellers despite limited production runs. The store's employees are equipped with technology that enables them to order local bestsellers while they are still available. This ability to react to local demand further adds to the brand's competitive advantage; by ensuring bestseller stock is available, trust in the brand is maintained and the cost of stock holding can be managed effectively.

Activity: Research the organizational structures of differing fashion retail business models. What makes each one suitable for its segment of the market?

SUMMARY

The escalating competitive pressures brought about by globalization, the easing of trade restrictions, technological supply-chain advances and increased consumer wealth have facilitated the entry of new businesses into an already crowded fashion retail market. In benign economic weather where the seemingly relentless rise of retail sales is matched by improvement in supply, many fashion businesses succeed. Some do not, though, and when good economic times turn to bad, many more fail. Product management is central to the success of a fashion business, and in such a fluid industry, where success is not guaranteed, ensuring product ranges respond to consumer demand is pivotal. This, however, cannot be at any cost, and ensuring the product range is profitable to allow further investment in new ranges is central to the role of product within a fashion business. Managing these key deliverables lies at the heart of a good fashion range.

SELF-DIRECTED STUDY

1. Using Mintel or Verdict research, assess the current macro trends affecting a particular segment of the UK fashion industry. Understand its total size and product types within it, and compare these to the same data for the industry in total. Is your chosen segment stronger or weaker than the average?
2. Assess ten different retail businesses. Identify if they have a competitive advantage and define what you think it is.
3. You should complete a competitive shop of your local high street to analyse which of the stores reviewed are international brands. Use this to assess the mix of home and international fashion brands available to you.
4. Log on to several online retail websites. Assess how much technology is required to present the site, manage transactions, develop social-media activities, deliver customer orders, handle returns and have a facility for you to communicate with them. Collate your findings and assess the number of skills and roles required to operate a successful online retail store.

Further Reading

Christopher, M. (2011) *Logistics and Supply Chain Management 4th ed*. Harlow: Pearson

De Chernatony, L and McDonald, M (2003) *Creating Powerful Brands 3rd ed*. Oxford: Elsevier

Varley, R. (2001) *Retail Product Management*. London: Routledge

Bibliography

Asos (2011) *Company report* [Internet] London. Available from http://www.asosplc. com/investors/results-reports/2011.aspx [Accessed 20th January 2014].

BBC (2005) *No breakthrough in China – EU talks* [Internet] Available from http://news. bbc.co.uk/1/hi/business/4478101.stm [Accessed 20th January 2014].

British Fashion Council (2010) *The value of fashion report* [Internet] London. Available from http://britishfashioncouncil.com/content.aspx?CategoryID=1745 [Accessed 20th January 2014].

Christopher, M. (2011) *Logistics and Supply Chain Management 4th ed*. Harlow: Pearson.

De Chernatony, L and McDonald, M (2003) *Creating Powerful Brands 3rd ed*. Oxford: Elsevier.

Goldfingle, G. (2013) *Footfall plunges 5.2% as March cold snap keeps shoppers away*. Retail Week [Internet] Available from: http://www.retail-week.com/footfall-plunges-52-as-march-cold-snap-keeps-shoppers-away/5048177.article [Accessed 20th January 2014].

Jeacle, I. (2009) *Accounting and everyday life: towards a cultural context for accounting research*, Qualitative accounting and research, volume 6, number 3. Available from http://www.research.ed.ac.uk/portal/files/8519560/Accounting_and_everyday_ life.pdf [Accessed 20th January 2014].

Kantar Worldpanel. (2012) *Quarterly report*,

Mintel (2011) *Clothing retail* [Internet]. London. Available from http://gmn.mintel. com.arts.idm.oclc.org/snapshots/GBR/333/shares/single [Accessed 20th January 2014].

Mintel (2012) *Clothing retail* [Internet]. London. Available from http://gmn.mintel. com.arts.idm.oclc.org/snapshots/GBR/271/performance/single [Accessed 20th January 2014].

Office of National Statistics (2013) *Retail sales* [Internet]. London. Available from http://www.ons.gov.uk/ons/rel/rsi/retail-sales/march-2013/index.html [Accessed 20th January 2014].

Porter, M. (1985) *Competitive advantage*. New York: Free Press

Thompson, J (2013). *Creditors pay £1bn for retail failures*. The Independent [Internet]. Available from http://www.independent.co.uk/news/business/news/creditors-pay-1bn-for-retail-failures-8566658.html [Accessed 20th January 2014].

Thomson, R. (2012) *The changing face of fashion retail*. Retail Week [Internet]. Retail Week, London http://www.retail-week.com/the-changing-face-of-fashion-retail/ 5037465.article [Accessed 20th January 2014].

Varley, R. (2001) *Retail product management*. London: Routledge.

Westfield Shepherds Bush (2012) *Westfield London Directory* [Internet]. Available from: http://uk.westfield.com/london/directory/search/ [Accessed 20th January 2014].

2 Fashion, Business and Product

INTENDED LEARNING OUTCOMES

1. An appreciation of the demands of fashion and business definitions.
2. Discussion and examples of the role of product within a fashion business.
3. The concept-to-carrier bag model – a process of product management.
4. Understanding and defining buying and merchandising.

INTRODUCTION

The previous chapter recognized that there are many opportunities within the fashion retail industry. However, they come with ferocious competition, requiring the best possible response in the form of balanced and relevant product ranges to compete effectively within their markets. As this chapter progresses, two fundamental product characteristics – qualitative and quantitative – will be offered as being central to this competitive ability. From there, the chapter will begin a discussion of the buying and merchandising (B&M) functions as the guardians of these characteristics which will be developed further in Chapter 3.

The management of the various activities of creating a product range can often feel as if one is trying to rescue a runaway lorry that is swerving at high speed along long and winding roads. The constant stream of data collation, review of options and decisions to follow a particular course of action and prevent disaster feel similar to the day-to-day life within B&M. Decision-making safety can be found in the various skilled roles that together are involved in the product creation process, particularly those of buyer and merchandiser, which work together to co-ordinate the complexities of taking a product concept through to creation, sourcing, manufacture, delivery and sale. This process can be costly in terms of the time it takes to be completed, and there is significant room for error, so all players need to be well organized with a planned approach. This organization, planning and co-ordination are the subject of this chapter, which will firstly discuss the role that product plays within a fashion business, and secondly provide a summary of the process of product management.

This chapter will present a theoretical concept-to-carrier bag process model that outlines the sequential activities which, when linked together, take initial product research and turn ideas and concepts into delivered commercial ranges.

There are various generic models of this kind, but the one chosen here will help explain the B&M roles and processes, and sets the scene for the detailed review of the merchandising function in Part Two. As a result, the model has been interpreted within the context of the book subject and is not presented as authoritative.

FASHION BUSINESS – A PARADOX?

As a starting point, if one considers the definitions of the two words *fashion* and *business*, it is possible to emphasize succinctly the context in which the B&M function operates.

- Fashion
  - 'The prevailing mode or style, especially of dress; custom or conventional usage in respect of dress, behaviour, etiquette, etc.' (OED 2013)

Fashion is therefore fluid and ever changing. By being 'prevailing', current fashion is just that: current. What is in line with culture, style, taste and mood this season will not last for ever and so carries a limited timeframe in which to be relevant and in demand. While fashion trends will emerge and fade, some to be revisited in the future, the exact moment in which each fashion trend becomes the prevailing trend will never happen again. The opportunity that fashion offers is elusive and difficult to capture. While capturing and interpreting a fashion trend as it emerges is difficult, knowing at which point in time to let it go and move on to the next trend is harder still.

- Business
  - 'A person's regular occupation, profession, or trade, an activity that someone is engaged in, a commercial activity.' (OED 2013)

The business definition by contrast suggests something quite different. It is an activity that will generate a specific result: wealth creation. This route could comprise one or many activities, but whatever the routes used, each would be undertaken to generate an income, a benefit for an individual or group of individuals. This would be done either within a specified timeframe, or more likely with an implication that the wealth creating activities will continue into the future with an unspecified end date.

If one considers the two definitions, a number of key words come to mind that help describe and interpret each definition:

- Fashion – presumptive, uncertain, current, visual, emotional, subjective, creative
- Business – long-term, financial, procedural, calculating, risk-managed, structured.

The paradox of fashion business is that the appropriate merging of uncertainty while generating wealth is a difficult feat to perform. The ideal trading conditions of certainty, safety and managed risk that would enable a business easily to navigate the uncertain waters of fashion do not exist; there are too many variables within an individual season to deliver a cast-iron guarantee that all decisions made will be accurate. In fact, the regular occurrence of end-of-season sales and the multitude of enticements during a season – such as one-day sales, gift with purchases and loyalty reward schemes to consumers – indicate how prone fashion ranges are to not fully satisfying consumer wants. Within fashion the risk of failure is very real: markdown, brand dilution, lost profit and potentially business closure.

Effective decision making in fashion encompasses a wide range of variables, but when consistently achieved well it ensures great success both commercially and financially. It is the management of the natural tensions between these two elements and the finding of a balance between them which are at the heart of a good product range and which in effect fuse the two competing definitions together to present a cohesive range to the consumer.

THE ROLE OF PRODUCT WITHIN A FASHION BUSINESS

In general terms, it is the B&M role that is charged with the delivery of product ranges that will reflect the creative direction and wealth creation needs of a fashion retailer. This places the understanding of the role of product in delivering these dual requirements as central to the individual activities of the buyer and merchandiser and their management of this asset is fundamental to the success of the function.

Cohesive balanced product ranges that can offer value to the customer do not happen by chance. The iconic Burberry trench coat, or a heavily branded Superdry hoodie or even a £2 T-shirt from Primark, all exist within a wider product collection. All pieces within a range must communicate to a target market, by reflecting its attitudes to fashion, trend and value for money. The products also have to be functional, fit for purpose and reliable. Not all pieces need to be highly embellished or deeply interpretive of trend. The delivery of a commercial balance within the range to offer diversity of choice is paramount to its visual and creative role within a fashion business.

Such qualitative aspects of product are ones that the customer uses to assess product suitability. For the customer, these aspects must match their desired end use at a price and quality that is acceptable to them. For the retailer, meanwhile, product is the opportunity to speak to the world and demonstrate its personality and values through a balanced and structured product offer. This meshing of different qualitative aspects is in simple terms the remit of the buyer. The business also has another requirement of product, a quantitative one – to make acceptable financial returns. The second role therefore is to be a wealth creator; generating profitable sales levels within the budgetary limits set for the life of the season concerned. The management of these quantitative aspects of the product range lies within the remit of the merchandiser.

BALANCED PRODUCT RANGES

As the establishment of a product range that can best communicate the mix of influences that have gone into its creation is the overriding principle behind the buying role, it is worth giving this point further practical thought. The sum of the qualitative role of product is 'to be a problem solver' (De Chernotony and McDonald 2003: 4) and must satisfy the consumer's particular need that motivated them to shop. A little black dress for a cocktail party, a pair of tights to replace a laddered pair, or a simple white blouse to match any number of skirts and trousers already in a wardrobe, a product range must offer an easily understandable set of solutions, the sum of which equal or exceed the consumer's identified need. For fashion retailers this presents difficulties; fashion is time-constrained, the life cycle of trends can be short and seasons are measured in weeks or months rather than years. A fashion range has a small window of opportunity to tempt consumers and once closed its role is at an end. The range has to be able to communicate to consumers easily and effectively.

Varley emphasizes this point by asserting that 'retailers capture their customers' interest by the nature of their product range' (Varley 2001: 9) and goes on to discuss the differing elements which add value to the customer experience, stressing diversity within product ranges. This is the key creative role of product – to be a suitable mix of product types, prices and trend to communicate and entice a broad range of consumers; in so doing, acting as a solver of their fashion problems.

Understanding that diversity and so creating product ranges that are an effective route to communication comes from using a hierarchy system of attributes that can be applied to products based on their problem-solving capabilities. Attributes have become a vital tool in identifying the correct composition of a product range to match identified needs of the target customer. One such example is the fashionability attribute. This determines different rankings of fashion interpretation so that, when constructing a range, the buyer will ensure it comprises a suitable mix of fashionabilities which reflects the positioning of their business. As with most aspects of product management, different businesses use different names to describe the fashionability attributes, but Table 2.1 provides a three-type example.

The correct mix of each will vary by retailer and consumer types targeted. High-street chains such as Gap, Next and Primark would likely target a greater percentage mix of core basic and fashion products as their customers' needs are simple and

Table 2.1 *Examples of fashionability attributes*

Fashionability	Definition	Product example
Core basic	Non-trend-led and has wide customer appeal and sales volume	Basic T-shirt
Fashion	Product that interprets current trends for a target customer	T-shirt with trend-led trim
High fashion	Directional trend product ranged often for fashion credibility	Laser-cut T-shirt with slogan

easy-to-understand products. A more fashion-forward business such as a luxury or premium brand would place a greater emphasis on fashion and high fashion products as their target customer need is to purchase of the moment prestige fashion within their shopping need.

A second example is the use of a price architecture attribute to plan a diverse mix of price points within a range. Table 2.2 gives an example of possible pricing structures using a system known as good, better and best pricing. Again the correct mix will depend on the business model and target customer type.

Table 2.2 *Examples of pricing attributes*

Price	Definition	Product example
Good	Opening price points of the range. Competitive pricing	Basic T-shirt
Better	Mid-price points of the range to reflect trend and design	T-shirt with trend-led trim
Best	Top price points of the range to reflect directional product	Laser-cut T-shirt with slogan

The use of hierarchy planning to construct product ranges allows buyers to offer a mix of style/colours and prices enabling the range to satisfy the widest range of potential problems for the customer – a core basic white T-shirt that has many end uses at a good price can be matched with a fashion pair of jeans or skirt to be worn on separate occasions. In doing this, the range becomes versatile and the customer is given options with which to use the style/colours available. Each option will be unique in its combination of qualitative characteristics, commercial strength and thus place in the range.

These two attribute examples are the tip of the iceberg; there are many more possible routes to matching the product to the overall problem-solving needs of the customer. Attributes such as end use (what the product will be used for – for example: everyday use, occasion wear or work wear) or fashion story (the fashion trend reflected in the option) are two further examples. Whichever attribute is used, linking them to a perception of the target customer and their needs puts a significant emphasis on the buyer's role and activities to deliver balanced product ranges.

FOCUS POINT 2.1: THE ROLE OF PRODUCT – THE USE OF ATTRIBUTES

With the development of powerful information technology, the ability to understand product performance and how each option contributes to business success or failure has been facilitated by the development of management information systems (MIS). Within the retail context, MIS allow the capture of product data at the point of sale and this in turn allows retailers to improve their stock inventories by reporting sales and stock data against various defined attributes that are applied to each product record as it is created. For B&M this has meant a far wider range of analysis possibilities to enable better and more accurate planning and trading decisions.

In the recent past, product analysis centered on simple attributes such as product type, colour, size and location of stock. While useful, if one considers the role of product to be a problemsolver for a customer, the limited value of these attributes becomes clear. To know if a product is fulfilling its role, buyers need to know if the presumptions made about its strengths translate into sales evenly achieving a balance across the product range. The ability to attach numerous attribute codes against products meant that any number of questions could now be posed about the range during the planning process to ensure the required balance of product; and once in store, comparisons could be made between that plan and actual selling results.

Over time, a number of proprietary software solutions have been developed to bring attribute planning to B&M. Central to the workings of these is the defining of suitable product attributes that will allow targeted data mining of product performance. Attributes such as fashionability, customer profile, product themes and stories are often used, but as retail business models have diversified, so too have the attributes used. One such attribute is end use. The end use attribute is increasingly favoured by retailers such as Debenhams, as its puts the problem-solving role of product at the centre of analysis through defining which option in the range will provide which problem-solving end use to its customers. Such end uses could be functional – such as raincoat and occasion coat – as opposed to coats or cultural such as smart career wear versus the wonderful up-to-a-mile wear, meaning leisure wear in which to pop to the shops or go to the gym.

Activity: Review a product range in several stores and identify the problem-solving role played by each option. Define in your mind the attributes you would use to best analyse performance.

CASE STUDY 2.1: WONDERBRA – FROM CORE BASIC TO FASHION

By 1992, after 27 years of trading in the UK market, the Wonderbra was a permanent if unspectacular product within most lingerie departments of any credible department store or specialist retailer. The Wonderbra was manufactured under licence by Leighton Buzzard-based Gossard, while in its North America home it was still manufactured by its creator Canadelle, in turn owned by the Sara Lee corporation. The Wonderbra was marketed as such because, through detailed engineering, 44 individual components and commercial intuition, it was a push-up plunge bra that created a fabulous cleavage, enhancing those that existed and creating new ones for those whom nature had otherwise endowed.

Despite a number of differing versions of bras being manufactured under the brand name of Wonderbra over the years, by 1992 style 1,300, a deep plunge laced push-up design, was the core piece that had entrenched itself on the shelves of UK retailers. Its functional problem-solving capacities remained, as did its USP. However, fashion trends had moved on, cheaper alternatives has emerged in the form of own-label ranges such as Presence for Debenhams and the Marks & Spencer lingerie juggernaut which continued to be the nation's favourite destination for its lingerie needs. Offered in standard underwear colours, the Wonderbra was a true core basic product. Steady regular demand that changed little was matched with steady re-orders from retailer to Gossard. Trends came and went but the 1,300 never changed. It had a small following who knew its secret well.

In 1992 everything changed and a revolution in the fashionability of the Wonderbra occurred which was to lead to a gargantuan battle for business control of the Wonderbra and its market. Having fallen out of fashion as clothing became less structured over the course of the 1960s, structure had re-emerged with the power dressing of the later 1980s and early 1990s. Fashion magazines such as *Vogue* picked up on the trend, leaving the reader fully aware that visible cleavage was back. Cultural icons such as Kylie Minogue and Kate Moss were soon devotees of the brand. Kate Moss was quoted as saying in 1994, 'I've got a couple of those Gossard Wonderbra's. They are so brilliant, I swear, even I get cleavage with them' (Baltimore Sun 1994).

The fortunes of the Wonderbra changed almost overnight. Sales rose and rose, quadrupling in a two-year period. Major department stores vied for dominance to cash in on demand. Debenhams emerged as an early winner in the battle and was so confident that it had captured the market that it chose to discount the Wonderbra to maximize sales volumes, much to the anger of competitors House of Fraser and John Lewis. Before long, new Wonderbra products emerged: the balcony bra, options in the jewel colours of red, purple and green that reflected current trends were ranged. The Wonderbra had made its transition from core basic to fashion style effortlessly.

The story did not end there. The UK licence for the Wonderbra expired in 1994 and Gossard lost out to Playtex in the business battle for the brand. Despite Gossard fighting back with its new Ultrabra, the Playtex team took the product on to new height; the Hello Boys advertising campaign, the development of the product into a brand and – possibly most important – business longevity.

Activity: Visit any fashion retailer. Assess the product range and define which products are core basic, fashion and high fashion.

BALANCED BUDGETS

No matter how unique and balanced a product range is, it must also support a second role of creating wealth for the business. To navigate towards this, all businesses operate within financial budgets that shape and direct the buyer to ensure that balanced ranges are also profitable ones. The ultimate responsibility for accurate budgeting lies with the finance team, who ensure that the businesses finances are transparent, accurate and follow all legal accounting requirements. Within financial budgeting there are two separate ledgers to do this. All income, expenses and profits are recorded and managed through a profit and loss (P&L) account, while the business records its financial assets, liabilities and worth within a separate balance sheet. Tables 2.3 and 2.4 give generic examples of each.

Table 2.3 *A profit and loss account example*

Sales turnover	£100,000
Cost of goods sold	£43,000
Trading profit	£57,000
Overheads costs	£42,000
Operating profit	£15,000
Interest and tax	£5,000
Net profit	£10,000

Table 2.4 *A balance sheet example*

Assets	
- Debtors	£5,000
- Cash	£10,000
- Stock	£40,000
- Other assets	£5,000
Total assets	£60,000
Liabilities	
- Creditors	£20,000
- Borrowing	£15,000
- Equity	£15,000
- Other liabilities	£5,000
Total liabilities	£55,000
Net worth	£5,000

If one reviews the P&L and balance sheet, the quantitative elements of the role of product within wealth creation becomes clear. The sale of product and associated costs such as supplier costs, markdown activity and stock loss all drive fashion retailers' gross trading profits. These in turn are used to support their overheads such as salaries, store and marketing costs. While on the balance sheet, the stock owned – or in other words, product that has been bought but is yet to be sold – sits as a valuable asset of the business.

The implication is that the management of the financial capabilities of a product range directly influences business success and so is equally important to get right as fashion credibility and range balance. This point raises a further one: it would be wrong to dismiss the relevance of a companywide finance team in the budgeting process, as ultimately they are the experts in managing P&L accounts and balance sheets. They are also the guardians of the debts routinely taken out to fund the cost of purchasing product, and without their approval no product range would be bought. However, the natural remoteness of the finance team from the commercial realities of the market requires a quantitative financial dimension within product management to at least influence, and at most direct, the shape of relevant product budgets. To ensure that product budgeting decisions are appropriate and achievable within the context of prevailing trends and market conditions, that influence and activity are provided by a third role: the merchandiser.

The question that remains to be answered at this point is what business budgets within the P&L and balance sheet fall within the influence of the merchandiser? Taking the P&L first, they are:

- Sales turnover – the cash value of monies paid by the customer for product that goes into the business bank account. For example, one shirt sold for £50 would represent £50 cash value paid to the business.
- Cost of sales data that record the costs incurred in generating the sale of product. There are two costs that are common to all retail business types:
  - Intake margin percentage – the budget between the cost and selling prices of product. This difference allows the business to work out the cost of purchasing product to sell to its consumers and to add a suitable profit margin to pay for overheads.
  - Markdown spend – the cash cost of reducing selling prices to achieve a sale. For example, if the £50 shirt were reduced by 50 per cent, every shirt sold would register a cash sales turnover of £25 but in doing so would also incur a cash markdown cost of £25 to the business.

In addition to the examples above, some businesses will also include stock loss (the cost of theft, misplaced stock) and supplier discounts (rebates for late deliveries, long-term incentive schemes).

Within the planning of a balance sheet, there is one budget to influence – stock budgets. The stock of product that a fashion business owns presents both an asset and a liability, and so budgeting for a suitable amount to hold at any point within a season is important.

- Stock level – the value of stock owned by the business at the end of the financial period.

CASE STUDY 2.2: MARKS & SPENCER – HOW POOR PRODUCT PLANNING CAN AFFECT FINANCIAL PERFORMANCE

In April 2012, in the midst of a protracted retail recession, one of the UK's largest and most influential retailers, Marks & Spencer reported to the city its sales for the fourth quarter of its financial year. Since the late 1990s, the business had developed a reputation for having mixed fortunes with its financial results, and the 2012 set of results was disappointing. Headline like-for-like sales were down 0.7 per cent on the previous year, led by a poor performance within its womenswear category.

This result was, however, not the key headline that was reported in the financial and trade press. M&S chief executive Marc Bolland, in explaining the poor performance, admitted to a fundamental error in the businesses B&M function. *The Daily Telegraph* commented that 'It stocked up for a more downmarket, cash-strapped shopper than it needed to, so increasing its stock of lower-margin togs. But it failed to buy enough of the pricier stuff they really wanted – and then lacked a supply chain quick enough to react to the demand' (Daily Telegraph 2012).

As a result, the business failed to satisfy the demand from its customers. Examples were given of knitwear where sales of 100,000 units could have been as high as 300,000, and ballet pumps where actual sales of 10,000 units were dwarfed by demand for 17,000 units.

Bolland was quoted as saying that 'That was a miss in our merchandising planning. We were bang on-trend but we should have had a bit more of some of our lines' (City AM 2012).

Activity: Regularly review the business sections of broadsheet newspapers. Assess which fashion retailers are successful and which are not.

WORKING TOGETHER – BUYING AND MERCHANDISING

With two clear roles for product identified, the complexity of successful product management begins to take a strategic as well as operational context. Quite apart from the actual processes of product development, the product has to be profitable, on-trend and communicate to its target customers. There are also other less obvious complexities. As brands develop images and personalities, restrictions begin to be placed on the rules within which product range development can be carried out. Decisions such as display criteria within store, the mix of products or use of promotional markdown become more formal and influential within the planning and trading of product ranges.

As a result, modern B&M has the potential to confuse and jeopardize business fortunes. One can speculate about whether the early 21st-century troubles of the likes of Burberry through excessive use of its house check or the overexposed FCUK logo T-shirts of French Connection were caused by overambitious designers and buyers pushing to expand ideas beyond balance, or if in fact it was the merchandisers and financiers pushing to develop more of the safe easy winners within the product ranges. Or were they both at fault, neither listening to nor advising one another when the ranges created became imbalanced and uncompetitive?

Ensuring that both roles within the management of product have an equal influence, the process of range planning and trading is of paramount importance. The relationship between buyer and merchandiser is often likened to a marriage in which the two players work together to create their ranges. They will not always agree, but a good buyer and a good merchandiser will listen and influence each other every step of the way.

The creation of a fashion product range is therefore multiskilled, and the many decisions required within the process by both roles must be made in tandem with each other. This is important as neither role can deliver its remit without the other. A buyer, for example, cannot buy a range without a buying budget, and a merchandiser cannot define the size of a product range without knowing which trends will require development into a larger mix within the range. To be effective, a chain of activities is required that link the roles together to deliver a cohesive product offer to the customer that is consistently in line with their expectations and those of the business. This linkage of activities means that the buyer and merchandiser do not and cannot work independently of each other, and must fulfil their roles within the context of an orderly sequential process.

THE CONCEPT-TO-CARRIER BAG MODEL

It should not be a surprise that fusing buyer and merchandiser together into a process, taking initial product ideas for the season ahead and translating them into a range available within a retail environment is complex and broad in its activities. The co-ordination of matching product to a target market within the confines of a requirement to deliver profit requires organization and clarity as to how the differing activities work to link their thought processes and actions together.

There are many ways of doing this, dependent on the business model applied. A luxury business may, for instance, place a greater focus on design, fabric and trim sourcing whilst a high-street volume retailer such as Primark may focus on efficiency, logistics and supply management. No matter where individual businesses place their emphasis, all businesses will follow a sequential process around which a product range is created. This section presents one such process model which will articulate how the B&M roles contribute to the successful delivery of product.

There have been many simplified supply chain models devised to demonstrate the totality of the product management process. A 'concept-to-carrier bag' model used within this book is shown in Figure 2.1, which identifies ten sequential steps that take relevant product research to develop a product concept and turn that into a product range, available for sale to a target customer. In doing so, the model neatly demonstrates a generic process and so it is presented as a guide template to then further demonstrate the B&M roles and activities required within the process model. The concept-to-carrier bag model above is a visual representation of distinct activities which, if followed, turn product ideas into a physical garment available for sale in a retail outlet. By its design it is linear, and takes no account at this stage of how or when the activities or indeed the roles that are responsible for them are carried out (Table 2.5).

Within the model, one can see a flow of activities that starts with collating and sorting through a breadth of relevant fashion information to identify relevant facts that facilitate the concept and direction of the new range. With a direction decided, the model moves on to the practical interpretation of the concept through the development of product ranges, the sourcing of suppliers, manufacture and delivery of a physical range to the retailer. Beyond this, the model also identifies that the remit of B&M does not finish at that point, but moves on to the allocation of product to different markets, support for the range in the form of packaging,

Figure 2.1 *The ten sequential steps of the concept-to-carrier bag process model*

Table 2.5 *The definition of each process step within the concept-to-carrier bag model*

Concept-to-carrier bag activity	Definition
1. Research	Undertaking and collation of relevant fashion research
2. Concept	Creation of product range concept and design direction
3. Product development	Finalization of concept as a product range
4. Sourcing	Sourcing of suppliers and manufacturers for the range
5. Manufacturing	Manufacture of the product range
6. Shipping	Shipping and delivery of the product range
7. Warehousing	Receipt of the product range, its allocation to store and storage
8. Distribution	The process of delivering initial store allocations
9. Retail	Display, sale, promotion and stock replenishment
10. Carrier bag	Purchase of the product by a consumer

display collateral, product information, stock replenishment and price management. It ends with the sale of a product to a customer who has identified the product as their own personal problemsolver.

As useful as it is, the model presented here lacks a key element: the length of time it takes to be completed, and the process takes time from beginning to end. Take London Fashion Week (LFW) in September as an example.

The autumn LFW is part of the buying season for the following spring season. When buying new ranges, buyers must have formulated product ideas (qualitative) and have financial budgets for the new range (quantitative). Within the concept-to-carrier bag model, the research and concept activities that decide these product ideas and budgets must therefore occur in advance of September. Typically, these activities will begin as early as July.

With a July date as the starting point for the first activities in the concept-to-carrier bag model, it is possible then to create a timeline identifying a critical path to research, plan, source, deliver and sell a fashion range (Table 2.6).

For an autumn/winter season, the approximate timescales would be the same, beginning in December to January and concluding 12 months later (Table 2.7). Knowing the length of time that the process can take is important as both buyer and merchandiser must co-ordinate their activities to make sure the flow of decisions is in line with the product's critical path rather than their own. Putting the product at the centre of the decision-making process is sensible for several reasons:

- Different products will have different timescales within the concept-to-carrier bag process. An exclusive silk fabric with limited availability may take longer to source than griege cotton to be coloured at a later date.

Table 2.6 The concept-to-carrier bag process timings for a spring/summer season

Concept-to-carrier bag step	Definition	Approximate timing
1. Research	Undertaking and collation of relevant fashion research	July to August
2. Concept	Creation of product range concept and design direction	July to August
3. Product development	Finalization of concept as a product range	September
4. Sourcing	Sourcing of suppliers and manufacturers for the range	September
5. Manufacturing	Manufacture of the product range	October to December
6. Shipping	Shipping and delivery of the product range	October to December
7. Warehousing	Receipt of the product range, its allocation to store and storage	January
8. Distribution	The process of delivering initial store allocations	January
9. Retail	Display, sale, promotion and stock replenishment	February to July
10. Carrier bag	Purchase of the product by a consumer	February to July

Table 2.7 The concept-to-carrier bag process timings for an autumn/winter season

Concept-to-carrier bag step	Definition	Approximate timing
1. Research	Undertaking and collation of relevant fashion research	December to January
2. Concept	Creation of product range concept and design direction	December to January
3. Product development	Finalization of concept as a product range	February
4. Sourcing	Sourcing of suppliers and manufacturers for the range	February
5. Manufacturing	Manufacture of the product range	March to April
6. Shipping	Shipping and delivery of the product range	March to April
7. Warehousing	Receipt of the product range, its allocation to store and storage	May
8. Distribution	The process of delivering initial store allocations	May
9. Retail	Display, sale, promotion and stock replenishment	June to December
10. Carrier bag	Purchase of the product by a consumer	June to December

- Manufacturing of different products within the range will require co-ordination to ensure they can be delivered as one collection.
- Products will have different life cycles (when and for how long a product will be available). Core basics are likely to be available at all times, while fashion or high fashion styles will be phased in at different times over the course of the season.

In addition to these examples, the development of improved supply chains as discussed in Chapter 1 has meant that product can be phased into stores during a season; product decisions therefore can be made at different times within the total model. Multiple phasing approaches where product ranges are regularly replaced result in the buyer and merchandiser juggling multiple concept-to-carrier bag processes within an overall planning process. Table 2.8 demonstrates this for a two-product-phase season; for fast fashion, meanwhile, the model would become mind boggling in its potential size and complexity.

AN INTRODUCTION TO THE BUYER AND MERCHANDISER ROLES

Having established an overview of the process and the order in which it is carried out, the concept-to-carrier bag model can be further interrogated to summarize the buyer and merchandiser roles within it. These are presented within Tables 2.9 and 2.10 which provide a summary description of the activities undertaken at each stage of the model. A more detailed review follows in Chapter 3.

Table 2.8 An example of a two-phase concept-to-carrier bag model

Concept-to-carrier bag step	Definition	Phase 1 approximate timing	Phase 2 approximate timing
1. Research	Undertaking and collation of relevant fashion research	July to August	November to December
2. Concept	Creation of product range concept and design direction	July to August	November to December
3. Product development	Finalization of concept as a product range	September	January
4. Sourcing	Sourcing of suppliers and manufacturers for the range	September	January
5. Manufacturing	Manufacture of the product range	October	February
6. Shipping	Shipping and delivery of the product range	October	February
7. Warehousing	Receipt of the product range, its allocation to store and storage	November	March
8. Distribution	The process of delivering initial store allocations	November	March
9. Retail	Display, sale, promotion and stock replenishment	December to March	April to July
10. Carrier bag	Purchase of the product by a consumer	December to March	April to July

What emerges from the summaries is that both roles have relevance throughout the process and at each stage their activities support, inform or direct the other in the completion of their own tasks. A second point is the similarity in tasks; taking the research step as an example, the research process is the same: the review of past and present information, but the focus of the research is different. For the buyer, the focus is on the information needed to make qualitative product decisions, while for the merchandiser their focus is on the quantitative ones; this delineation of roles is evident throughout the summaries presented. There is also commonality in the delivery of the activities throughout – negotiations with key contacts, liaison with various common or role-specific stakeholders, and towards the end of the season the joint learning by review and adjustments to ideas and preconceptions about customers, trends and initial product concepts.

Product management and its associated activities ultimately rely on the effectiveness of the relationship between the two roles to engage in dialogue to create a product range in which they have each had an appropriate level of input. That dialogue requires effort and an understanding of the rationale for each other's role, and a willingness to listen and debate as much as having a particular technical skill or personality trait.

The complementary nature of the two roles results in a planning approach that is thorough but also questioning. The different approaches and skill sets means that each segment of the decision-making process has an equilibrium between buyer and

Table 2.9 *The buyer activities of the concept-to-carrier bag model*

Concept-to-carrier bag step	Definition	Buyer activities
1. Research	Undertaking and collation of relevant fashion research	Review of past ranges, competitors, future product and cultural trends
2. Concept	Creation of product range concept and design direction	Articulation of research into a product concept, mood boards and product range ideas
3. Product development	Finalization of concept as a product range	Creation of option range plans, product specifications and price strategies
4. Sourcing	Sourcing of suppliers and manufacturers for the range	Negotiation and agreement with suppliers to produce products within cost and quality requirements
5. Manufacturing	Manufacture of the product range	The oversight of the creation of samples and bulk production
6. Shipping	Shipping and delivery of the product range	Liaison with suppliers to finalize product production and approve final production samples to allow shipment
7. Warehousing	Receipt of the product range, its allocation to store and storage	Final review of received product and authority to either release to allocation or return to supplier
8. Distribution	The process of delivering initial store allocations	Provision to retail stores of product information, training or look books for the season
9. Retail	Display, sale, promotion and stock replenishment	Review of current ranges, competitors and trends to make necessary changes to future production for the season
10. Carrier bag	Purchase of the product by a consumer	End of the successful season with the sale of the last unit of the range

merchandiser that has to be achieved before the next activity can be started. As both roles are clearly intertwined and cannot function fully without the other, it seems more appropriate to find a single definition for both that reflects the importance attached to the role of product, which after all provides the physical manifestation of a brand's personality and the route to creating sustained wealth for its many stakeholders.

Table 2.10 *The merchandiser activities of the concept-to-carrier bag model*

Concept-to-carrier bag step	Definition	Merchandiser activities
1. Research	Undertaking and collation of relevant fashion research	Review of past ranges, competitors, future product and economic trends
2. Concept	Creation of product range concept and design direction	Articulation of research into a financial budgets and open to buy budgets
3. Product development	Finalization of concept as a product range	Creation of option range plans and unit buys within open to buy budgets
4. Sourcing	Sourcing of suppliers and manufacturers for the range	Negotiation and agreement with suppliers to produce products within delivery phasing budgets
5. Manufacturing	Manufacture of the product range	Oversight of the status of orders compared to delivery phasing budgets
6. Shipping	Shipping and delivery of the product range	Liaison with the buyer to finalize product production and to allow shipment
7. Warehousing	Receipt of the product range, its allocation to store and storage	Creation of allocation plans for the product to be distributed to stores
8. Distribution	The process of delivering initial store allocations	Oversight of the authority to allocate product to stores and the creation of replenishment plans
9. Retail	Display, sale, promotion and stock replenishment	Review of current ranges, competitors and trends to make necessary changes to future production for the season
10. Carrier bag	Purchase of the product by a consumer	End of the successful season with the sale of the last unit of the range

Using the discussions within this chapter, the core messages are that the components of the B&M roles out of which any definition must come are:

- Strategic – the roles have a direct influence on achieving a fashion business strategy;
- Creative – they plan and create the qualitative characteristics of a physical product;
- Financial – they plan and create the quantitative characteristics of a physical product;
- Operational – they engage in operational activities to deliver, sell and trade a product.

Taking the above together, the combined role of B&M defined for the purposes of this book is:

'A role that connects the creative and financial product requirements of a fashion brand through strategic range planning and operational trading that optimizes a fashion business opportunity.'

It is with this overall definition of the B&M function that the next chapter will review the buyer role and others and assess their interaction with the merchandiser in their role.

FOCUS POINT 2.2: THE BUYING CYCLE AND DIFFERENT BUSINESS MODELS

The concept-to-carrier bag model defines a linear process of taking the output of relevant research and turning it into a delivered product available to purchase through a retail channel. However, like the myriad of other retail business models, while useful for exemplifying the buying cycle process, it is not definitive. The question therefore remains: Is there a definitive process that is followed? In some ways there is and in some not. The intellectual process will be broadly the same and follow the same logic as the process presented in this chapter, as after all the concept of B&M to turn capital into product to retail and so turn back into a higher valued capital is common across all business models. Where the differences in approaches emerge is in the execution of the physical process.

Within a typical own-label buying cycle, the B&M department will own the entire planning process and buy in the skills involved in the manufacture of product from the suppliers from whom they will source product. In comparison, wholesale brands' B&M departments will be presented with finished collections from which products to be ranged are selected, meaning little or no involvement within the sourcing and manufacture of the ranges that they sell within their stores. Different again are vertical fashion businesses which will own the skills and activities of manufacture in-house.

What will be common across all business models is the focus on the outputs of the various buying cycles employed. The product that results from the buying cycle must reflect the brand and its personality; the fabrics and trim-sourcing process in a luxury buying cycle is likely to be more complex and time-consuming than that of a high-street supermarket. However, perhaps the single biggest focus within the buying cycle is time; the advent of fast fashion and the success of brands like Zara is testament to the importance of speed of supply within fashion retailing and the ground-breaking buying cycles that they possess.

The fast fashion model owes much of its principles to that of Quick Response (QR) supply chain strategies; developed to remove time thus inefficiency from the manufacturing process of US textile businesses. Its principles expanded into the fast fashion concept to remove excessive time from the entire buying cycle from initial planning through to the sale of the last garment in the product range. Tactics to achieve this include the integration of new technologies, reductions in the presumed life cycles of product ranges, the recycling of silhouettes throughout a season and the simplification of the manufacturing process to enable entry to a new season with only small amounts of buying budgets spent, allowing multiple buying cycles throughout a season rather than just relying on one.

Activity: Design a fast fashion concept-to-carrier bag process with 13 phases, and assess how much shorter each step in the concept-to-carrier bag process becomes compared to the introductory model of this chapter.

SUMMARY

The rationale for this chapter has centred on introducing concepts that inform the decision-making process of the merchandiser that will be then be demonstrated in the second part of this book. By discussing the conflicting nature of fashion and business and emphasizing twinned qualitative and quantitative characteristics, the first evidence of separating the B&M function into the distinct roles of buyer and merchandiser has been established. The concept-to-carrier bag model has shown that through an ordered process, both roles are equally critical throughout product management, relying on each one's different focuses to make relevant and balanced product decisions.

What is still required is a fuller review of the roles within the context of the concept-to-carrier bag process to identify suitable job descriptions for both players. This will be the subject of Chapter 3.

SELF-DIRECTED STUDY

1. Conduct a thorough competitive shop of a fashion retailer's product range. Understand how you think the range has been put together. Review each option and define what you think the fashionability, end use and price attributes are. Is there too much or too little of a specific attribute type? Or is it a balanced range?
2. Consider the concept-to-carrier bag model. How might it be varied for an e-retail business?
3. Think about the simple P&L model described above. Visit a store that is promoting its product by using markdown. Count the number of units on display of several marked-down products. Then:
   - calculate the value of the stock to the business at its original selling price;
   - calculate the value of the stock at the reduced selling price;
   - calculate the value difference between the two and identify the markdown cost to the business;
   - repeat for several other products that have different markdown offers and assess the scale of the loss of profit to the business of each one.

Further Reading

De Chernatony, L and McDonald, M (2003) *Creating Powerful Brands 3rd ed.* Oxford: Elsevier

Jackson, T and Shaw, D (2001) *Mastering Fashion Buying and Merchandising Management.* Basingstoke: Macmillan

Varley, R (2001) *Retail Product Management.* London: Routledge

Bibliography

De Chernatony, L. and McDonald, M. (2003) *Creating Powerful Brands 3rd ed.* Oxford: Elsevier

Jefford, K. (2012) *Marks and Spencer sales hit by stock shortages.* City AM [Internet]. Available from http://www.cityam.com/article/marks-spencer-sales-hit-shortage-stock [Accessed 20th April 2014]

Marbella, J. (1994) *Popular bras boost the not-so-savage breast.* The Baltimore Sun [Internet]. Available from http://articles.baltimoresun.com/1994-05-13/features/1994133183_1_wonderbra-push-kate-moss [Accessed 20th January 2014]

Oxford English Dictionary (2013) *The Oxford English Dictionary.* Oxford: Oxford University Press

Osborne, A. (2012) *Marks & Spencer Chief Marc Bolland may need to prepare for humble pie next Valentine's Day.* Daily Telegraph [Internet]. Available from http://www.telegraph.co.uk/finance/comment/alistair-osborne/9210318/Marks-and-Spencer-chief-Marc-Bolland-may-need-to-prepare-for-humble-pie-next-Valentines-Day.html [Accessed 20th January 2014]

Varley, R. (2001) *Retail Product Management.* London: Routledge

3 The Roles of Buyer and Merchandiser

INTENDED LEARNING OUTCOMES

1. A review of the buyer role within the concept-to-carrier bag model.
2. An introductory understanding of the B&M roles within the concept-to-carrier bag model.
3. An appreciation of the differing skill sets of the B&M roles.
4. Knowledge of generic job descriptions for the B&M roles.

INTRODUCTION

The concept-to-carrier bag model discussed in Chapter 2 demonstrated sequential B&M processes, around which a top level summary of the roles of B&M was defined. This chapter reviews the detail of the two roles, provides example job descriptions and, in the case of the merchandiser, the subject of this book, two current merchandisers present a short review of their own individual impressions of the jobs they do.

One theme that has been consistent so far is that there is no one single type of fashion retail business, product range or B&M process. Not surprisingly, this means that there is no single method by which buyers or merchandisers undertake their roles. The contents of this chapter are by necessity generic, to provide knowledge of the principles of the roles which can be interpreted in different ways throughout the industry.

The roles will be discussed in line with the concept-to-carrier bag process using an own-label environment as its theme. Branded B&M follows a similar path for much of the process and a short section at the end of the review will discuss key differences between the two.

BUYING AND MERCHANDISING REVIEW

At the end of Chapter 2 the B&M function was defined as being:

A role that connects the creative and financial product requirements of a fashion brand through strategic range planning and operational trading that optimizes a fashion business opportunity

This definition puts B&M at the heart of a fashion retail business, having the power to affect its strategic direction via its product ranges, whilst the aggression with which those ranges are worked once in store impacts the company's day-to-day operations. This dual impact is known within B&M as planning and trading, and, as the review of the concept-to-carrier bag process below shows, both feed from one another into in a continuous cycle of planning a range, trading it and then using the knowledge gained to influence future planning and trading.

This dual approach also makes the buyers and merchandisers very versatile within their roles; over time their experiences turn them into much sought after, multi-skilled retail professionals able to influence a business's strategic direction. There is invariably a place for B&M professionals amongst the board of directors, with a high prevalence of CEOs, such as Stuart Rose, Belinda Earl or Jane Shepherdson, for whom B&M was their forte.

THE ROLE OF THE FASHION BUYER

Despite this book focusing on the merchandiser, it is useful to present a short review of the buyer's activities to draw comparisons between the two, and so justify the rationale for a distinct merchandiser role. Definitions of the role of the fashion buyer have been discussed many times. Jackson and Shaw assert that the role is 'to ensure that the products bought for sale by the retailer are appropriate for the target market and can sell in sufficient quantities to achieve the profit margin expected by the business' (Jackson and Shaw 2001: 13). They place the emphasis of the role very clearly on three elements:

- product range creation
- within an appropriate target market
- that will deliver commercial strength.

Goworek concurs, writing that fashion buyers are 'responsible for overseeing the development of a range of products aimed at a specific type of customer and price bracket' (Goworek 2007: 5). Finally, Varley defines the buyer as being 'more concerned with the qualitative side of buying' (Varley 2001: 23). Comparisons of these definitions with the summary of the buyer in Chapter 2 allows us to show in Table 3.1 a summary of how these relate to the concept-to-carrier bag model in practical terms.

- Research – The buyer, and where appropriate their designer, undertake research activities prior to making decisions about the product range. This research has five elements to it:
  - A review of the previous season's range to identify which product categories, styles, colours and price points sold well and which were unsuccessful. This enables the buyer to understand strengths and weaknesses of past ranges, but also the direction of the business and its target customers.

Table 3.1 *The summary activities of the buyer.*

Concept-to-carrier bag step	Definition	Buyer activities
1. Research	Undertaking and collation of relevant fashion research	Review of past ranges, competitors, future product and cultural trends
2. Concept	Creation of product range concept and design direction	Articulation of research into a product concept, mood boards and product range ideas
3. Product development	Finalization of concept as a product range	Creation of option range plans, product specifications and price strategies
4. Sourcing	Sourcing of suppliers and manufacturers for the range	Negotiation and agreement with suppliers to produce products within cost and quality requirements
5. Manufacturing	Manufacture of the product range	Oversight of the creation of samples and bulk production
6. Shipping	Shipping and delivery of the product range	Liaison with suppliers to finalize product production and approve final production samples to allow shipment
7. Warehousing	Receipt of the product range, and its allocation to store and storage	Final review of received product and authority to either release to allocation or return to supplier
8. Distribution	Delivering initial store allocations	Provision to retail stores of product information, training or look books for the season
9. Retail	Display, sale, promotion and stock replenishment	Review of current ranges, competitors and trends to make necessary changes to future production for the season
10. Carrier bag	Purchase of the product by a consumer	End of the successful season with the sale of the last unit of the range

- A review of competitor product offers to build up a picture of their strengths and weaknesses and identify potential gaps in the market. This review goes beyond direct competitors; directional shopping trips to key retail locations such as New York or Milan are often undertaken.
- Knowledge of the trends emerging from cool hunters, haute couture fashion brands and editorials all help to build up ideas of what the world that surrounds the business is doing, so identifying what is either currently, or likely to be, in demand.
- Identification of key aspects of the target customer's life such as their demographic, personal likes, dislikes, attitudes and lifestyle allows a portrait to emerge of who they are, how they live, and their attitude to fashion.

- Awareness of macro market trends such as overall economic conditions, future events – e.g. cultural, sporting or national – and announced plans of competitor activity will all have a potential impact on future demand.
- Concept – Once the research process is completed, the buyer will use the information gathered to formulate a concept around which product ranges can be built:
    - The range concept includes an interpretation of relevant trends into mood boards to capture the inspiration behind the product range.
    - The identification of range stories or themes that product ranges will be built around. This will include initial ideas of price point strategies, colour palettes, key product types and shapes for the season.
    - The possible purchase of example products from directional shopping trips for design inspiration.
- Product development – At this point the buyer, alongside the merchandiser, develops the range concept into an initial range plan. Range plans vary in scope, but will generally list all the options to be ranged and against each one list:
    - an option description (often with sketch and fabric swatch attached);
    - the trend or theme that it belongs to
    - the fashionability level of the option (core basic, fashion or high fashion)
    - supplier name and country of origin
    - cost and selling prices and resultant intake margin percentage
    - number of stores that the option will be ranged within
    - unit buys for each option and calculated cost and selling values.

This initial range plan will in turn evolve and change shape over the course of this planning stage as ideas are developed and budgets decided. Some early product ideas will be developed and grow in importance, while others may be discarded. As the process moves on, prototype designs are created and suppliers will submit mock-up samples, fabrications, trims, linings, cost prices, shipping details and delivery dates for approval by the buyer.

- Sourcing and manufacture – The buying role throughout the sourcing process is one of negotiation and direction. To ensure that delivered options match the technical and aesthetic concept of the range, the buyer, in conjunction with technical support from the quality assurance team, will:
    - oversee fabric and trim testing (for quality and performance tests), colour testing (for colour fastness and colour matching), garment labelling approval, size and fit assessments. At each stage of the manufacture process, prototype garments to pre-production samples (to check make and components), post-production samples (to check the final manufactured garment) will require approval to ensure the supplier has manufactured products to agreed designs, and that they adhere to various legal and trading requirements placed on the retailer
    - negotiate payment terms, cost prices and delivery dates that are in line with margin and stock-phasing budgets and company policies
    - raise purchase orders to confirm all product details, size ratios and delivery terms.

- Shipping and warehousing – With the manufacture process completed and the product compliant with technical, aesthetic and trading concept, the product can be shipped and delivered:
  - In agreement with the merchandiser, authorise shipment of the product from factory, via its port of origin, to the retailer's warehouse or distribution centre.
  - Once received into the warehouse or distribution centre, the buyer will, in conjunction with quality-assurance personnel, review the delivered product. This enables any quality issues or damage while in transit to be spotted and corrective action taken. This could include an order cancellation should the damages be thought unsalvageable, or a negotiated in cost price.
- Distribution and retail – Once checked, the product is allocated to stores (physical or online), becoming the responsibility of the marketing and retail teams to promote and maximize selling potential. The buyer contributes to this by:
  - providing product information, samples for the press office, visual merchandising guidelines, look books, and, if necessary, facilitating the provision of product training
  - constantly reviewing the performance of the product range and where necessary liaising with suppliers to manufacture repeat orders of options which sell well, cancelling or reducing the units supplied of options that have yet to be delivered should sales of similar options be poor
  - discussing with the merchandiser suitable markdown policies for the end-of-season sale (ESS), where appropriate seeking markdown funding from suppliers.
- Carrier bag – As the products are sold at the end of the season, the buyer will review the entire process by:
  - assessing the product range performance to make any required immediate changes to the next season's range plans
  - reviewing supplier performance to assess quality, delivery performance and ethics within the manufacturing process
  - review feedback from stores and customers to influence future product range direction.

THE SKILL SET OF GOOD FASHION BUYERS

To deliver a targeted product range clearly requires various skills. First, the buyer must understand the product development process, the influence of fashion and cultural trends on product ranging, and have the ability to interpret these into balanced ranges for a particular target market. Second, they must be able to articulate this creativity through persuasion and negotiation with internal and external stakeholders to ensure all aspects of the planning and trading process are completed. Third, the buyer must be flexible and resilient to manage the inevitable changes of mind and unforeseen problems that occur. These could include a supplier not being able to manufacture a particular product at the cost price requested, an emerging trend requiring that a range's creative direction be amended, or the finance director requiring cost savings which require a change to budgets.

The buyer's skill set centres on their knowledge and understanding of product and creativity; however, they must also be analytical in order to understand the impact of their decisions on the commercial strength of a business, and possess unlimited enthusiasm and passion for their industry.

FASHION MERCHANDISING – THE RATIONALE FOR THE ROLE

The merchandiser role in working alongside the buyer is relevant throughout the concept-to-carrier bag process and has evolved since the late 20th century to fulfil a unique activity within fashion retail by offering:

- an involvement with and understanding of fashion, its trends and influences
- a financially and detail-minded approach to the product creation process.

The role can be described at its core as being like a bridge, connecting not two banks of a river, but the two disciplines of buying and financial management. Buyers need time to develop new and exciting product ranges. This naturally means that they are busy within their roles focusing on trends and product development and so lack focus on the logistical and financial specialisms required within the planning process. In many businesses the finance director will carry out this duty; however, with their focus on P&L accounts and balance sheets, they are often not well placed to understanding the priorities and language of product management. By setting and influencing the financial parameters of the product range, the merchandiser can ensure that product-ranging decisions make commercial sense, and articulate to the finance director why this is the case. This helps prevent the setting of budgets based on quantitative logic and past seasons' experience only, rather than forward-looking trends and competitive reality.

The merchandiser role is of particular benefit in large complex businesses. In small retailers where ease of communication and a smaller infrastructure will mean that the product range and finance decisions can be made easily, the role of the merchandiser can be subsumed between the buyer and finance. In larger complex businesses where communication and decision making are more remote, the business case for the merchandiser as a bridge role becomes compelling (see Figure 3.1).

The merchandiser therefore has a clear complementary role to the buyer. Neither can function without the other where the business size dictates that both roles are required. In large-volume businesses such as Debenhams, the merchandising role is very much on an equal footing with the buying function due to its strong influence in stock management. In others, such as design-led luxury brands, the role could be argued as being secondary to the buyer, as those businesses trade on unique ideas and designs that could defy logic and sense. However, the rationale of the role rests on the presumption that it works alongside the buyer in a fashion business and they work together to create and develop fashion product ranges.

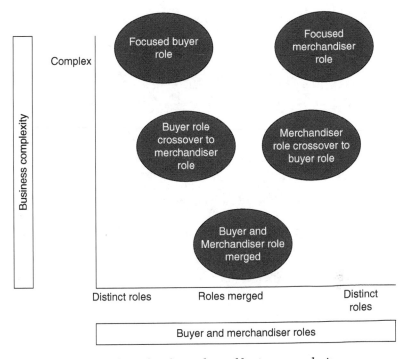

Figure 3.1 *The buyer and merchandiser roles and business complexity*

THE ROLE OF THE FASHION MERCHANDISER

As with the outline of the buyer role, the concept-to-carrier bag process allows details of the merchandiser role and its activities to be developed and its personality traits and natural skill set identified. Again, academics have provided differing definitions of the role. Jackson and Shaw describe it as being 'total process of stock management' (Jackson and Shaw 2001: 26) while the Goworek definition is 'responsible for setting the financial parameters of a garment range' (Goworek 2007: 9). Varley defines merchandising as being 'concerned with the quantitative aspects of buying, and [...] usually responsible for estimating sales, planning deliveries and distribution of goods to the stores' (Varley 2001: 25).

Interestingly, there is less common ground within these three definitions to pull together a consistent theme. The definitions feel narrow, leaving the reader with unanswered questions; for example, the Jackson and Shaw one suggests a process that is relevant throughout a concept-to-carrier bag model but does not elaborate beyond stock management. Goworek meanwhile, suggests a much more narrowly focused role, while the Varley definition is the fullest, but that too feels limited as it makes no definitive reference to product.

As with the buyer role, Chapter 2 was able to describe the merchandiser activities within the concept-to-carrier bag (see Table 3.2) and this section will build upon this initial description and give a fuller review of the role. As it does so, what

Table 3.2 *The summary activities of the merchandiser*

Concept-to-carrier bag step	Definition	Merchandiser activities
1. Research	Undertaking and collation of relevant fashion research	Review of past ranges, competitors, future product and economic trends
2. Concept	Creation of product range concept and design direction	Articulation of research into a financial budgets and open to buy budgets
3. Product development	Finalization of concept as a product range	Creation of option range plans and unit buys within open to buy budgets
4. Sourcing	Sourcing of suppliers and manufacturers for the range	Negotiation and agreement with suppliers to produce products within delivery phasing budgets
5. Manufacturing	Manufacture of the product range	Oversight of the status of orders compared to delivery phasing budgets
6. Shipping	Shipping and delivery of the product range	Liaison with the buyer to finalise product production and to allow shipment
7. Warehousing	Receipt of the product range, its allocation to store and storage	Creation of allocation plans for the product to be distributed to stores
8. Distribution	Delivering initial store allocations	Oversight of the authority to allocate product to stores and the creation of replenishment plans
9. Retail	Display, sale, promotion and stock replenishment	Review of current ranges, competitors and trends to make necessary changes to future production for the season
10. Carrier bag	Purchase of the product by a consumer	End of the successful season with the sale of the last unit of the range

becomes clear is that product is central to the merchandiser role, something that is not explicit in the definitions so far presented.

- Research – The research and analysis undertaken by the merchandiser analysis differs not in approach but in its focus to that of the buyer. It has four main elements:
  - Initially, research takes the form of a thorough interrogation of the existing product range's financial strengths and weaknesses, by reviewing performance against budgets that have been set for it. Over- and underperformances against each budget are noted to ensure a full review of the reasons behind the product range's financial contribution to the business.
  - A second, more detailed focus will be on individual product performance to identify which product trends worked and which did not. This review is similar to the buyer's, but the focus is on understanding which options sold well and which did not. The merchandiser assesses this by reviewing unit volumes, sales versus buy and stock levels.

- Like the buyer, the merchandiser will review the macro trading environment and will look for evidence of relevant economic and market trends. If the economic outlook is good, then this is reflected in ambitious future planning budgets. If poor, then budgets will be tightened and possibly reduced to manage any associated trading risk.
- The merchandiser also reviews the competitive landscape, the competition and their ranges to build up a picture of the risk within the market to help influence the budgeting process.

- Concept – As the buyer articulates fashion trends into product concepts, the merchandiser works to calculate appropriate financial budgets to enable the finalization of the product range. The budgets are the sum of the research undertaken by both roles, and are reviewed by the finance department to ensure that the business can support the plans of the B&M team:
  - The merchandiser will work with senior management to understand any strategic initiatives that will influence the product budgeting process (for example: new stores opening, changes in trading strategy such as reduced markdown activity).
  - Product budgets will be created mixing past financial history with strategic initiatives and product trend data into a realistic plan from which a buying budget can be identified for the buyer, while finance can assess the impact of the products contribution to the P&L and balance sheet.

- Product development – With a financial budget set for the season, buyer and merchandiser will work closely at this point to finalize the product range plan. The buyer is responsible for a large part of the range plan identifying the options, fashionabilities, countries of origin, pricing and store distribution. The merchandiser will, however, determine the final element of the range plan:
  - Unit buys for each option and calculated cost and selling values. This will be calculated to ensure the correct unit amount is bought for each option, supporting its expected commercial strength, size ratio and period of availability within stores.

- Sourcing and manufacture – This stage in the process is very much the domain of the buyer; however, the merchandiser will contribute by deciding the phasing of deliveries in line with stock budgets:
  - A master delivery schedule is created to track deliveries of new ranges and direct timely contact with suppliers during the manufacturing process. Identified issues and changes to delivery dates can all be reviewed against stock budgets, and are agreed or negotiated if not suitable to the retailer.
  - Updates on stock intake will be discussed with finance in case of any impact on cash flow and debt requirements.

- Shipping and warehousing – With the supplier confirming that the product is ready to be shipped, the merchandiser will oversee the tracking of deliveries and expected delivery dates:
  - In agreement with the buyer, the shipment of the product from factory, via its port of origin, to the retailer's warehouse or distribution centre will be authorized.
  - The merchandiser will liaise with the logistics team to update them on delivery dates, quantities and any special priorities that the product may have.

- Initial allocations will be calculated and provided to the warehouse/distribution centre for despatch of stock to stores.
- Distribution and retail – This is possibly the most exciting part of the role – trading the product. With the product delivered, sales data become available and the merchandiser will actively look to trade the range to its maximum potential:
  - Review on a weekly basis of individual options performance to assess opportunities to place repeats or if necessary, cancel orders.
  - Discuss the financial performance of the range with the buyer and finance to assess the impact on end-of-season targets being met.
  - Liaise with suppliers to manage the flow of outstanding orders into the business.
  - Organize any promotions designed to manage stock levels during the season.
- Carrier bag – Inevitably the season will come to an end and the merchandiser will work on the end of season sale to clear residue stocks.
  - The most effective percentage reductions to clear stocks will be identified and the cost quantified to finance to assess the impact on the P&L and balance sheet.

At this point, with the season ended, the season is closed with a final review of the product range's performance against financial budgets to assess how well it performed, to quantify the gross trading profit achieved and to calculate if a bonus could be expected!

THE SKILL SET OF GOOD FASHION MERCHANDISERS

As with the buyer, the merchandiser role requires much resilience and enthusiasm to be effective, with similar pressures to those on the buyer but at a different pace. At the heart of the role is an understanding of the two disciplines that influence the success of a product range – product and finance – and how they weave into one another. This means the role is more methodical, requires clear logical thinking, with an almost dispassionate temperament to be able to make sense of the required decision making. In this skill, the merchandiser is often quite different to the buyer.

Quite obviously, the merchandiser must be numerate, not just able to use a calculator but also able to understand the implication of the figures that they create, manage and review. This understanding of numbers is articulated in the commercial acumen that a merchandiser must possess, understanding and acting upon data to maximize the potential opportunity that is presented.

Similarly to the buyer role, there is a strong requirement to possess good communication and persuasion skills. The merchandiser, like the buyer, spends a great deal of time negotiating to get their ideas understood, or simply to persuade another stakeholder in the concept-to-carrier bag chain to do a deal or grant a favour.

The role does focus heavily on process and analytical review, but, no matter how good a merchandiser is at that, they have to have a relationship with the buyer that is supportive of one another and open to being persuaded to look at things from a different angle.

CASE STUDY 3.1: THE RATIONALE FOR THE ROLE OF THE MERCHANDISER

At the core of the merchandiser role is the influence that it has on the financial characteristics of range planning. Within this remit, the accurate management and manipulation of markdown budgets by the merchandiser could be argued to have the biggest impact on maintaining a fashion range's suitable profitability. Mark down product too early and the range will not maximize the profit potential for the season. If the business were to markdown too late it would run the risk of missing the bulk of the opportunity to clear old and obsolete stock.

The role of markdown within the fashion industry is extensive, with businesses using it actively to manage stock levels. Research undertaken by Anya Media in 2012 found that 19 per cent of fashion retailers use markdown to get rid of excess stock inventory, while a further 31 per cent marked down because the stock that they held was not suitable for future seasonal trends (Anya Media 2012). Anya Media's managing director Christina Grzasko commented that 'Many companies are reading the market poorly and are confused about what their customers are looking for. As a result, they are overbuying, and buying in products that don't match what their customers actually want to buy' (Anya Media 2012).

The discipline of the merchandising functions can support buyers by analysing, and planning in a logical almost unemotional way can add real value to a fashion business. Interestingly, Anya Media's survey also revealed widespread confusion about what merchandising is. Less than half of respondents (43 per cent) said that to them it meant ensuring 'they had the right products in place at the right time for their customers'. Nearly a quarter (23 per cent) claimed it was about promotional products and 17 per cent associated it with electronic point of sale technology (Anya Media 2012).

According to Grzasko, 'It is worrying that so many retailers equate merchandising with promotional products. If they think that merchandising is all about the products themselves, rather than selling the right products to the right customers, they will struggle to understand the market, boost their margins and drive up their profits'. (Grzasko 2012) In addition, the survey revealed that some retailers still take the old 'be your own customer' saying a little too seriously. Some 16 per cent said that personal choice helped them decide which products to sell, whilst well under half, 36 per cent, claimed their decision was based on the product matching the profile of their customers and prospects (Anya Media 2012).

The development of the merchandiser role and proprietary software solutions to aid the merchandising planning process is evidence of the importance attached to the role by both fashion businesses and software houses such as Anya Retail.

Activity: Create and analyse a survey to identify the extent of understanding of the merchandiser role within a targeted group of people

OWN-LABEL VERSUS BRANDED BUYING AND MERCHANDISING

The role of B&M does have a further element to it that requires consideration – the difference between own-label and branded product management. Within a fashion business, the rationale for the B&M function is the same regardless of business model. The differences between the two are found in the application of product development knowledge, predominantly affecting the buyer. For the merchandiser, the impact that they feel lies within the management of stock flow.

Working within a branded environment for the buyer means that there is less of a need to understand the technical aspects of product design and manufacture. This is because they will select product from a wholesale collection rather than be part of creating it. In practical terms, this places more emphasis on market research to be fully aware of trends, new emerging brands, competitor ranges and most importantly the branded customer and their lifestyle. The role of the buyer becomes one of matching brand and the product within it to the target customer type. This changed emphasis also changes the skill set of the branded buyer compared to an own-label buyer. Relationship building between buyer and brand becomes vitally important to first persuade a brand to trade with the retailer, but then to retain and nurture the relationship beyond a single season.

For the merchandiser, the concept-to-carrier bag process is more or less the same between the two. The key difference lies within the challenge of matching the retail business strategies to those of the wholesale brand. Often, brands impose minimum order quantities, restrictions on markdown policies and even delivery dates quoted across several months rather than a specific day or week. This makes the budgeting process more complicated, as the full implications of potential restrictions have to be assessed and judged acceptable or not.

Despite the seeming restrictions, branded B&M also offers opportunities. The adjusted focus means that deep long-term business relationships can be developed, while buyers and merchandisers can widen their skill set into other disciplines. The buyer can facilitate the development of store layouts and shop fits, while the merchandiser can be part of the development of supply chain strategies to link the two businesses together. Ultimately, though, the requirements of the concept-to-carrier bag process remain for both types of B&M, and the ease with which merchandisers in particular can move between the two is evidence of this.

PROFILE 3.1: THE ROLE OF THE OWN-LABEL MERCHANDISER – FREYA BAXTER

I call own label merchandising the spreadsheet behind the glamour. I have many spreadsheets that I use in my day-to-day working life, but I am also glamorous enough to understand product and what makes a successful range from a customer as well as business perspective. The core part of my role is to make sure that everything we do as a team has a good dose of common sense and reality built into it. I split my week into two categories: planning and trading.

The planning activities that I undertake include identifying sales, markdown, stock and open to buy budgets for the season being planned. Using these, I can budget for a gross trading profit for my department which the company uses to pay for its overheads. I will spend a lot of time range planning – working out how many options the buyer can buy with the agreed buying budget. Buyers often try to buy more options than I have planned. If they do we have to have a chat and I point out that the more options they buy, the fewer units can be bought of each which runs the risk of bad size ratios and allocations to stores. Once all the buys have been made, I will create a delivery schedule that shows all the orders placed and when they are due to be delivered. I monitor changes to the delivery schedule as suppliers update us on how production is going.

I use the wizzy (WSSI) to give me an overview of each week's budgets and amend it with updated delivery information to assess the risk to the business achieving its targets if deliveries slip. This brings me onto the second part of my role: trading. Once orders are delivered, I analyse how well the products are selling and place re-orders for the best sellers and cancellations for the poor sellers. Being own label, we can control stocks better than branded departments, and so can usually make easy changes to the ranges and orders. We have lots of phases of stock intake in a season and so tend to mark down poor sellers as we go through the season, another advantage we have over the branded departments who are restricted by their agreements with brands. The trading of an own-label department is fun as I really am in control of the success or failure of the season's profit targets.

I also spend a lot of time working with my assistant merchandiser and allocator developing them and helping them learn the tools of the trade, as teamwork and mutual support are vital within merchandising!

PROFILE 3.2: THE ROLE OF THE BRANDED MERCHANDISER – LIZZIE CLARK

In my role as a branded merchandiser the activities that I undertake and the process that I follow is similar to that of an own-label merchandiser. What is different is the emphasis placed on the various tasks. There is a greater focus, for example, on developing relationships with brands, deal negotiation and internal meetings with various other functions within the organization that I work for.

At any one time I will be working on three seasons: the current one, the next and the one after that. Depending on where we are in the season, the sort of activities that I would undertake for the current season would be to review sales, markdown, stock levels and trading profit data to assess our position against the budgets set for the season. If we are beating the budgets, then my focus would be to try and do even better by calling in orders of best sellers, asking brands for repeat buys and discussing with the buyer the implications of the success on future planning. If we are not doing well, then the focus changes a bit. I still chase the best sellers, but I also review stocks and future orders for brands that are not doing well and try and negotiate stock cancellations, cost price reductions or contributions to the cost of markdown needed to liquidate the stock. Often success within branded businesses is dependent on relationships between the retailer and the brand, and so if there are any difficult negotiations to be had, the buyers are involved as they have the main relationship with the brands.

Once a month, I will prepare a sales and profit review where I update the WSSI with our trading performance and then forecast forward my view on how trading will continue to the end of the season. This reforecast is central to my liaison with the finance team as this gives them visibility of likely changes to cash flow planned.

At the same time as doing this, I will be planning the next season ranges with the buyer, setting the budgets for the brands and identifying the open to buy available. This part of the role takes time as often we have to negotiate with brands how much business we will do with them and I have to check that we are not agreeing to anything we cannot afford. The budgeting process takes ages and I have to present my budgets to my director several times during the planning round. Once they are finalized and the buys are made, I can work through size ratios and allocation plans for stores. Finally, the buyer and I will be thinking about the following season, talking to brands about our plans and theirs, looking for new brands to work with and setting the planning strategy that will dictate everything we do.

The job is pressured and there are days when you do not know whether you are coming or going, but I like it that way. I also prefer branded merchandising to own-label as I can influence not just the success of the business, but also the brands that we work with.

THE FASHION BUYER AND MERCHANDISER JOB DESCRIPTIONS

The complementary nature of the two roles of the buyer and merchandiser result in a planning approach that is thorough but also questioning. The different approaches and skill sets means that each activity must acquire equilibrium between B&M before the next can be started. As the two roles are so intertwined, job descriptions for them can also be bound together. Given so many unique business structures and strategies within the fashion industry, it is not possible to create definitive job descriptions. What is possible, though, is a generic template split into the roles' three core competencies.

The job descriptions are presented in three sections and then subdivided in the order of the concept-to-carrier bag model:

- planning the product range
- trading the product range
- managing the B&M team.

Joint tasks are presented under the B&M headings and separate tasks will then follow for both buyer and merchandiser.

Planning the product range

This refers to the planning and creation of the overall size and shape of the product range. The activities within this section of the job description will be the most extensive and will be relevant throughout the concept-to-carrier bag process.

The activities include those required to analyse past performance, forecast influences for the future, propose the characteristics of the product range and develop the supporting decisions and documents needed for the process of creating the product range.

- Research and concept
  - Buyer and merchandiser
    - o Understand the required critical path for the season ahead to ensure all defined deadlines throughout the concept-to-carrier bag process are met on time.
    - o Communicate the requirements of the critical path to all relevant personnel within the value chain and take responsibility for its delivery by deadlines.
  - Buyer
    - o Review past season product performance using relevant attribute analysis to understand which products were successful and which were not, using this information to shape the concept of the new season product range direction.
    - o Review current and forecast competitor, consumer, price, product and fashion trends to identify new opportunities to develop within the product range concept for the new season.
    - o Review past season supplier performance to understand which suppliers provided the best and most reliable services to deliver product in line with cost, quality and delivery requirements.
    - o Create in conjunction with the merchandiser a trend, product, price and consumer strategy for the new season product range.
  - Merchandiser
    - o Review past season financial performance to understand the sales turnover, densities and profit contributions of each product type, and use this information to influence the new season's financial budgets.
    - o Review current trends for the macro environment to include economic, market share and consumer confidence trends and identify a risk assessment for the new season's financial budgets.

- o Create – in conjunction with the buyer – budgets for the product range to include sales turnover, markdown, intake margin, stock and trading profit budgets.
  - Buyer and merchandiser
    - o Propose and discuss the initial product range concept and financial budgets for the new range to the B&M and finance directors and make any required changes to the proposals.
    - o Propose and discuss the promotional activities to support the new range with the marketing and retail directors. and make any required changes to the proposals.
    - o Create a final product range concept and financial budget strategy for the new season.
- Product development
  - Buyer
    - o Create an initial product plan to identify growth or decline that the merchandiser can refer to while creating product category budgets.
    - o Create – in conjunction with the designer – option designs and specifications for each product type, and facilitate these designs being distributed to potential manufacturers for costing and sampling.
    - o Create draft option plans detailing the option description, relevant attributes such as theme, fashionability and end use, its target cost and selling prices, supplier, fabric type and its proposed store distribution.
    - o Review initial manufacture responses to proposed option designs and negotiate proposed sampling, cost prices, delivery dates and trading terms.
    - o Review draft option plans and compare to merchandiser-created range plans and buying budgets.
  - Merchandiser
    - o Create product budgets that add up to the agreed business budget strategy for the new season.
    - o Using the product budgets, create buying budgets (open to buy, OTB) budgets for the buyer.
    - o Create range plans and option details using OTB budgets to plan the number of options and unit quantities to be bought by the buyer.
    - o Create a phasing document to use to phase new product intake by week or month for the new season.
  - Buyer and merchandiser
    - o Work together to create a final agreed option range plan that reflects the buyers product concept, the product and OTB budgets and calculated range plans.
    - o Propose and discuss the agreed product OTB, range plan and sizing plans for the new range to the B&M director, and make any required changes to the proposals.
    - o Create a final product OTB and option detail plan for the new product range.

- Sourcing, manufacturing and shipping
  - Buyer
    - o Agree the final specifications for the options to be ranged to include product design, fabrications, trims, labelling, hangers, ticketing, size ratios, shipping details and costs.
    - o Undertake the final negotiation of cost prices, delivery dates and trading terms for the finalized option range plan.
    - o Manage the product purchase-order-raising process and delivery of required standard labelling, hangers and ticketing on behalf of manufacturers.
  - Merchandiser
    - o Support the buyer in their negotiations with manufacturers by providing any relevant financial information as required.
    - o Create proposed size ratios for all product types based on previous seasons for the buyer to review and use when placing orders.
    - o Support the buyer with the management of the product purchase-order-raising process and delivery of required standard labelling, hangers and ticketing on behalf of manufacturers as required.
    - o Create the delivery schedule for the new season and liaise with manufacturers on delivery requirements in line with stock budgets, and authorize delivery shipments when required.

Trading the product range

This details the trading and optimization of the product range once it has been delivered. The activities within this section are limited in number, but are repeated throughout the season – usually on a weekly basis – that the product is on sale.

The activities include those required to analyse current performance, take action to maximize the good performance and minimize the worst by taking proactive decisions to support the product range. The activities are split into three subheadings: performance management, stock management and promotional management.

- Warehousing and distribution
  - Buyer and merchandiser
    - o Ensure all supplier and delivery records are at all times up-to-date so that all deliveries, warehousing activities and store deliveries are delivered on time.
  - Buyer
    - o Review all deliveries to ensure that bulk production is as final approved samples and in line with quality assurance guidelines.
    - o Provide relevant look books, product training and range support materials as required to retail operations and marketing.
    - o Provide relevant product samples or photographic materials to the press office for editorial.

- Merchandiser
  o Create initial allocation quantities for stock to be distributed to stores or reserved for e-stores.
  o Liaise with the warehouse and logistics teams to ensure stock is delivered on time to correct stores.
  o Update retail stores on stock deliveries, and ensure all store space allocated to the product is fully stocked and utilized.
- Buyer and merchandiser
  o Communicate weekly or monthly trading strategies such as promotions, new product range launches or range cancellations to retail operations and marketing to allow them to plan their activities.

Retail and carrier bag

- Buyer and merchandiser
  - Action the agreed promotional activities to promote product ranges to the consumer throughout the season.
  - Decide on product re buys and cancellations based on actual product performance and finalize unit quantities, delivery dates and purchase orders.
- Buyer
  - Review competitor ranges and promotional activities throughout the season, and discuss with the B&M director.
  - Assess product performance against planned assumptions within the finalized option range plan and update the merchandiser and directors on product performance.
  - Share and update manufacturers and suppliers of product performance and discuss possible repeats or cancellations of purchase orders.
  - Negotiate with the relevant supplier suitable terms for product re buys and product cancellations.
  - Liaise with manufacturers to ensure all technical and quality requirements of any new product ranges are met and compliant with legislation.
  - Liaise with the retail operations and marketing to provide details of new product ranges to be delivered.
- Merchandiser
  - Assess business performance against agreed financial budgets on a weekly basis and update buyer and directors on business performance.
  - Update and reforecast the product budgets for the season on a monthly basis to assess impact of product performance on business finances.
  - Communicate re-forecasted product budgets to B&M and finance directors and obtain approval to work to revised OTB budgets created as a result.
  - Provide regular stock delivery updates to relevant warehouse or logistics teams based on changes to OTB budgets or product delivery plans.
  - Decide the suitable replenishment criteria for product ranges and communicate these to the relevant warehouse or logistics teams.
  - Calculate the financial cost of a suitable promotional calendar and ensure that it is within the markdown budget for the product range.

- Create an ESS proposal that is within agreed markdown budget and liquidates excess stock as efficiently as possible.
- Buyer and merchandiser
  - Ensure all business activities are updated with changes to the product ranges as a result of stock management decisions.

Managing the buying and merchandising team

This refers to the management of the team of people who support the buyer and merchandiser. For the buyer, they may be supported by an assistant buyer and a buying administration clerk. The merchandiser may be supported by an assistant merchandiser and allocator (also known as a distributor). The activities in this section centre on being a good manager of these support roles, the development of their individual careers and the delivery of efficient B&M activities. The responsibilities of buyer and merchandiser will be the same in this third section and so are given as one.

- Supporting a balanced team
  - As required, source and interview candidates for vacant positions within the B&M function.
  - Ensure all new members of staff are inducted into the business and are aware of their job description, role and responsibilities.
  - Develop team members to achieve career goals to their own and the business's benefit, and recommend promotion as appropriate.
- Day-to-day management of the department
  - Deliver on-the-job training and support to all team members.
  - Identify off-the-job training needs for team members and source suitable training events.
  - Set clear personal and professional objectives for each team member at an annual appraisal.

SUMMARY

What becomes clear when reviewing B&M and the presented job descriptions is that the creation of a product range is as much about finance and science as it is about fashion trend and art. The merchandiser role, as an important influence within a fashion retailer, gives it a clear role within the concept-to-carrier bag model, whilst its decision points are as much strategic as they are operational.

The merchandiser, like the buyer, cannot work alone and indeed should not; they do not possess enough knowledge to singlehandedly plan and trade a product range. The role is by its activities separate to that of the buyer, but also not part of the finance team. It sits in the middle of the two and adds a unique skill to retail buying and fashion businesses as a whole.

The final chapter in Part One will take this final thought and review the place of B&M within a retail structure, before proceeding into Part Two and the practical demonstration of the merchandiser role.

SELF-DIRECTED STUDY

1. Presume you are a fashion buyer and undertake the research and concept stages of the concept-to-carrier bag process for your favourite brand:
   a. Create a small 12-option (style/colour) range plan.
   b. How easy was it to create a range that you feel is right for the brand?
   c. Would you buy your range if you were a customer?
2. Follow the same process again but this time for a brand that you would not normally shop with:
   a. Review your range – would you buy it?
   b. If not, how easy was it to understand the brand and its customers?
   c. If yes, is that the right answer? Ask yourself if you are being objective in your buying decisions.
3. Presume you are a fashion merchandiser:
   a. How might you assess the financial value of the product ranges?
   b. What information do you think you would need to help you decide their financial value to a business?

Further Reading

Goworek, H. (2007) *Fashion Buying*. Oxford: Blackwell

Jackson, T. and Shaw, D. (2001) *Mastering Fashion Buying and Merchandising Management*. Basingstoke: Macmillan

Varley, R. (2001) *Retail Product Management*. London: Routledge

Bibliography

Anya Media (2012) *Retailers confused about merchandising and 'killing their margins' on discounts*. [Internet]. Available from http://www.anyamedia.co.uk/news/rbte2012-survey-results.php [Accessed 20th January 2014]

Goworek, H. (2007) *Fashion Buying*. Oxford: Blackwell

Jackson, T. and Shaw, D. (2001) *Mastering Fashion Buying and Merchandising Management*. Basingstoke: Macmillan

Varley, R. (2001) *Retail Product Management*. London: Routledge

4 Organizing the Buying and Merchandising Function

INTENDED LEARNING OUTCOMES

1. An introduction to the value chain and its application within a fashion retail business.
2. A discussion of the structure of the B&M team.
3. The identification of the key contacts of buyers and merchandisers.
4. The use of planning and trading meetings to inform B&M decision making.

INTRODUCTION

With a discussion of the roles of B&M in place, this chapter reviews the structure of the function, and its place within the wider retail business. Organizational hierarchies are not necessarily the most exciting of topics, but they do facilitate the efficient, effective strategic and operational management of business. They are relevant within the identification of how the different functions that comprise the business operate together to achieve its set strategic and operational objectives.

Organizations must be structured to optimize trading activities and there has been much academic thought given to this topic. Michael Porter provided seminal work in the development of the value chain concept, and this will be reviewed within the context of fashion retail to identify the importance of B&M, but also to help identify the key contacts who work with buyers and merchandisers in the course of their duties. The chapter concludes with a discussion of the various planning and trading meetings that buyers and merchandisers hold to enable them to undertake the roles.

THE VALUE CHAIN

A concept-to-carrier bag model, as a linked set of sequential steps, is in effect a simple supply chain. Its effectiveness in supporting the flow of product ranges and wealth creation is central to the delivery of the aims of a retail business, but also the expectations of the target customer. A truly inspirational and dynamic fashion range will never make it to a shop floor if the supply chain process cannot deliver it on time!

Michael Porter recognized that an enduring competitive advantage is achieved through all the activities within a supply chain operating to ensure that each delivers optimal value benefit to the business. In recognizing that a supply chain comprises different activities means that while product range responsibility rests with B&M, its delivery relies upon a number of roles working collaboratively within the business. A second discussion point is the meaning of optimal value. A generic concept-to-carrier bag process can be applied to most retail businesses; however, an optimal one will be shaped around the values and practicalities of the brand and its personality. Zara would not get optimal benefit if its supply chain did not broaden the scope of the responsibility of manufacturing activities within its process, whilst a fashion leader luxury brand would place a greater emphasis on sourcing activities to hunt down specialist fabrics within theirs.

Recognizing that product management is a chain of activities which work appropriately together to deliver product ranges to market led to Porter's articulation of the value chain in his seminal 1985 text *Competitive Advantage*. In summary, the value chain identifies the activities required to create product and then divides them into two types – primary or support. Figures 4.1 and 4.2 present the generic value chain model devised by Porter in 1985, split between the two differing types of activity.

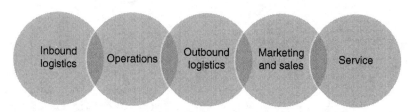

Figure 4.1 *The value chain – primary activities*

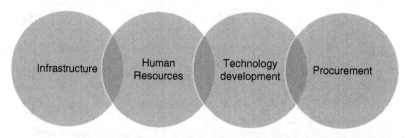

Figure 4.2 *The value chain – support activities*

Porter articulated that businesses require nine activities in total, five of which related to product management and were defined as being primary within the value chain. A further four activities were defined as supporting the primary ones.

For example the primary activities link together as follows:

- Inbound logistics – activities that co-ordinate the components of a product.
- Operations – activities that create a product.
- Outbound logistics – activities that co-ordinate the delivery of a product to the customer.
- Marketing and sales – activities that inform and sell a product.
- Service – activities that provide services that support the sale of a product.

Secondary activities support the primary activities as follows:

- Infrastructure – activities of general management (for example: Finance, Estate management).
- Human Resource management – activities relating to recruiting and retaining employees.
- Technology development – activities that develop best practice and information technology (for example, implementation of improved ICT systems).
- Procurement – activities that ensure the purchase of resources to support business activity (for example, the provision of computers to the workforce).

The model, and its modern-day relevance, have been much discussed and dissected. As a model, it is generic and its original focus lay within the manufacture and delivery of product as opposed to being led by the expectations of the end consumer. It also does not explicitly place the research and concept activities as defining the product to be manufactured within the chain. Its use within the context of this subject is that its template shape can be interpreted within the wider fashion context, so helping to identify the totality of the process of creating balanced product ranges.

Using Porter's model as a start point, it is clear that the creation of product ranges, and therefore the B&M activities, are primary within a retail fashion business. The model's logic can also be useful to define an example template of the primary activities that work with B&M through the concept-to-carrier bag process:

- Inbound logistics – activities that co-ordinate the components of a product.
  - Design – the process of research, design and selection of ideas for the range and the sourcing of appropriate fabrics, trim, labelling and suppliers.
- Operations – activities that create a product.
  - Suppliers – the process of product approval, sampling, sizing and manufacture and pre-retailing of product.
- Outbound logistics – activities that co-ordinate the delivery of a product to the customer.
  - Suppliers, logistics – the process of planning delivery, shipping, delivery, warehousing and allocation to retail.

- Marketing and Sales – activities that inform and sell a product.
  - Marketing, retail selling – the process of communicating and selling key trends, themes and products.
- Service – activities that provide services that support the sale of a product.
  - Retail selling – the process of providing services to enhance the retail and purchase of fashion product.

By superimposing the principles of the value chain onto a generic retail concept-to-carrier bag process, two conclusions can be drawn. First and most obvious is that the B&M role does not work alone within product management, and effective delivery of a product concept to store relies on an alignment between a range of roles and their activities. Good practical examples of this could be that there is no sense in the buyer creating a product offer that comprises 1,000 style colours if the retail shops can only accommodate 500 style colours, or alternatively if a buyer decided to source suppliers in China without being aware of whether the logistics function is able to manage the delivery of product from that location. A second conclusion is that using Porter's accepted definitions, finance is not primary within the value chain, meaning the quantitative merchandising activities within B&M become crucial to connect finance into the process, so reinforcing the merchandiser roles' relevance and expertise within a retail business.

CASE STUDY 4.1: SUPERDRY – THE IMPORTANCE OF ALL VALUE CHAIN ACTIVITIES WORKING TOGETHER

Supergroup was founded and developed by two men – Julian Dunkerton and James Holder – who merged their differing skills and life experiences to launch a truly unique and exciting brand. Once established, the business grew fast and found its own special niche within the fashion industry. However, some doubted the genius behind the label as shown later when, reviewing Superdry for her column in the *Daily Telegraph*, Mary Portas commented that her experience 'makes me wonder whether Julian's super brand was a stroke of genius or a stroke of luck' (Portas 2010).

The news in April 2012 that Supergroup shares had plunged 33 per cent after its third profit warning in six months emphasized the importance of support functions contributing to the delivery of business success. The third profit warning came as a result of blaming arithmetic errors and stock delivery timing issues in wholesale division, as well as lower margins in its retail business. The arithmetic issue was a simple human mistake, but misjudging wholesale customer actions is perhaps a reflection of poor management. The meteoric rise of the brand had led to structural problems within the business, as City analysts in London noted as rafts of share price downgrades were prepared.

The brand – whose clothes are a favourite of celebrities such as David Beckham – has grown fast and the number of styles available has grown significantly. In 2008, the autumn collection comprised 700 styles and by 2011 this had grown to 2,500. The brand introduced a short order service in 2011 to further expand its market share, but many stockists were growing concerned about spasmodic deliveries, growing competition from nearby House of Fraser concessions and company-owned stores, as the business's relentless expansion continued.

Concerns that the business support functions could not fully support the brand were heightened in October 2011 with the issuing of a first profit warning by the group, when the implementation of a warehouse IT system upgrade left its stores short of replenishment on core styles. This poorly executed upgrade was estimated to have cost Supergroup £9 million in lost profit, when the newly installed system authorized the delivery to store of products in sizes small and extra-large only. Supergroup described this as 'an unwelcome temporary setback' (Retail Week 2011).

Activity: Use the value chain model to define a flow chart of primary activities within a fashion retail business, and consider how all the activities in the chain rely on each other.

THE STRUCTURE OF BUYING AND MERCHANDISING DEPARTMENTS

The focus of the past three chapters has been on defining the role of B&M as a function, and this section reviews how the function can be structured to enable it to deliver its wide remit. With different fashion businesses placing differing emphasis on activities within their value chains, the top-level structures that influence the hierarchy within B&M will be different. Some businesses will head their B&M function with a B&M director who will be responsible for all the activities of their teams, others may have a Commercial director whose remit expands to include other functions such as supply chain or retail operations. The exact nature of the directorship that B&M operate under will be driven largely by what is right for the brand to ensure, as Porter discussed, that optimal value is generated for the business. Over time there have been unusual interpretations of this with some businesses placing B&M under the remit of the design director or retail director to name but a few.

The organizational hierarchy of the B&M function itself it is not uniform throughout the industry. This is a further reflection of the many different business models that operate in the diverse and complex fashion market of today. The classic structure of a B&M function is presented below in Figure 4.3 .

The buying and merchandiser director will oversee the activities of a function across a defined product group; for example, a department store may have up to five directors to cover womenswear, menswear, childrenswear, beauty and homewares. In a fashion multiple such as a womenswear retailer, there may be directorships split by product type – clothing, accessories or lingerie, for example. The number of

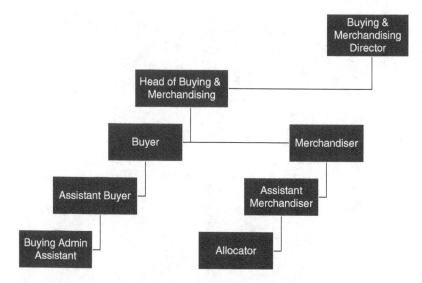

Figure 4.3 *A classic buying and merchandising office structure*

directorships will be dependent on the size of the business and often one director may cover more than one distinct product group.

The role of the B&M director is predominantly strategic; usually sitting on the board of directors, they will be influential in the setting of the business strategy and its delivery by the B&M teams. They will also act as a high-level link within the value chain and work closely with other directors such as finance, marketing or retail operations to ensure accurate and timely decisions can be made across all roles within the business.

In their role they are supported by a head of B&M, who will help with the day-to-day operations of the function by directly managing the individual buyers and merchandisers and feed down information from the director to the teams and vice versa. Again dependent on the size of the business, there may be one or more heads of department reporting to the director; and where there is more than one, they would be divided by discrete product group. In beauty, for example, there may be a head of perfumery and one for body and bath.

The B&M teams will work together as one, headed by a buyer and merchandiser, each with their own teams below them. Leaving aside the roles of the buyer and merchandiser which have been discussed in Chapter 3, the responsibilities of the remaining team members are detailed below.

Assistant buyer

This role works closely with the buyer at all stages of the concept-to-carrier bag process and often will be given responsibility of a specific product area to buy. They will be involved in the research and development of a product concept and then oversee the sourcing and manufacturing process on a day-to-day basis.

Whilst the ultimate decisions lie with the buyer, the assistant buyer has the role of implementer; approving lab dips and other technical aspects of product, managing the sampling process, reviewing range plans for balance by attribute, and overseeing the purchase order-raising process. The assistant buyer role is significantly different if the business model follows that of branded buying. In this case there is no need for the product development elements within the role and this is replaced by working closely with branded partners. This facilitates the business relationship by putting together product information, ensuring that the brand values of the supplier are upheld through display guidelines and the marketing and retail of the product range is appropriate.

PROFILE 4.1: A DAY IN THE LIFE OF AN ASSISTANT BUYER – KAYLEIGH JACKSON – OFF-PRICE RETAILING

There is no such thing as a typical day in the life for an assistant buyer! One day I could be finalizing buys and writing orders, whilst the next day I may be in a showroom viewing products with brands or manufacturers and negotiating a mutually acceptable deal in the interests of both businesses.

What *is* typical, though, as with every other fashion business, is that Monday is analysis day. Here we all pause to review company and departmental performance (being the best performer is always grand!), product winners and losers, and finally store rankings. Brands that are performing well will need meetings to be organized to view newly available stock to buy. Poor performing products need to be reviewed – ideally in store, to understand why (for example, price point, fashion, sizing, quality). Once assessed, liaison with the merchandising team ensures a plan will be put in place to trade the failing products out of the business.

A very big part of my role is travel to see our suppliers. We are always sourcing new products and by visiting suppliers we can make decisions there and then in real time rather than spending ages deliberating over a decision back in the office. This means I can expect to be travelling every other week, visiting fashionable showrooms or a dirty warehouse the next. I get to meet so many people and visit so many different places that I have built up a list of contacts, useful for my future career, as well as a night out!

Our business is all about contact. Hand in hand with being out of office, the best part of the job role, it is key to liaise with and update my colleagues in the merchandising department. I also must not forget to update the distribution centre with stock arrival information and processing requirements, brand suppliers regarding the purchase of goods and order statuses, other buying teams for their takes on their latest deals and thoughts of the market, and most importantly of course the buying administrators who know anything and everything and who regularly have to tell me what I am doing, and why!

Buying administration assistant (BAA)

The BAA role is the entry level into a buying career and is focused on managing the heavy administration created by the buying role. The BAA will ensure range plans are fully updated with all relevant information, and that this is input onto category management computer systems to generate purchase orders. Once orders have been placed, they will ensure sampling is completed by the suppliers within the time requirements of the concept-to-carrier bag. After the ranges have been delivered, they will often provide weekly analysis of performance to the team and pull together the best and worst sellers to present at relevant meetings.

PROFILE 4.2: A DAY IN THE LIFE OF A BUYER'S ADMINISTRATION ASSISTANT – EVIE BAXTER – PREMIUM HIGH STREET

Monday, and Monday morning in particular, is the most important day of all as it is the day when the trade from last week is analysed and action for the following week is decided. On a typical Monday I get into work for 8.00 am, check my e-mails for any significant messages that may affect the business, and then work on my Monday responsibilities. These are to create a summary of purchase orders raised the previous week to add to our outstanding stock commitments, tracking deliveries of these and chasing suppliers to ensure stock deliveries are on time.

The buyer will attend the company trade meeting, feedback any relevant sales and product information that we need to know about. This is followed by a departmental meeting to review the best/worst performing stores and products, and decide action we would like to take in terms of changes to stock levels, markdowns, promotions or product ranges. After this, I do the everyday jobs like creating purchase orders, contacting suppliers, replying to store enquiries, and have meetings with the assistant buyer to plan my activities for the week ahead.

By Tuesday we have moved onto implementing our decisions of the previous day. It is the day when all trade actions are uploaded to the system. For example, markdown and price changes go live and all relevant information about these have to be communicated to all affected stores. The rest of the week is devoted to supplying a high level of accurate administrative support to the team with the responsibility of data management, including style definitions, descriptions and attributes, price changes and purchase order entry, as well as attending any meetings that are put in the diary and working towards finalizing and agreeing the latest product buys for the season ahead.

On an hourly basis I talk to and interact with many people in the business, from buyers assistants from other departments, through store staff and suppliers up to the directors of the business. It is a role of many faces and styles – so wide and interesting I cannot help but love it.

Assistant merchandiser

The assistant merchandiser, like the assistant buyer, works closely with their line manager, the merchandiser, and will often be given their own product area to plan and trade. The assistant merchandiser collates and presents to the merchandiser relevant information to create budgets for the range and the range planning process. The activities of merchandising have a high degree of linkage between them, and so often – once key planning decisions have been made – the assistant merchandiser will create the various planning documents and manage their use and accuracy. The assistant merchandiser will take the lead with the trading of the product range by reviewing business performance, identifying rebuy and cancellation opportunities, and managing the flow of product into the business. Part of this trading activity will be to propose products to be marked down either on a rolling process through the season or at the end in the final clearance sale period.

PROFILE 4.3: A DAY IN THE LIFE OF AN ASSISTANT MERCHANDISER – ELEANOR JEWELL – DEPARTMENT STORE

Being an assistant merchandiser is like balancing an operational role with a strategic one and never quite knowing which to prioritize! I have to keep an operational eye on the day-to-day running of the department; overseeing the Monday morning chaos of collating and understanding the financial results of the previous week's trade and from there assessing the implication for the week ahead as well as the impact on our sales, stocks and profit plans for the season. At the same time, I may be heavily involved in the research analysis and planning of the next season and finding time to work with the merchandiser, buyer and assistant buyer to finalize product ranges, buy quantities and intake phasing dates. It really is all systems go all of the time.

Monday mornings are the trading day – once we have a good assessment in place of the previous week's trade, I will set about identifying the priorities for the week for the allocating team. I always prioritize the opportunities first; which products need to be re-bought, which delivered early, which to be extended to more stores or given a greater online profile. With the allocators sorting out the opportunities, I will assess the threats – which products to mark down, which to cancel and which to transfer around our store estate. I will also find time to reforecast stock orders for continuity products. This emphasis on stock management is important. I will have to update and reforecast the WSSI with my latest best guess of future sales and OTB requirements. This forward-looking aspect of my role is a way of protecting the business and our profit objectives so as we can assess the likely effect of current trading patterns on our business and take any corrective action to ensure we hit all of our financial budgets and so achieve a bonus!

On the other hand, I am also always looking beyond the end of the current season by planning the new season; identifying and setting budgets, creating the seasons WSSI, range planning and deciding unit buy quantities and creating a delivery schedule of placed orders so we can keep an eye on committed buys versus our OTB budget. I do this under the guidance of my merchandiser, who often delegates some of the decision making to me which is both challenging but also motivating. I have such real responsibility and get a real kick out of telling friends and family that I spend millions of pounds a year on fashion!

Allocator

The allocator is managed by the assistant merchandiser and implements both their and the merchandiser's decisions. Similar to the BAA, the role is heavily administrative with responsibility for liaising suppliers to deliver stock, maintain all stock management records and flag any potential issues that may result in stock targets being missed. The largest part of their role is to ensure that the allocation process is complete by inputting allocations into the relevant stock management system, allocating replenishment stock to stores, and managing stock allocations for specific events such as new store openings. Finally they will manage the files and records of the merchandising team.

PROFILE 4.4: MERCHANDISE DISTRIBUTION ASSISTANT

Each day, above all else I have to send out the sales data for our department from the previous day to the rest of the team to review and assess. This early intelligence alerts us to any opportunities or risks to our achieving our budgeted sales plans, also allowing the merchandiser and myself to assess work priorities for the day ahead.

We all as a team have to get in early on Monday mornings to put a weekly profit, sales, stock and product analysis pack together, so a detailed analysis can be made of how we performed the previous week which we can then discuss as a team and with category management. Often, decisions are made as a result of these meetings such as making changes to deliveries or repeats and cancellations to outstanding orders. These decisions help me to manage one of my key documents – the delivery schedule.

The delivery schedule gives me an up-to-date assessment of recent deliveries, upcoming deliveries and also any new orders that have been raised and approved by the buying team. The flow of stock into the business is of vital importance and I can assess stock budget requirements against what is likely to happen. This knowledge allows me to decide which suppliers to chase to deliver and support if there are any problems with the supply chain team. Beyond this practical element to delivery management is the customer relationship aspect. Deliveries have to be on time to meet live on website deadlines which is when new products are launched to the waiting customers, who could be literally anywhere in the world. This element to my role means that I have to have to have a close relationship with the logistics team, so I always meet with them at least once a week, often daily, so we can discuss and catch up on any updates or issues.

The other role that I love to work very closely with is the buyer's assistant, and life wouldn't be the same without him. For example, in the weekly trade and trends meeting – where we show what our best and worst selling lines are – the BA shows the products, and I explain the sales and stock data of the products.

The other area where we work closely together is the use of SEO (search engine optimization) to ensure that our products rank highly when searched by the global customer – I monitor where in the rankings the brands I am responsible for are when searched on Google. I spend a lot of my time over the course of the year trying and keep them and the business at the top of the searches.

It is exhausting, but the thought that something I have done could mean an order being placed by a customer anywhere in the world gives me a real buzz!

Reorganizing the B&M structure

This classic B&M structure and role responsibilities is often reinterpreted where it is suitable to do so. Some larger more complex business may create a split in reporting structures between B&M by having separate heads of B&M as shown in Figure 4.4.

The benefit of organizing the B&M function in this way is that it allows both buyers and merchandisers to be focused on their roles and work within an environment of specialists. This can mean that they are able to manage larger business units of perhaps several product types, as their roles are narrower in definition. The obvious disadvantage of this is that it can encourage a silo mentality to develop where decisions are made within a narrow context, unaware of or not taking into account other activities in the value chain.

A second more extreme example of the above separation of roles is where stock management and allocation are hived off into a third role of distribution. The Burton Group, now known as Arcadia, moved to this mode of organization in early 1993 as a way of harnessing the increasing technological capabilities of stock management systems. With easier and more effective mobility of stock, an increased focus was placed on branch merchandising, a form of micro-merchandising, where stock was able to be allocated with short lead times or easily moved from one store to another. The greater stock efficiency required an individual focus, leading to the removal of the allocator role and reduction in the scope of the assistant merchandiser role to

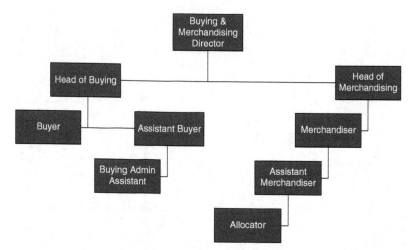

Figure 4.4 *B&M structure with buying and merchandising roles separated*

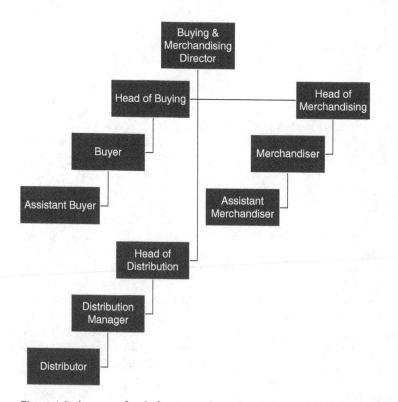

Figure 4.5 *An example of a buying and merchandising and distribution structure chart*

a greater focus on planning. This approach had strong business benefits, but again promoted silo mentalities and, at times, confusion between buying, merchandising and distribution as to the correct priorities within stock management. An example structure chart of this hierarchy is shown in Figure 4.5 .

THE BUYER AND THEIR KEY CONTACTS

The key contacts of the buyer are presented in Figure 4.6 and are summarized into five roles. Before summarizing each, it is worth noting that using value chain definitions, all of the roles would be regarded as primary activities. A second point to note is that contact with the roles is spread throughout the buyer's concept-to-carrier bag process, from the very beginning to the very end when product ranges are in store and available to buy.

Figure 4.6 *The buyer and their key contacts*

The relationship that the buyer has with their key contacts will vary depending on the business model and the requirements of the product management process. The relationship with the design role, for example, will be more intense in an own-label environment where the buyer and designer will work closely throughout the season, whereas in a branded business the input of the designer will be more muted, offering guidance into trend and moods for the season only. There are some general themes which can be used to demonstrate the five key relationships that the buyer has.

- Buyer and designer – The role of the designer is to identify trends and moods and interpret them into a number of product designs from which the buyer will select the ones to be ranged. The buyer will work with the designer to match trends and moods to the product concept that has been devised in tandem with the merchandiser. The designer may work across several product groups, having the benefit of ensuring that a single design handwriting across these groups results in a cohesive offer to the customer.

- Buyer and supplier – The buyer will source suppliers to manufacture the product range and it is not unusual for strong long-term relationships to be formed. The buyer will liaise with the supplier on a continuous basis through the design, approval, sampling, manufacturing and delivery processes. The operational working relationship has to be well managed and with mutual respect. However, at a strategic level, there is much evidence that retailers have squeezed suppliers with imposed changes to trading terms. In 2013, for example, Selfridges, Laura Ashley and John Lewis were all highlighted as engaging in this activity.

- Buyer and quality assurance – Quality assurance (QA) will confirm a product's suitability from a garment construction, legal and practical perspective, and will heavily influence the design of product. QA work with both buyer and supplier through the sampling process and, once product is delivered, will also ensure that deliveries are in line with approved specifications. The QA role is of great importance, and some retailers – such as Target in the USA – have used it to build deep relationships with suppliers, delegating this responsibility to the suppliers to speed up decision making.

- Buyer and retail operations – the relationship between buyer and retail operations is perhaps the least defined of all. The buyer could, for example, organize and facilitate product training for store staff, or develop point-of-sale materials for stores or possibly create visual merchandising guidelines. In some businesses, the buyer may also be involved in deciding how stores will be laid out or which brands or product groups will be displayed. However, whatever the level of contact, and in large organizations it can be quite limited, the ultimate responsibility for the delivery of retail standards will of course rest with the retail operations teams, either in store or head office.

- Buyer and marketing – With the development of brands and the importance attached to their communication to the outside world, the marketing department will work closely with the buyer to understand the product, its strengths, its value to the business and how the customer responds to it. This relationship is based on communication; the buyer has to inform the marketing team about the direction of the range, while marketing have to update the buyer on the reaction to it. At a practical level this may be in the form of the buyer providing samples for press days, editorial shoots or online sites, and marketing providing summaries of editorial comment and press-day feedback.

There is one other key contact that the buyer has and which – as detailed in Chapter 3 – forms the deepest and most important relationship of all: the merchandiser. They rely 100 per cent on each other. Failing to build a mutually respectful relationship can be hugely damaging to the product range, the business and each other.

THE MERCHANDISER AND THEIR KEY CONTACTS

Apart from the buyer relationship, the merchandiser also has key contacts with whom they liaise on a regular basis. Figure 4.7 outlines what those relationships are.

Figure 4.7 *The key contacts of the merchandiser*

Like the buyer, the merchandiser has five key contacts, but interestingly in this case one of them, finance, is a support activity of the value chain. This point is worth noting, as it adds another dimension to the idea that the role acts as a bridge that connects buying to finance. In communicating with finance, the merchandiser is feeding upwards to the business vital financial information that allows the planning of support activities such as warehousing and human resources to be budgeted and implemented. This link between primary and support activities is probably the single most compelling rationale for the role of the merchandiser. Beyond the relationship that they have with the buyer, this link is therefore strategically the most important one that the merchandiser fulfils.

- Merchandiser and finance – At an operational level there is a deep working relationship between the two. The finance team communicates down the chain to the merchandiser any financial requirements that the business has – growth targets, stock management requirements. The merchandiser meanwhile will communicate up the chain their views of the financial strengths and weaknesses of the proposed product range. This top-down, bottom-up planning approach allows both sides to understand the requirements of the other, allowing any differences of opinion to be discussed and resolved. Once delivered, the merchandiser will regularly feed upwards product performance against the agreed budgets and discuss opportunities to develop successes and negate losses that will have a financial implication (for example, more buying budget or markdown spend).

- Merchandiser and suppliers – This relationship tends to be operational in nature as the strategic relationship with the supplier rests with the buyer. The merchandiser will ensure deliveries are on time and able to be worked through the warehouse as efficiently as possible. The same will apply for repeat orders. The merchandiser will also provide forecasts for future for orders on core basic products that flow between seasons, allowing the supplier to plan production efficiently. Where there is a long-term supplier relationship, the merchandiser will also facilitate the agreement of best-practice policies, and give regular updates of product performance during the season.

- Merchandiser and logistics – The efficient flow of stock is the responsibility of the logistics team who receive and distribute product deliveries to retail stores, as well as store any replenishment stock. This process is fraught with potential difficulties, so the merchandiser provides accurate stock flow forecasts to enable the most efficient use of their resources. As there is a finite amount of resource available to unpack deliveries, sort into store allocations and deliver, interruptions to this process are costly in terms of time and finance, put an added impetus on the relationship. Allocation plans must be communicated in good time by the merchandiser, as must intelligence updates about any delays to deliveries that may need to be accommodated.

- Merchandiser and retail operations – The merchandiser will update the retail teams on delivery information, allocation quantities and summaries of sales performances so that best sellers can be identified across the store estate and moved to prominent locations in store. As part of the planning process, the merchandiser, as will be seen, will have the responsibility of creating sales turnover budgets which will act as the sales targets that store teams will work to. A good knowledge of the stores and a good working relationship with the retail operations teams ensures that these sales targets are realistic and achievable.

- Merchandiser and marketing – This relationship is probably the loosest of all as much of the operational liaison is between buyer and marketing. The merchandiser will influence the choice of products that will be chosen for marketing use, by providing the marketing team with details of the value of products to them – how much has been bought, how many stores have been ranged, which ones will feature heavily in the end of season sale etc.

Pulling together the nature of the relationship between the merchandiser and their key contacts together – such as the buyer – shows there is a mix of strategic and operational links and activities. Key to these is ease of regular communication and discussion which take the form of informal chats at desks or in more formal planning and trading-themed business meetings, a discussion of which forms the next section.

MEETING SCHEDULES – HOW B&M WORK WITH OTHER ACTIVITIES IN THE VALUE CHAIN

It is natural that, for a total process that can take up to one year to complete, there will be reason to hold meetings to discuss issues as they arise. Many of them are ad hoc, or part of the operational activities of product development. Meetings between the buyer and supplier for fit sessions to review samples are examples of these, and will be undertaken as and when they are required. However, throughout the process there are two overriding formal meetings that guide the planning and trading activities of the buyer and merchandiser. The former is regulated by the range meeting process that covers the period between the research activities through to the distribution ones. The second are the trading meetings which start at the distribution activity and occur through to the end of the concept-to-carrier bag process, the end of the season.

These meeting cycles carry much weight within B&M as they are seen as staging posts in the life cycle of a product, and are opportunities for all the relevant players within the value chain to meet and discuss the product range to agree together how to proceed for the benefit of the business. As a result, great emphasis is placed on these meetings and much work goes into preparing for them. This section provides an insight into their contribution to the workings of B&M.

The planning cycle can be lengthy and subject to much change. A benign economic environment at the beginning of the cycle may suddenly change to a malignant one requiring a change in planning presumptions, or a trend may suddenly emerge that merits a place in a product range in development. The range review process is therefore designed to bring some order to the planning process, but also to offer opportunities for reflection and review of the work completed to date to ask if decisions made are still valid or not. The schedule is split into up to five meetings and is laid out in Figure 4.8 .

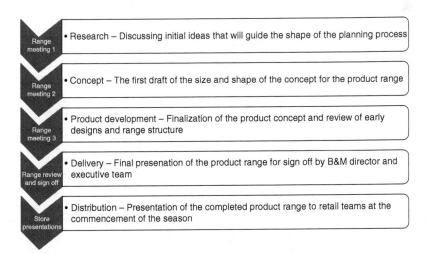

Figure 4.8 The planning schedule of meetings

The first three planning meetings will be led by the buyer and merchandiser, both of whom will have prepared documents for discussion. The assistant buyer and merchandiser will support in the preparation for the meetings, contributing where relevant their own information and analysis. The usual audience will comprise the head of B&M, and the design and QA teams, and together the meetings will consider the following:

- Range meeting 1 – The buyer will present data on predicted trends and moods and discuss which are felt to be relevant to the business. Early ideas for colour palettes, silhouettes and fabrics are discussed, and, if a branded business, the discussion will also assess which brands are likely to be on-trend and if there are any brands that should be actively courted. The merchandiser will present initial budget proposals and discuss the influences such as projected economic strength, financial guidance from the finance team or simply the gut feel that led to their creation. The output from the meeting is confirmation from the head of B&M that the team can progress to the next stage of the planning process.
- Range meeting 2 – Approximately one month later, the team will meet again and this time review the more detailed planning that has resulted in a product range concept. Discussion will be had about the size and shape of the range, the number of options to be ranged, how much will be bought of each and which suppliers will be manufacturing them. This work of the buyer will have been undertaken in conjunction with the merchandiser, who will present a draft budget that reflects the detailed product concept and a calculated OTB. The output from this meeting is confirmation of the product concept and proposed budgets to allow the first orders to be placed.
- Range meeting 3 – This is the final range meeting between the original members of the planning group. It is used to recap on any changes to plans since the last meeting and reviews early samples of the product range provided by suppliers. The meeting is usually held another month after the second meeting and in that time the first of a finalized buying budget will have been spent with the agreement of the finance team. In a branded product range, this meeting will finalize the brand matrix which details the distribution of brands to stores and the buying budget to be spent on each.

At this point the buyer and merchandiser will work to complete the planning of the range and prepare for the last two planning meetings, which tend to occur just before the beginning of the new season.

- Range review and sign-off – This meeting is the opportunity for the buyer and merchandiser to present their finalized product range to the executive group of the business for approval. The various directors of the business are given a preview of the collection and its direction, along with its budgets and value to the business. This allows directors of the business to assess how their own teams can maximize the range when it goes on sale.
- Store presentations – The final planning meeting is between the buying team and retail store staff. This is led by the buyer, who will present the product range

or brands to stores, discuss the inspiration behind the product and give tips on display and delivery timings. The merchandiser will be on hand to discuss allocation quantities and, if relevant, sales budgets and timings of promotional activities.

Timings of the planning meetings will vary depending upon the overall timings of the concept-to-carrier bag process that the retail business operates. However, in general, as shown in Figure 4.8, the meetings will occur at the point when the research, concept, product development, delivery and distribution stages of the model occur.

By contrast to the planning period, the schedule of meetings during the trading period is far more intense. There is at least one weekly meeting that involves the B&M team, each of which has immediate outcomes that need actioning as quickly as possible. The pace of trading the product range provides the equivalent of an adrenaline rush; instant decisions, sudden changes to priorities and much negotiation to ensure the opportunities of that day can be maximized. With potentially frenetic decision making, the meeting structure is designed to give time to pause and consider the most suitable next steps. There are three regular meetings that are held and these are detailed in Figure 4.9 .

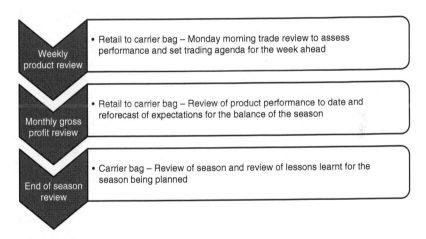

Weekly product review
- Retail to carrier bag – Monday morning trade review to assess performance and set trading agenda for the week ahead

Monthly gross profit review
- Retail to carrier bag – Review of product performance to date and reforecast of expectations for the balance of the season

End of season review
- Carrier bag – Review of season and review of lessons learnt for the season being planned

Figure 4.9 The trading schedule of meetings

The meetings are led by the buyer and merchandiser, and they present trading updates to both the B&M director and head of B&M. The focus of the meetings is as follows:

- Weekly product review – these are held every Monday morning without fail and review the previous week's performance to the budget set and the previous year. Comparisons are made between product groups to assess which are performing well and which are not. The buyer will present the best and worst sellers from the range and an immediate plan of action for the week ahead will be agreed.

- Monthly gross profit review – this meeting is dominated by the merchandiser, who will present the business's performance to date against the budgets that had been created during the planning process. This is used to assess the emerging financial trends and the likely trading performance during the remaining weeks of the season. To do this accurately requires some skill, but the output of it is an informed assessment of impacts on the budgeted gross trading profit and the stock position at the end of the season. With forward visibility of this nature, any corrective actions or changes to the remaining product to be delivered can be agreed by the team.

- End of season review – this final meeting of the season reviews where the business ended at the end of the season against its original qualitative and quantitative concepts agreed at the beginning of the planning process. At this final point, nothing can be done to alter the performance of the product range as it fades into history, and the meeting is in effect a post mortem of what happened, designed to inform the best course of action for following seasons.

With a regular flow of key planning and trading meetings, the burden of which are shared equally between buyer and merchandiser, the control mechanisms to ensure well-timed and accurate decision making are in place. An explanation of how those decisions are made will begin in Part Two.

CHAPTER AND PART ONE SUMMARY

This chapter completes Part One of this book. Part Two will concentrate on the role of the merchandiser and present a detailed step-by-step review of their concept-to-carrier bag process. Before that, though, what has Part One discussed?

Fashion is big business and subject to constant evolution either by accident or design. Its growth has been achieved on the back of equilibrium between the forces of supply and demand, in a generally benign macro-trading environment since the Second World War. This has made it an exciting but very competitive industry. To survive, levels of professionalism amongst its stakeholders have risen to combat the increasing risk of being left behind as the industry develops still further. As this chapter alone has shown, the route to successful product management is multifaceted, and involves many stakeholders within the retail value chain, one of whom is merchandiser.

The role of the merchandiser is well hidden. Consumers buying product are unaware of how the merchandiser has contributed to the process of product management, but contribute they have, and in a unique way that adds real value to business success. The concept-to-carrier bag process has shown that there is a place for the merchandiser, and this chapter has reinforced that view by adding texture to the argument that the role acts like a bridge connecting two potentially opposing forces; buying and finance. The importance of the role is proven; the detail will come in Part Two and the next six chapters.

SELF-DIRECTED STUDY

1. Review the chapter and devise job advertisements for a fashion business looking to recruit a merchandising team.
2. Review Chapters 1–4 and write a short 1,000-word review of the B&M function. Outline the key differences between the buyer and merchandiser roles.
3. Research the value chain and list all the roles that contribute to the creation of product range. Which of those you have identified would fit within primary activities and which are support activities.

Further Reading

Goworek, H. (2007) *Fashion Buying*. Oxford: Blackwell

Jackson, T. and Shaw, D. (2001) *Mastering Fashion Buying and Merchandising Management*. Basingstoke: Macmillan

Porter, M. (1985) *Competitive Advantage*. New York: Free Press

Varley, R. (2001) *Retail Product Management*. London: Routledge

Bibliography

Goldfingle, G. (2013) *SuperGroup supply chain glitch 'shows risks of rapid expansion'*

Retail Week [Internet]. Available from http://www.retail-week.com/sectors/fashion/supergroup-supply-chain-glitch-shows-risks-of-rapid-expansion/5029904.article [Accessed 20th January 2014]

Portas, M. (2010) *Shop! Mary Portas at Superdry*. Daily Telegraph [Internet]. Available from http://fashion.telegraph.co.uk/news-features/TMG8140569/Shop-Mary-Portas-at-Superdry.html [Accessed 20th January 2014]

Porter, M. (1985) *Competitive Advantage*. New York: Free Press

Introduction to Part Two

The second part of this book will outline the activities of the merchandiser, by providing a practical demonstration of the role. This will be accomplished through the use of a fictional case study used to discuss – but more importantly – example the role. A case study has been chosen as an appropriate approach as it acts as an anchor to enable each of the activities of the merchandiser to be linked together through both text and numerical exampling.

Exampling the role of the merchandiser is notoriously difficult for two reasons. First, many of their activities are hidden from public consciousness and cannot be visually exampled in the same way as those of the buyer. Mood boards, pen portraits, fashion shows can all be found within the public domain to demonstrate good or bad buying. However, for the merchandiser, their outputs – budgets, OTBs, phasing plans etc. – are not easily accessible as they are viewed as confidential by businesses, meaning replication within a theoretical context is difficult. Second, it is easy to become bogged down in numerical data and examples of calculations rather than focusing on their importance. A case study that flows between chapters will provide both the context in which the role operates, and provide a linked process within the numbers to show how they each rely on one another to be created, and the value that they bring to product management.

The approach will introduce Prentice Day, a fictional retailer and, as a starting point, presumes that it is at the beginning of planning for a new season product range. Inevitably, a fictional case study will mean that some given presumptions will have to be used to set the scene, as well as an element of oversimplification of scenarios to allow a flow to the chapters. The process laid out is not authoritative but a guide; not all businesses will follow it exactly or accept its outputs as being appropriate. What Part Two will offer is an example of a seamless process with each chapter flowing into the next, and in doing this it uses the shape of the concept-to-carrier bag process outlined in Part One.

5 Fashion Merchandising: The Prentice Day Case Study

INTENDED LEARNING OUTCOMES

1. Introducing the Prentice Day case study used throughout Part Two.
2. Initial research tools – gross trading profit and sales density analysis.
3. Understanding the relevance of macro environment research.
4. The relevance and benefits of a merchandiser's planning strategy.

INTRODUCTION

This first chapter of Part Two will introduce the Prentice Day case study that will be used over the next six chapters. The information presented within it sets the scene and uses various analysis tools to build an initial picture of the subject of the case study. To ease the journey ahead, assumptions have been made that in a real-life scenario might not be fully appropriate; however, the aim at all times is to present ideas in such a way as to enable a quantifiable output to be articulated within each chapter.

For the case study, a menswear retailer was chosen. This product category lends itself to clear product groups and the fashionability attribute which will be discussed extensively. The retailer is truly fictitious, and bears no known resemblance to an existing business. A business the size and scale of Prentice Day would be highly unlikely to have distinct buyer and merchandiser roles; however, to enable this second part to concentrate on demonstrating the merchandiser role, it is presumed that the two roles exist.

By the end of the chapter a business scenario will have been explained, with initial planning decisions made. As the chapters unfold, each will be cross-referenced back to this chapter, and as the case study develops, this will help with digesting the data still to come.

PRENTICE DAY MENSWEAR CASE STUDY

It is 1 July and another spring/summer season is coming to a close. The planning process for a new spring/summer collection, due to launch in the following January, is about to start for a small family-owned menswear fashion business called Prentice Day. The business trades out of one store located on busy Oxford Street, in the heart of London's West End. The business has traded for many years, is well established with a loyal customer base that comprises men who work locally, who are looking to buy simple and easy-to-understand product from Prentice Day. The store also benefits from the many tourists and out-of-town shoppers who regularly make their way to the premier shopping district of London, drawn by its many well-known retail businesses.

FOCUS POINT 5.1: THE MARKETING MIX

The marketing mix was developed by Neil Borden in the mid-20th century to act as a marketing tool to ensure that a business and its product offer are in line with the expectations and financial capability of a target customer. The mixing together of the 4Ps (product, price, place and promotion) into a consistent product and marketing strategy ensures that a business is easily understood by customers and marketing strategies are effective.

Over time, the 4Ps are giving way to the 7Ps – the original four components plus physical presence, people and process. These extra components have become more relevant as retailing has moved further towards a service-orientated brand experience.

The business has traded well for many years, and its success has been the result of strong attention being paid to ensuring its marketing mix is balanced and continually updated (see Table 5.1). The owners place emphasis on understanding their customers, making continual changes to the product offer as required. This is achieved by creating product ranges that are formed from detailed research not only of fashion trends, but also by analysing each range's performance to determine the best product strategy for forthcoming seasons.

Table 5.1 *The Prentice Day 4P marketing mix*

Product	An exclusive own-label product of co-ordinated easy pieces that attract men aged 20–35 years of age. The range takes key fashion trends and interprets them into simple-to-understand basic and fashion styles
Price	The pricing policy reflects the customer perception of quality product and exclusive designs. The price policy places Prentice Day in the same price bracket as Next and Gap
Place	The store is located within the Plaza on the east side of Oxford Street, London. The store benefits from its prime location and is particularly busy during lunch breaks on weekdays when office workers shop and all day at the weekend
Promotion	The store does not advertise itself and is reliant on a well-laid-out store, personal selling to customers and twice yearly end of season sales

Despite this balanced approach to planning, the owners of the business were disappointed by the reaction to the product offer for the spring/summer season just concluding. The product offer was organized within the business into a three-level hierarchy, designed to create cohesive product ranges that could easily be translated into defined store layouts that made best use of floor space. The product hierarchy followed a classic ranking approach with the three levels being defined as follows (Figure 5.1):

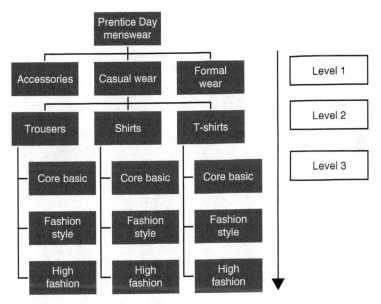

Figure 5.1 *The product hierarchy of Prentice Day*

- Level 1: Product group – e.g. casual wear
- Level 2: Product type – e.g. trousers, shirts, T-shirts
- Level 3: Attribute – e.g. fashionability.

Within the product hierarchy, the buyer felt that the product range had a competitive and cohesive mix of accessories, casual wear and formal wear. Over the course of the season, the casual wear product range had performed well and almost sold out, while formal wear seemed slow and required markdown to reduce stock levels in the ESS (end of season sale). The accessories range – a small additional product offer providing an incremental sales opportunity – was considered to be too small to be of any real consequence to the success or failure of the clothing ranges. The main disappointment, however, was the product range's failure to meet the businesses financial requirement of it. Sales turnover and gross profits missed their budgets, albeit by a small amount. However, the budgets had been considered to be very easily beatable, and overall trade in Oxford Street was buoyant; the owners had expected to end the season in a stronger financial position.

A strong financial position was certainly needed. The development of the West End of London, with new stores such as Primark opening for trade, meant that Prentice Day needed to generate good gross trading profits to support its overheads and enable investment in the store to keep it in line with its new larger, stronger competitors. The size and scale of these formidable competitors enabled them to introduce new retail concepts such as lifestyle shop fitting and the use of new point-of-sale techniques such as digital signage, as ways of enticing customers away from small independents. In addition, the continued growth of online trading was luring loyal Prentice Day customers to broaden their fashion purchasing beyond the little menswear shop upon which they had previously relied, promoting the owners to consider developing a transactional website in the future.

FOCUS POINT 5.2: THE SWOT

The SWOT analysis tool is used to identify the macro and micro situations facing a business at any one time. The micro, or internal strengths or weaknesses, are summarized and analysed to then influence the macro or external opportunities and threats that the business faces.

It is important that a SWOT has a ranking within it so the bullet-point summaries used to communicate to the reader should be written in priority order. This gives a sense of scale and for the buyer and merchandiser and helps them to prioritize their workload.

SWOTs can be dangerous, though. They are of the moment, and the factors that influence them can change at a moment's notice – they need regular review and updating.

Concerned by the disappointing reaction to the product range at a time when the best possible profitability was required, the Prentice Day owners spent time reviewing the business and articulated their thoughts in a SWOT (strengths, weaknesses, opportunities and threats) which is detailed in Table 5.2 below.

Recognizing research value, the owners of Prentice Day requested that the SWOT be incorporated into the new season planning process by the buyer and merchandiser. For their part, the merchandiser knew that to be in a position to create a successful planning strategy that would reflect the SWOT'S data, three initial steps would have to be taken.
These were:

1. Obtain an initial understanding of the strengths and weaknesses of the product range.
2. Consider the likely trading environment that the business would face in the season ahead.
3. Develop a merchandising-specific planning strategy to guide the decision-making process.

Table 5.2 The Prentice Day SWOT analysis

Strengths	Weaknesses
The store is established and well known within its trading location	The product range is not providing a suitable financial return
There is a loyal customer base for core basic product types	Customers consistently complain of issues with size availability within T-shirts
The product ranges follow in-demand trends	A strong focus on product management is not mirrored with a focus on product budgets
The supplier base is flexible with short lead times and so can support changes in product mixes	The lack of a transactional website is not liked by loyal customers

Opportunities	Threats
Challenge B&M to ensure sales, profits and cash flow improvements for the new season	Customers are increasingly cost-conscious and do not tolerate price increases well
Reshape the total product offer in line with demand patterns	There are new stores planned to open on Oxford Street which could poach customers
Develop a better sizing strategy for T-shirts	Online trading is relevant to our customers and may reduce footfall further
Grow and develop strong product types such as core basics for the transactional website	While London trade is strong, the rest of the UK and the world are less strong

INITIAL APPROACHES TO UNDERSTANDING A BUSINESS

Before commencing any detailed research activities, the merchandiser will under-take a short summary review of business performance to obtain an initial feeling of its strengths and weaknesses. This is achieved by reviewing two business metrics:

- actual gross trading profit
- sales densities.

The ultimate success criterion for any product range is its gross trading profitability. It is these profits that will support the businesses overheads, but also provide capital to invest back into the business. Knowing the levers of profitability at the beginning of the planning process not only informs the merchandiser, but can also lead them through the first vital research process step.

Table 5.3 identifies the three distinct product groups within Prentice Day; its accessories, casual wear and formal wear ranges. Each has delivered cash gross profits which combined add up to £35,005. The table compares these achieved gross trading profits to the equivalent budget and the previous year figures. To easily interpret the data, the table highlights performance using a colour coded traffic-light system with mid-grey for good, light grey for average and dark grey for poor profit performance.

Table 5.3 *Gross trading profit by product group compared to budget and the previous year figures*

Spring/summer season	Actual gross trading profit	Budget gross trading profit	Trading gross profit % variance budget	Previous year gross trading profit	Gross trading profit % variance previous year
Men's accessories	£4,125	£4,125	0%	£3,850	+7%
Men's casual wear	£18,823	£13,813	+36%	£12,864	+46%
Men's formal wear	£12,057	£17,750	–32%	£16,250	–26%
Total gross trading profit	£35,005	£35,688	–2%	£32,964	+6%

The table tells the merchandiser that casual wear not only outperformed its gross trading profit budget, but almost made up the deficit recorded by the formal wear product group. Accessories, while small in its cash profit contribution, did perform in line with budget and, like casual wear, recorded profit growth against the previous year.

Sales density, by contrast, measures the efficiency of use of retail space to generate sales. It is particularly useful in identifying where particular product groups are over- or underperforming against the business average. Acceptable density values vary by business model type, but a general rule of thumb is that businesses will aim to achieve as high a sales density as possible, meaning that the maximum sales turnover is being generated on the store space available. Its calculation is very simple and uses two variables; sales turnover and floor space employed.

- Sales turnover/floor space employed = sales density
- £250,000/1,000 square ft = £250 sales density

Accurate density analysis requires that the two components are accurate to be effective. Recording accurate cash sales turnover is a standard activity within a retail store, but the management of floor space can be more difficult. While the total size of a store may not change, the use of space within it often does and so the use of density analyses requires an accurate measurement of the division of floor space between product groups to be of use.

The Prentice Day store was small in comparison to the large multiple businesses such as Next, Burton and Gap trading nearby. The store was 1,500 square ft in total (150m²) of which 1,000 square ft was used as trading space. Figure 5.2 shows the store and its layout.

Table 5.4 meanwhile identifies sales densities generated by each product group within the Prentice Day store after the merchandiser had completed the density analysis.

Table 5.4 shows that the accessories product range drives the highest sales density – it may be a small cash product group, but its retail execution appears highly efficient. Casual wear too, outperforms the £90 average sales density, while it falls

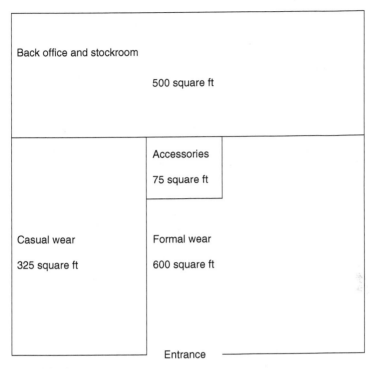

Figure 5.2 *Prentice Day store layout*

Table 5.4 *Prentice Day sales densities*

Spring/summer season	Actual cash sales turnover	Floor space employed	Sales density
Men's accessories	£10,000	75 square ft	£133
Men's casual wear	£40,000	325 square ft	£123
Men's formal wear	£40,000	600 square ft	£67
Total sales density	£90,000	1,000 square ft	£90

to formal wear to significantly underperform, suggesting its space allocation in store is too big to justify its contribution to sales turnover.

With two analyses reviewed, the merchandiser already has a feel for the strengths and weaknesses in the product range, which are both clear in message and also go some way to explaining the detail within the SWOT. Formal wear is weak and the main cause of the disappointing overall financial performance. Casual wear meanwhile appears very strong, with its performance supportive of the buyer view that customers have a preference for it. Accessories, while thought of as an add-on product range, may be worth further review – its financial performance is good, and its sales densities are in line with the powerhouse that is casualwear.

UNDERSTANDING THE MACRO ENVIRONMENT

There is a tendency to view merchandising as being introspective, always reviewing and checking internal financial data, whilst the extrovert buyer travels the world looking for inspiration and fresh approaches to fashion. There is some truth in this view; however, the role does have an outward-looking element to it that can be forgotten. An introspective role alone will not provide a rounded approach to understanding the context within which data are reviewed and acted upon. Reliance on a past season trading history is limiting, and the conditions that came together to influence the previous season are unlikely to occur in exactly the same way again. The addition of an assessment of forward forecasts of the macro environment facing a business highlights external influences that could impact the quantitative aspects of the product range, just as trend and cultural influences could impact upon the qualitative ones.

The relevance of macro data will vary by market sector, business model type and size, but relevant knowledge offers a fresh perspective within the planning process, and gives a real-world context, adding flavour to what budgetary numbers suggest. Recognising that macro environment research will vary by business type, it is possible to identify some common analysis tools and their relevance to the merchandiser at this point in the planning process.

- Competitor trends

Competitor trends data that link product ranges to financial strength can provide vital intelligence to a business. Which competitor holds the greatest market share? Which competitors are growing their share and which are facing a decline? This different dimension to competitor trends allows the planning process to take into account the power and influence competitors have within the market, so identifying opportunities or limitations that the fashion business has in attracting consumers to their stores.

- Economic trends

Prevailing economic trends significantly impact the budgeting decision-making process. Reviewing indices such as gross domestic product (GDP) growth, inflation forecasts and specific forecasts for individual market types provides a feel for the risk within the market, growth opportunities and also forewarning about possible inflationary pressures. The well-communicated response by many fashion businesses – such as Next – to the phenomenal growth of inflationary pressures in 2011 due to raw material prices increasing indicated their strong grasp on the realities of the macro market.

- Product trends

Product trend analysis is a natural research area and is used not just to identify fashion trends, but also the financial size of the market, growths against previous years and/or specific trading periods (e.g. Christmas or Valentine's Day). A good example of the balance that such analysis can provide could be seen in 2009, when the Christmas season occurred during the worst of the banking crisis. Being able to benchmark performance against the dreadful market trend as a whole gave true insights to a retail business's performance within the market, rather than relying simply on internal financial data.

• Price and volume trends

Price and volume trend analysis reviews the relationship between market value and unit volumes. A growing market in value is not always an indication that all is well within a particular product segment. The growth of discount fashion ranges and intense competition has reduced retail price inflation, meaning that any recent market growth has come from unit volume growth. Understanding this relationship is vital in setting retail selling prices and setting suitable financial budgets.

The depth to which such macro data are reviewed varies, and in the case of a small single store business, wide ranging national data could have less resonance than data which are related to its specific market – in this case London. With this in mind, the Prentice Day merchandiser, after reviewing a wide range of data, summarized their findings and these are presented in Table 5.5.

Table 5.5 *Prentice Day macro environment research summary*

Competitor trends	The development of Oxford Street and the growth of malls such as Westfield Shepherd's Bush will increase competition
Economic trends	Retail sales growth in London is forecast to be at least 10 per cent next versus the UK average growth rate of 5 per cent
Product trends	Casual wear is on-trend and predicted to continue growing market share next year
Price and volume trends	Strong retail sales growth is forecast to be driven by unit volume growth rather than increasing retail prices

IDENTIFYING A PLANNING STRATEGY

Without yet undertaking a comprehensive review of the product range, the merchandiser is already equipped with rich data which can act as a set of signposts directing their future decision making. Such signposts are invaluable as they can give shape to the analysis when confronted with a potentially detailed and labour-intensive review. Taking each element in turn, a picture is built up of the key themes and messages from each, and from there priorities emerge. Table 5.6 summarizes the findings from the research undertaken by the merchandiser up to this point.

Table 5.6 *Initial research summary*

SWOT summary
Prentice Day has strength in the core basic product offer – Is there potential to develop this?
The supplier base is flexible – changes can be made to the product hierarchy as appropriate
There is an issue with T-shirts that requires investigation
Gross trading profit summary
Casual wear is performing very strongly – What is causing the strong gross profit performance?
Formal wear is the opposite – What is causing this?
Accessories are in line with expectation and do not appear a priority
Density analysis summary
Accessories are the strongest product group, which conflicts with the gross profit summary
Formal wear appears to be overspaced and so have too many options in the product range
Macro environment review
There is growing competition in a buoyant retail market
Growth is driven by volume growth rather than price increases
There is a clear opportunity with the strong growth forecast within the London economy

Reviewing the table, the first signposts to guide the planning process can be summarized into an initial planning strategy to be discussed with the buyer, the finance team and the business owners. From the summary, three key topics emerge as being central to the strategy.

1. Gross trading profit: All gross profit levers must be reviewed and understood.
   a. There is wild variation in gross profit by product group which needs to be understood and corrected.
2. Product: The performance of the product range needs to be understood.
   a. What is the correct mix of product groups for next year?
   b. Attention needs to be paid to T-shirts and accessories to understand their potential.
3. Competition is strong.
   a. Prentice Day is strong in core basics which work well in a volume-driven trading environment.
      i. What is the true potential of core basics?
   b. Unit volumes must increase as a result of the planning process.

This defining of a planning strategy direction will shape thoughts and actions, and this is no different for the Prentice Day merchandiser. This quantitative planning strategy is also useful for the buyer, as within it there will be precious information on possible priorities for them to consider in advance of more formal discussions when finalizing the product range for the new season.

SUMMARY

This chapter has acted as a prologue to Part Two of this book, which will lay out the merchandiser role and its activities through a practical demonstration using the

Prentice Day case study. As such, it has set the scene and established a shape for the activities to be reviewed over the remaining chapters of Part Two. The concepts introduced while simplified for the purposes of the text and ease of discussion are industry-standard. The skill, as with the other chapters in Part Two, is in the interpretation, knowing what to look for and spotting inconsistencies in data.

A second requirement at this point is to have an open mind. As humans we tend to remember anecdotes and conversations, and it is very common to believe strongly about a particular event or action over the course of a season as being definitive in the ultimate performance of the product range. Time and time again, good research proves many of these beliefs wrong, and so open minds lead to open research and effective reflection and understanding of what really happened.

SELF-DIRECTED STUDY

1. Create a 4P and SWOT analysis for a national retail fashion brand of your choice.
    a. Using Mintel and Verdict research, understand the macro environment facing the brand.
    b. Undertake a full comparative shop review of your chosen brand.
    c. Review the competitors of your band and note their strengths and weaknesses.
    d. Research trade and national press for details of your brand's financial position.
2. Create a planning strategy for the brand based on your research

Further Reading

Goworek, H. (2007) *Fashion Buying*. Oxford: Blackwell

Jackson, T. and Shaw, D. (2001) *Mastering Fashion Buying and Merchandising Management*. Basingstoke: Macmillan

Jackson, T. and Shaw, D. (2009) *Mastering Fashion Marketing*. Basingstoke: Macmillan

6 Fashion Merchandising: Research and Analysis

INTENDED LEARNING OUTCOMES

1. An appreciation of the process of analysing key performance indicators (KPI) budgets.
2. An appreciation of the process of analysing product performance.
3. A demonstration of how to draw conclusions from analysis.
4. A demonstration of the creation of a financial product strategy for Prentice Day.

INTRODUCTION

As discussed in Chapter 1, there are many differing fashion business models, all of which will plan, organize and analyse themselves in a way that is suitable for their own successful pursuit of business strength. This process, and the resulting creation of commercial product buying strategies, will therefore vary, and so identifying a single research process that is applicable to all retail businesses is impossible. It *is* possible to simplify a number of approaches into a single generic example as presented in this chapter. The result is not exhaustive, but it does demonstrate the value of good research.

In the presentation of a research and analysis approach, this chapter clarifies the merchandiser role as a bridge between the established and well-understood buying and finance roles. The financial and product awareness of the business possessed by the end of the research process is an invaluable resource. It can help both buyers and finance to make holistic fact-based decisions rather than mixing fact with a liberal dose of anecdotal personal thought. The chapter will do this by developing the Prentice Day case study to review and analyse budget and product data, concluding with the formulation of a budgeting strategy which will continue into Chapter 7, where product budgets will be created. Each chapter, including this one, will start with a reminder of the concept-to-carrier bag model to set the scene. This chapter then starts at the beginning of the model, the activity of research and analysis (Table 6.1).

Table 6.1 *The concept-to-carrier bag model*

Concept-to-carrier bag step	Definition
1. Research	**Undertaking and collation of relevant fashion research**
2. Concept	Creation of product range concept and direction
3. Product development	Finalization of concept as a product range
4. Sourcing	Sourcing of suppliers and manufacturers for the range
5. Manufacturing	Manufacture of the product range
6. Shipping	Shipping and delivery of the product range
7. Warehousing	Receipt of the product range, and its allocation to store and storage
8. Distribution	Delivering initial store allocations
9. Retail	Display, sale, promotion and stock replenishment
10. Carrier bag	Purchase of the product by a consumer

RETAIL MATHEMATICS VERSUS COMMERCIAL ACUMEN

Being the first activity apportions significant importance to the research process. Once a planning season moves towards defining a product concept, both buyer and merchandiser must be able to work on their individual tasks secure in the knowledge that they are working to a single vision and strategy. This can only be true where research has accurately informed the decision-making process, and so it must be skilfully completed by being mathematically correct, but also commercially relevant to the following stages within the planning process.

The former requirement is easy to deliver. The beauty of mathematics within fashion merchandising is that the variables within the calculations are limited in number, are simple to carry out and big in effectiveness. The commercial relevance of financial research can be more difficult to articulate. Numerical analysis can focus too much on the absolute answer rather than what the true meaning is. A common example of this is undertaking research at the end of a season and reviewing data to assess where a product range ended up. This approach is flawed as a business can only retail the stock that it has offered for sale, research should be used to identify facts but also identify potential. Selling out of a product is good – sales presumptions maximized, markdown avoided and stock holding reduced are all good metrics – but selling out also implies more could have been made of the product – bigger unit buys, improved stock availability and increased sales. Therefore, using research not just to identify what happened, but also to identify what should have happened, is important. Using mathematics to identify fact but also to be a tool to question data is a more appropriate method of attack, and is one with which the fashion merchandiser approaches the task.

To do this effectively, the merchandiser analyses and assesses the performance of the product ranges for which they are responsible throughout a fashion season. Daily, weekly and monthly research to highlight performance is a prerequisite of a retail business, and as a season progresses trends emerge, surprise reactions to products happen and lessons are learnt. With regular research throughout a season, the inclusion of a formal review of the previous season at the start of the concept-to-carrier bag model must deliver specific benefits. First, a total review of all budget and option performance of a comparable season gives a good strategic summary of the direction of the business, giving signposts to future product concepts and their budget requirements. Second, it allows all relevant data to be reviewed at a single point in time, providing uniform research that gives a good sense of ranking the range into good, average and poor performances which then can influence the buyer and their new season buying strategy. This approach is mirrored by the use of defined retail calculations, meaning that all analysis uses a standard set of calculations, generating comparisons on equal terms and no subjective favouritism for a particular product type will cloud the judgements of either buyer or merchandiser.

BUDGET ANALYSIS

The management of the finances of a product range is the core of the merchandiser role, and so understanding budget performance is an appropriate place to start the research process. Budget analysis within B&M is most effective when it is used to signpost direction, posing questions that can be answered by a more detailed product analysis. The analysis reviews the budgets introduced in Chapter 2 for which the merchandiser has responsibility, and they are summarized below:

- sales turnover
- markdown spend
- intake margin percentage
- stock level (inventory).

Each one is reviewed throughout the product category hierarchy and is related to the initial gross trading profit and sales densities analyses previously completed. The analysis is guided by the use of two standard calculations, those of percentage mix and variance.

The mix calculation is used to identify the quantitative contribution of a variable within a collection of related variables, and is useful to demonstrate each one's importance. For example, if a jumper were available in two colours, red and blue, each colour would represent 50 per cent of the total (Table 6.2).

Table 6.2 The percentage mix calculation

Style	Quantity	% Mix	Calculation
Red	1	50%	(red jumper/total number of jumpers)*100 = 50% or (1/2)*100 = 50%
Blue	1	50%	(blue jumper/total number of jumpers)*100 = 50% or (1/2)*100 = 50%
Total	2	100%	

The variance calculation is used to identify positive or negative changes in size between two related variables. In the example below, stating that jumper sales turnover is 33 per cent above its budget gives an easy-to-understand sense of scale to the success of the product type (Table 6.3).

Table 6.3 *The percentage variance calculation*

Product	Actual sales	Budget	Calculation
Jumpers	£20,000	£15,000	((actual sales – budget sales)/budget sales)*100 = 33% or ((£20,000–£15,000)/£15,000)*100 = 33%

The budget review starting point is to be aware of the period and the product categories that are to be analysed. In the Prentice Day case study, the budget analysis will cover:

- a spring/summer season of 26 weeks' duration between 1 January and 30 June
- all three product categories ranged within the store – accessories, casual wear and formal wear.

With the starting point set, the first activity would be to analyse the overall shape of the range by understanding each product budget contribution to the total business by using the percentage mix calculation. This summary is presented in Table 6.4.

Table 6.4 *Overall business shape analysis*

	Actual sales turnover mix	Actual markdown spend mix	Actual stock mix	Actual gross trading profit mix
Men's accessories	12%	4%	22%	12%
Men's casual wear	44%	24%	17%	54%
Men's formal wear	44%	72%	61%	34%
Total	100%	100%	100%	100%

Table 6.4 presents a rich source of data to the merchandiser which is summarized below:

- Sales turnover – Casual and formal wear are equal in size (44 per cent of the mix), while accessories represents a small but still significant 12 per cent mix.
- Markdown spend – Formal wear accounts for 72 per cent of all markdown spent. This concentration of markdown implies its ranges were weak and needed price reductions to stimulate demand.
- Stock – All product categories stock holding mixes are out of line with sales mixes, suggesting that none is being bought in line with sales potential. Accessories and formal wear both appear to carry excessive stocks whilst the casual wear stock mix at 17 per cent is far lower than its sales mix, implying stock shortages.

- Gross trading profit – The mix of profit generated demonstrates the success of casual wear. Of all profits, 54 per cent came from its casual wear products. Accessories mix was in line with sales, but formal wear generated just 34 per cent of gross trading profit, well down on its sales mix.

The owners are correct in their thinking that accessories are a smaller part of the product mix, however; it contributes 12 per cent to sales turnover, which is not insignificant. The bigger implication of the mix analysis is the influence of casual wear within the business. Its sales and profit mixes are high, but its markdown and stock mixes are low, implying it is not being bought to potential. Conversely, formal wear appears to be overbought with high stock and markdown mixes compared to casual wear.

The initial mix analysis has posed some interesting questions to be answered. A greater detail of analysis reviewing each budget individually will answer the initial presumptions more fully. To do this, each one will be reviewed comparing actual data to the following variables:

- budget set for the season;
- the previous year.

The first budget to review is the sales turnover budget shown in Table 6.5 below, which is colour coded – mid-grey for good, light grey for average and dark grey for poor.

Table 6.5 Sales turnover analysis

	Actual sales turnover	Sales turnover budget	Sales turnover % variance to budget	Sales turnover previous year	Sales turnover % variance to previous year
Men's accessories	£10,000	£10,000	0%	£9,500	+5%
Men's casual wear	£40,000	£33,000	+21%	£31,500	+27%
Men's formal wear	£40,000	£50,000	−20%	£47,500	−16%
Total sales turnover	£90,000	£93,000	−3%	£88,500	+2%

Using the mid-grey, light grey and dark grey colour coding system, the merchandiser can assess strengths and weaknesses within the sales turnover budget.

- Good
  - The only product category to exceed its sales turnover budget was casual wear (+21 per cent).
  - Accessories and casual wear sales turnovers both exceeded the previous year cash figures. At +27 per cent, casual wear sales growth was very strong.
  - Accessories and casual wear were the reason that sales turnover in total at £90,000 was +2 per cent greater than the previous year.
- Average
  - Accessories sales turnover met its sales turnover budget.

- Poor
  - Formal wear sales turnover of £40,000 was −20 per cent below its budget and −16 per cent below the previous year.
  - The poor formal wear sales turnover meant that sales turnover in total was £3,000 lower than budget, representing a −3 per cent underperformance.

Accessories, while representing a small sales turnover, appears to be a stable product category that has performed in line with original expectations. This stability makes the product category worth retaining as it offers relatively risk-free sales turnover to the business.

Casual wear appears to be highly successful and could be developed further. The sales turnover analysis also supports the SWOT analysis, which described casual wear as running out of stock. Formal wear, on the other hand, has performed poorly and the analysis backs up the perception that customers do not understand or like the formal wear range.

As informative as it is, the sales turnover analysis cannot be relied upon in isolation to set a product strategy. Sales performance can be highly influenced by markdown. Markdown is reviewed next, to assess the depth of its influence on business performance. Table 6.6 presents the markdown budget analysis.

Table 6.6 *Markdown spend analysis*

	Actual markdown spend	Budget mark-down spend	Markdown spend % Variance budget	Previous year markdown spend	Markdown spend % Variance previous year
Men's accessories	£1,000	£1,000	0%	£1,100	−9%
Men's casual wear	£5,250	£7,500	−30%	£7,750	−32%
Men's formal wear	£16,000	£14,500	+10%	£15,000	+7%
Total markdown spend	£22,250	£23,000	−3%	£23,850	−7%

This table compares by product category the actual cash markdown spend that was needed to liquidate unsold stock at the end of the 26-week season.

- Good
  - Because markdown is a cost, casual wear by underspending markdown is the only product category to be better than its budget. Actual cash markdown spend of £5,250 was −30 per cent compared to budget.
  - The good casual wear markdown spend meant that the total markdown spend of £22,250 was also below budget at −3 per cent.
  - Both accessories (−9 per cent) and casual wear (−32 per cent) had less markdown spent clearing stocks than the previous year.
  - The good accessories and casual wear markdown spends resulted in the total £22,250 markdown spent being −7 per cent lower than the previous year.

- Acceptable
  - Accessories markdown spend was in line with budget.
- Poor
  - Formal wear markdown spend of £16,000 was +10 per cent higher than budget and also +7 per cent higher than the previous year.

The underspend of a cost of sales item in the P&L account is good, but has been delivered by a very strong casual wear range only. All of the budget provision for accessories was spent and formal wear significantly overspent – a reflection of its poor sales turnover. Reviewing the sales and markdown tables together implies that significant rebalancing of buying budgets between the product categories is required.

The merchandiser will next want to review the impact of sales turnover and markdown spend on the stock position at the end of the season under review. This is presented below in Table 6.7.

Table 6.7 *Stock level analysis*

	Actual closing stock	Budget closing stock	Closing stock % Variance budget	Previous year closing stock	Closing stock % Variance previous year
Men's accessories	£12,500	£12,500	0%	£12,500	0%
Men's casual wear	£10,000	£16,000	−38%	£16,000	−38%
Men's formal wear	£33,000	£25,000	+32%	£27,000	+22%
Total stock at end of season	£55,500	£53,500	+4%	£55,500	0%

The actual stock holding valued at retail selling at the close of the season shows the effectiveness of the use of markdown to clear stocks to budget.

- Good
  - Stock holding below budget implies good stock management. Casual wear held less stock (−38 per cent) at the close of the season to budget and also in comparison to the previous year.
- Acceptable
  - Accessories again was in line with budget and in this case was also in line with the previous year stock holding.
  - The strong casual wear and accessories stock holdings-enabled actual stock at the end of the season was in line with the previous year at £55,500.
- Poor
  - Formal wear stock holding of £33,000 was +32 per cent greater than budget and +22 per cent greater than the previous year.
  - As a result of the poor stock management of formal wear, total stock holding of £55,500 was greater than budgeted by 4 per cent.

The trends identified by the sales and markdown analyses – that accessories was a stable product category, casual wear had development potential, whilst formal wear was a poor performer – are confirmed by the stock level analysis. One key message emerges which is that casual wear quite clearly ran out of stock. Formal wear, on the other hand, missed its sales budget and even with the use of excessive markdown ended the season grossly overstocked. Formal wear was overbought and unappreciated by customers, the effect being to put a financial strain on the business as a whole.

One way of preventing poor trading from impacting upon business finances is to manage the intake margin percentage so that it is as high as possible. Knowing this is useful as a check to prevent any budget analysis from pushing the new season budgets towards low margin product types. In the case of Prentice Day, Table 6.8 presents an intake margin analysis.

Table 6.8 *Intake margin analysis*

	Intake margin %
Men's accessories	55%
Men's casual wear	65%
Men's formal wear	60%
Total	62%

Intake margin is expressed as a percentage and is the difference between cost price from the supplier and the selling price offered to the customer. The intake margin is declared exclusive of value added tax (VAT).

- Good
  - Casual wear intake margins are above the average for the business.
- Average
  - The average intake margin is 62 per cent.
- Poor
  - Both accessories and formal wear intake margins are lower than the average.

The compelling argument to develop the casual wear range is augmented by the strong intake margin achieved by the product. Accessories offer a safe and reliable contribution to the business but carry a low intake margin. The 60 per cent intake margin delivered by formal wear is below the average and so any opportunities to improve its finances – through, perhaps, selling price reductions – will be limited as reducing intake margin could put profitability at further risk.

The overall impact of the product budget's strengths and weaknesses on gross trading profitability is summarized in Table 6.9. For a fuller discussion of gross trading profit, refer back to Chapter 5.

Table 6.9 shows the gross trading profit delivered by the product ranges that was used to pay for the overheads of the business. It shows the ultimate effect each product category had on the financial strength of the business.

Table 6.9 *Gross trading profit analysis*

	Actual gross trading profit	Budget gross trading profit	Trading gross profit % variance budget	Previous year gross trading profit	Gross trading profit % variance previous year
Men's accessories	£4,125	£4,125	0%	£3,850	+7%
Men's casual wear	£18,823	£13,813	+36%	£12,864	+46%
Men's formal wear	£12,057	£17,750	−32%	£16,250	−26%
Total gross trading profit	£35,005	£35,688	−2%	£32,964	+6%

- Good
  - Casual wear is the only product category that has exceeded its budgeted gross trading profit. At £18,823, this is an increase of +36 per cent above budget.
  - Both accessories and casual wear profits are higher than the previous year.
  - The strength in accessories and casual wear has enabled total business profit of £35,005 to be +6 per cent higher than the previous year.
- Acceptable
  - Accessories profit of £4,125 is in line with its budgeted gross trading profit.
- Poor
  - Formal wear profit of £12,057 is −32 per cent below budget and −26 per cent lower than the previous year.
  - As a result of formal wear being such a poorly performing product, the total gross trading profit delivered by the business was −2 per cent lower than budget.

The ultimate success criterion for any range is its profitability. The excellent performance of casual wear across all KPI budget measures was of vital importance to the business. Casual wear not only outperformed its budgets, but the business relied upon it to make up for the poor formal wear performance. Accessories, while small in the mix of product, did perform in line with budget and was consistent in achieving its budgets. Accessories are unique in that they represented stability and a safe, if unspectacular, product for the business.

Reviewing each product budget individually, step by step, builds a picture of the business, its strengths and weaknesses, and, in the case of Prentice Day, has highlighted the following conclusions.

- Accessories
  - Safe and stable with no compelling reason to increase or reduce its sales mix. There is an opportunity to improve its stock management and intake margin percentage for the new season.
- Casual wear
  - The very high sales turnover growth, low markdown spend and stock levels suggest that the product range was underplanned initially and has much room to be expanded.

- Formal wear
  - The single reason that the business as a whole missed achieving its budgets. It is clear that with low sales turnover, high markdown spend and excessive end of season stocks that the product range has failed and needs a radical re-think.

PRODUCT ANALYSIS

To understand the reasoning of the budget review requires a detailed knowledge of the product range, the options within it and how each one contributed to the overall position at the end of the season. For such a specific analysis to be successful it must review product data using retail calculations that provide distinct information to inter-rogate the range's strengths and weaknesses. Relevant calculations to support this are:

- Rate of sale – measures unit volume and helps understand the sales turnover budget analysis

Unit sales for each product vary and the rate of sale analysis identifies the average rate at which each option sold whilst it was on sale. The calculation relies on three components: total unit sales of an option, the number of stores that ranged it and finally its life cycle – the number of weeks that it was available in store.

For example, presume a red dress sold 100 units, was ranged in five stores and had been available for ten weeks. The average rate of sale would have been two units per week in each store (Table 6.10).

Table 6.10 *The rate of sale calculation*

	Unit sales	Stores ranged	Life cycle	Calculation
Red dress	100	5	10	(sales units/stores ranged/life cycle) = 2 or (100 units/5 stores/10 weeks) = 2

- Sell through rate percentage – measures unit sales in relation to buy units and helps understand the markdown budget analysis.

The sell through rate calculation determines unit sales as percentage of the unit buy. Its calculation relies upon two components; total unit sales achieved and the unit buy.

Taking a grey pencil skirt as an example, if 200 units were bought by the buyer and it sold 150 units, the sell through rate would be 75 per cent (Table 6.11).

Table 6.11 *The sell-through rate calculation*

Option	Unit sales	Unit buy	Calculation
Grey pencil skirt	150	200	(unit sales/unit buy)*100 = 75% or (150 units/200 units)*100 = 75%

- Weeks cover – measures relationships between stocks and sales and helps understand the stock budget analysis.

The final and probably most universally used and understood is the weeks cover calculation. This is because it is probably the most versatile, quickest and easiest to use retail calculation within B&M. It measures the rate at which an option will sell out at current unit sales rates.

As an example, if a business holds 100 units in stock of a red shirt and is currently selling ten units of the shirt per week, it will sell out in ten weeks' time (Table 6.12).

Table 6.12 The weeks cover calculation

Option	Stock units	Sales units	Calculation
Red shirt	100	10	stock units/sales units = 10 weeks or 100 units/10 units = 10 weeks

Each of the retail calculations offers simple approaches to analysis, but intelligence as to why a range performed as it did, illuminating its financial performance within the business. They all identify size, scale and measurement of performance, which sold well, which were average and which were poor sellers. The budget analysis identified that casual wear, for example, was underplanned and the product analysis will identify the particular product types, price points, colours that enabled this conclusion to be drawn. The product review also gives a sense of the scale of opportunity and risk. For example, if analysis identified that all options sold erratically, with no meaningful trend established, this would suggest risk and a lack of stability in the range. Conversely, if all options sold equally well, with little extremes in the range, a conclusion may be drawn that the product range was stable, if unexciting in the way it was being bought by the buyer. A final reason to analyse option performance is that it is exciting to see the results of all the hard work undertaken to create a product range. As the concept-to-carrier bag process takes up to a year, it is impossible not to feel an attachment to the range and seeing it to its conclusion is always satisfying even if the range has not been as successful as hoped for.

For this next analysis process, the casual wear product range will be interrogated to assess why the category performed in the way that it did. The data will be presented in tables and use the mid-grey, light grey and dark grey coding to emphasize strengths and weaknesses that the analysis will identify. Table 6.13 begins with a presentation of the casual wear product range.

Table 6.13 presents details of the casual wear product category. The seventeen options are divided into three product types (trousers, shirts and T-shirts) and then by attribute (core basic, fashion style and high fashion). The table goes on to detail for each option:

Table 6.13 The casual wear range

Option	Product description	Option	Fashion attribute	1 Selling price	2 Stores ranged	3 Full-price sales units	4 Stock units remaining	5 Total buy units
1	5-pocket cotton Chino	Black	Core basic	£50	1	130	4	134
2	5-pocket cotton Chino	Natural	Core basic	£50	1	117	9	126
3	Combat jexans	Indigo	Fashion style	£70	1	48	14	62
4	Combat jeans	Light blue	Fashion style	£70	1	44	18	62
5	Punk jeans	Navy	High fashion	£90	1	10	9	19
	Trousers total					349	54	403
6	Plain shirt	White	Core basic	£35	1	111	12	123
7	Plain shirt	Blue	Core basic	£35	1	125	8	133
8	Flower shirt	Green	Fashion style	£50	1	36	23	59
9	Laser cut shirt	Yellow	High fashion	£60	1	7	11	18
	Shirts total					279	54	333
10	Basic T-shirt	Navy	Core basic	£15	1	222	0	222
11	Basic T-shirt	White	Core basic	£15	1	216	4	220
12	Basic T-shirt	Green	Core basic	£15	1	220	2	222
13	Raglan T-shirt	Navy	Fashion style	£25	1	73	20	93
14	Raglan T-shirt	White	Fashion style	£25	1	59	23	82
15	Raglan T-shirt	Red	Fashion style	£25	1	54	28	82
16	Skull print T-shirt	Blue	High fashion	£35	1	10	25	35
17	Skull print T-shirt	Yellow	High fashion	£35	1	6	30	36
	T-shirt total					860	132	992
	Grand total					1,488	240	1,728

- retail selling price
- number of stores ranged
- total full price sales units for the season prior to the ESS
- total stock units remaining at the end of the season
- total buy units (unit buy = sales units + stock units remaining).

Reviewing the product range further identifies that:

- Trousers
  - The basic chino options had the biggest unit sales (black 130 units and natural 117 units) and almost sold out. The punk jeans sold the least number of units (ten units). There seemed to be a pattern of core basic, opening price point products selling better than the other fashion attributes.
- Shirts
  - Sales of shirts follow the same pattern established within the trousers product group. One key difference to note is that the high fashion laser cut T- shirt sold less than half of its unit buy.
- T-shirts
  - With eight options, this is the largest product group in the casual wear range. The basic T-shirts have more or less sold out despite having more units bought of them than any other option. The high fashion T-shirt sales were very poor compared to the unit buys made.

This initial analysis identifies that the seventeen -option casual wear range comprises a mix of styles, colours and fashion attribute types. One early trend identified is the reliance on core basic opening price point options within the product range.

Having established the shape of the range, the first calculation to apply is the rate of sale analysis, shown below in Table 6.14.

For example the first option rate of sale is calculated to be:

- Five-pocket chino in black
  - (sales units/stores ranged/life cycle).
  - (130 sales units/1 Prentice Day store/20 full price weeks) = 6.5 units.

The table has the rate of sale for each option, product group and casual wear product category total added to it and shows that:

- Trousers
  - Rates of sale of the trouser options range from the highest of 6.5 units sold per week of the black chino to just 0.5 units sold on average of the punk jeans. The low rate of sale recorded by the punk jeans – at less than one unit per week – means that in some weeks of the season no sales were made of this option at all.
- Shirts
  - On this measure, shirts again mirror the performance of the trousers product group, with core basic options generating high rate of sale which reduces as each option becomes more fashionable.

Table 6.14 Rate of sale analysis

Option	Product description	Option	Fashion attribute	Selling price	Stores ranged	Sales units	Stock units remaining	Total buy units	Rate of sale
1	5-pocket cotton Chino	Black	Core basic	£50	1	130	4	134	6.5
2	5-pocket cotton Chino	Natural	Core basic	£50	1	117	9	126	5.9
3	Combat jeans	Indigo	Fashion style	£70	1	48	14	62	2.4
4	Combat jeans	Light blue	Fashion style	£70	1	44	18	62	2.2
5	Punk jeans	Navy	High fashion	£90	1	10	9	19	0.5
	Trousers total					349	54	403	3.5
6	Plain shirt	White	Core basic	£35	1	111	12	123	5.6
7	Plain shirt	Blue	Core basic	£35	1	125	8	133	6.3
8	Flower shirt	Green	Fashion style	£50	1	36	23	59	1.8
9	Laser cut shirt	Yellow	High fashion	£60	1	7	11	18	0.4
	Shirts total					279	54	333	3.5
10	Basic T-shirt	Navy	Core basic	£15	1	222	0	222	11.1
11	Basic T-shirt	White	Core basic	£15	1	216	4	220	10.8
12	Basic T-shirt	Green	Core basic	£15	1	220	2	222	11.0
13	Raglan T-shirt	Navy	Fashion style	£25	1	73	20	93	3.7
14	Raglan T-shirt	White	Fashion style	£25	1	59	23	82	3.0
15	Raglan T-shirt	Red	Fashion style	£25	1	54	28	82	2.7
16	Skull print T-shirt	Blue	High fashion	£35	1	10	25	35	0.5
17	Skull print T-shirt	Yellow	High fashion	£35	1	6	30	36	0.3
	T-shirt total					860	132	992	5.4
	Grand total					1,488	240	1,728	4.4

- T-shirts
  - While the same pattern emerges within T-shirts, there is a very pronounced difference in the rates of sale generated by the core basic T-shirts' rates of sale which – at 11 units for each option – are the highest of all options in the casual wear range.

The rate of sale analysis is clearly communicating that expanding the casual wear product range should be targeted towards core basic options. The high fashion options present a problem to the merchandiser as with the rate of sale averaging 0.4 a question as to their rationale being in the range is inevitable.

The next product analysis is the sell-through rate percentage which is shown below in Table 6.15.

For example the first option sell-through rate per cent over the same 20-week full price period is calculated to be:

- Five-pocket chino in black
- (unit sales/unit buy)*100
- (130 unit sales/134 unit buy)*100 = 97%

The table has the sell-through rate percentage for each option, product group and casual wear category total added to it.

- Trousers
  - The average sell-through was 87 per cent, with a sell-through higher than average recorded by the core basic chinos. The fashion style combat jeans' sell-through was in line with the trousers' total, while the punk jeans were poor sellers with a sell-through of just over half of the unit buy (53 per cent).
- Shirts
  - The shirts sell-through of 84 per cent was marginally lower than the total for the product category of 86 per cent. The core basic plain shirts sell-through rates were very good, but the other options had much lower and disappointing sell-through rates.
- T-shirts
  - The core basic T-shirts sold out with sell-through rates of not less than 98 per cent. Clearly more of these options could have been bought and sold. The sell-through rates of the fashion styles were reasonable at over 70 per cent sold-through, but again the high fashion options sold poorly, both selling less than 30 per cent of their unit buys.

The sell-through rate calculation is very useful within fashion as it gives a simple single percentage assessment of the strength of each option. The implication of this analysis is clear. Within casual wear, the business needs to buy more unit volumes of core basic options and reduce volumes for fashion and high fashion.

The final product analysis is weeks cover which is presented below in Table 6.16.

Table 6.16 has the average weeks cover for each option, product group and casual wear category as a total. The average covers have been presumed by the author.

Table 6.15 Sell-through rate analysis

Option	Product description	Option	Fashion attribute	Selling price	Stores ranged	Sales units	Stock units remaining	Total buy units	Sell through rate
1	5 pocket cotton Chino	Black	Core basic	£50	1	130	4	134	97%
2	5 pocket cotton Chino	Natural	Core basic	£50	1	117	9	126	93%
3	Combat jeans	Indigo	Fashion style	£70	1	48	14	62	77%
4	Combat jeans	Light blue	Fashion style	£70	1	44	18	62	71%
5	Punk jeans	Navy	High fashion	£90	1	10	9	19	53%
	Trousers total					349	54	403	87%
6	Plain shirt	White	Core basic	£35	1	111	12	123	90%
7	Plain shirt	Blue	Core basic	£35	1	125	8	133	94%
8	Flower shirt	Green	Fashion style	£50	1	36	23	59	61%
9	Laser cut shirt	Yellow	High fashion	£60	1	7	11	18	39%
	Shirts total					279	54	333	84%
10	Basic T shirt	Navy	Core basic	£15	1	222	0	222	100%
11	Basic T shirt	White	Core basic	£15	1	216	4	220	98%
12	Basic T shirt	Green	Core basic	£15	1	220	2	222	99%
13	Raglan T shirt	Navy	Fashion style	£25	1	73	20	93	78%
14	Raglan T shirt	White	Fashion style	£25	1	59	23	82	72%
15	Raglan T shirt	Red	Fashion style	£25	1	54	28	82	66%
16	Skull print T shirt	Blue	High fashion	£35	1	10	25	35	29%
17	Skull print T shirt	Yellow	High fashion	£35	1	6	30	36	17%
	T shirt total					860	132	992	87%
	Grand total					1488	240	1728	86%

Table 6.16 Weeks cover analysis

Option	Product description	Option	Fashion attribute	Selling price	Stores ranged	Sales units	Stock units remaining	Total buy units	Average weeks cover
1	5 pocket cotton Chino	Black	Core basic	£50	1	130	4	134	10.0
2	5 pocket cotton Chino	Natural	Core basic	£50	1	117	9	126	11.0
3	Combat jeans	Indigo	Fashion style	£70	1	48	14	62	16.0
4	Combat jeans	Light blue	Fashion style	£70	1	44	18	62	16.0
5	Punk jeans	Navy	High fashion	£90	1	10	9	19	35.0
	Trousers total					349	54	403	13.0
6	Plain shirt	White	Core basic	£35	1	111	12	123	13.0
7	Plain shirt	Blue	Core basic	£35	1	125	8	133	13.0
8	Flower shirt	Green	Fashion style	£50	1	36	23	59	20.0
9	Laser cut shirt	Yellow	High fashion	£60	1	7	11	18	40.0
	Shirts total					279	54	333	14.0
10	Basic T shirt	Navy	Core basic	£15	1	222	0	222	3.0
11	Basic T shirt	White	Core basic	£15	1	216	4	220	2.5
12	Basic T shirt	Green	Core basic	£15	1	220	2	222	3.5
13	Raglan T shirt	Navy	Fashion style	£25	1	73	20	93	12.0
14	Raglan T shirt	White	Fashion style	£25	1	59	23	82	12.0
15	Raglan T shirt	Red	Fashion style	£25	1	54	28	82	14.0
16	Skull print T shirt	Blue	High fashion	£35	1	10	25	35	40.0
17	Skull print T shirt	Yellow	High fashion	£35	1	6	30	36	48.0
	T shirt total					860	132	992	7.0
	Grand total					1488	240	1728	9.0

- Trousers
  - The average cover for trousers is 13 weeks. The core basic options are the best at ten and eleven weeks' average cover. The high fashion option of 35 weeks' average cover means that there was enough stock to last longer than the full price selling season (35-week average cover versus a 20-week season).
- Shirts
  - The same pattern is shown in shirts. The poor average cover of 40 weeks for the laser cut shirt is even worse than the 35-week cover for the punk jeans.
- T-shirts
  - T-shirts' total average cover of seven weeks is better than both the average covers for trousers and shirts. This is a reflection of the too-low covers for the basic T-shirts (approximately three weeks per option). Covers this fast can easily mean that core sizes are not available as stocks are limited.

The average weeks cover analysis suggests that the excellent performance of casual wear is due to two factors. First, core basic T-shirts have clearly sold well, with average covers implying that stock was in short supply throughout the season. Second, the average covers of all core basic options in the product range were the lowest weeks cover recorded, indicating that future ranges should emphasize these products.

Overall the review and analysis of the product performance of the range has highlighted the following conclusions:

- Overall, the strong casual wear product category performance was the result of excellent trading of core basic options.
  - There was consistency in the performance of each product group.
  - Core basic options performed the best, achieving the highest rates of sale and sell-through rates as well as the lowest average covers.
  - Fashion styles within the range did not stand out as being of note, and could be described as being of average performance.
  - Meanwhile, high fashion styles across all measures performed poorly.

Any product strategy for casual wear must therefore ensure that development and growth are directed towards the core basic option type, where opportunities for volume sales and managed stocks are possible. High fashion options would seem to need to be reduced either by reducing the number of options or by reducing the units bought of each.

SETTING A BUDGETING STRATEGY

The thorough and structured review of the performance of Prentice Day, its spring/summer range, and the understanding that it has brought, enables a clear and articulate interpretation of the reasons for the financial performance of the business. With this knowledge, buyer and merchandiser are able to discuss a product strategy and concept that needs to be developed for the new season. The buyer, too, through their own research and analysis, will have opinions about the strengths and weaknesses of the range and how new trends will affect them. By meeting and discussing these, they are able to hold a first 'range review' and from there agree the approach to be taken within the next step of the process: the creation of the product range concept.

Taking the analysis to date, the merchandiser will bring to the initial range review the following strategy proposals:

1. Recognize and protect the accessories product category. It may be difficult to manage, but it represents safe sales turnover and trading profit. In the world of fashion, such stability should be protected.
2. Casual wear needs budgets that reflect its strength and so should be proposed for expansion to the buyer.
3. Formal wear as an integral part of a menswear offer needs to be retained, but it must be reduced in the product mix to limit its influence whilst it is being restructured.

The creation of a planning strategy is important. A strategy is in effect a plan of action, a statement of intent as to where the product range should move in the long term. Good strong analysis identifies both the statement of intent – in this case a realignment of the product offer towards casual wear core basics and also the action needed to be successful – and development of unit buys that grow in the case of core basics while reducing fashion and high fashion options.

This planning strategy informs the merchandiser of the principles that should be adhered to during the budgeting process. But it also informs the buyer within their role. Initial ideas can emerge to support the change of business focus, suppliers sourced and new terms agreed on the likely changes to the size of production runs for different products. The importance of this first step within the concept-to-carrier bag process cannot therefore be overestimated.

SUMMARY

This chapter reviewed both budgets and product analysis and demonstrated how data can be interpreted, but also how the various analysis types can relate to one another to build a compelling analysis of a fashion product range. With a linked and articulate analysis completed, the buyer and merchandiser are able to work towards agreeing a concept strategy for the new season which, in turn, feeds into their next activities within the planning process.

A key point that the chapter discussed was the link between good mathematics and commercial acumen. This link cannot be emphasized enough. Good analysis that adds up is important, but understanding the answers within a commercial context is paramount.

At the end of the research process, the buyer will be in a position to begin to formulate design and product ideas, source potential suppliers and start to create first-draft range plans that will be refined later in the process. The merchandiser will meanwhile be able to create the budget shape for the new season and from there inform the buyer of the buying budget that is available for the season. Chapters 7 and 8 will review this process.

SELF-DIRECTED STUDY

1. Review the retail calculations to fully understand their calculation. If possible, use them to analyse product data of a retail business.
2. Refer to the companion website for Prentice Day case study exercises.

Furter Reading

Goworek, H. (2007) *Fashion Buying*. Oxford: Blackwell.

Jackson, T. and Shaw, D. (2001) *Mastering Fashion Buying and Merchandising Management*. Basingstoke: Macmillan.

Varley, R. (2001) *Retail Product Management*. London: Routledge.

7 Fashion Merchandising: Budgeting

INTENDED LEARNING OUTCOMES

1. A review of the KPI budgeting process within the concept-to-carrier bag model.
2. An example-led discussion of the KPI budgeting process.
3. A demonstration of the theory that lies behind the KPI budgeting process.
4. The review and discussion of the KPI budget summary for the Prentice Day case study.

INTRODUCTION

The analysis of financial and product performance in Chapter 6 identified the financial and product strengths and weaknesses of Prentice Day. This chapter takes this research knowledge and develops it into product budgets.

The budgeting process is perhaps the most challenging element of the merchandiser role, turning research into a set of product budgets that satisfy the twin demands of buying and finance takes time, with constant communication between the three roles. The merchandiser will need to articulate to finance how the budgets will be shaped in line with commercial reality, but also within the capabilities of the business's financial boundaries. At the same time, the buyer will be feeding in their own research and strategy requirements, which will need reflecting within the finalized product budgets.

This chapter is laid out to provide an overview of the linear process of budget creation. It does so by discussing each budget and uses a range of sources (Prentice Day case study, Chapter 4 research and the author's own presumptions) to build a budget summary sheet. By the end of the chapter, the practical demonstration laid out will flow into Chapter 8, which will take the created budget and develop it further into an OTB – the buying budget with which the buyer can proceed to buy product (Table 7.1).

Table 7.1 *The concept-to-carrier bag model*

Concept to carrier bag step	Definition
1. Research	Undertaking and collation of relevant fashion research
2. Concept	**Creation of product range concept and direction**
3. Product development	Finalization of concept as a product range
4. Sourcing	Sourcing of suppliers and manufacturers for the range
5. Manufacturing	Manufacture of the product range
6. Shipping	Shipping and delivery of the product range
7. Warehousing	Receipt of the product range, and its allocation to store and storage
8. Distribution	Delivering initial store allocations
9. Retail	Display, sale, promotion and stock replenishment
10. Carrier bag	Purchase of the product by a consumer

BUDGETS BECOME KPI BUDGETS

The importance of product budgeting cannot be overestimated. At its simplest, poorly planned budgets generate inaccurate buying budgets, and so imbalanced product ranges. If too high, the buyer could over-range products, confusing the customer, and if too low, they will be unable to create credible ranges, risking customer migration towards better product offers elsewhere. Poorly planned budgets are a double-edged sword for the finance team, too. Inaccuracies can result in poor overheads planning within the P&L account, while management of the balance sheet could be affected by a lack of focus on the debt regularly used to pay suppliers.

The budgeting process forms the bulk of Step 2 in the concept-to-carrier bag model and as a result is complex and often frustrating. To successfully navigate this time-consuming and often problematic process, one has to identify the relevant product budgets, as well as the process that lies behind their creation. Relevant budgets vary from business to business, but there are five that can be described as core to most fashion business types and these are:

- sales turnover (£)
- markdown spend (£ and percentage)
- intake margin (percentage)
- stock level targets (£)
- gross trading profit (£ and percentage).

The starting point will be the establishment of an overall strategic approach that combines merchandiser research with that of the buyer and the finance team. Following on from Chapter 6, the merchandiser identified:

- The importance of protecting the accessories product category. While difficult to manage, it represents safe sales turnover and trading profit.

- Casual wear is strong on all measures and should be expanded. Budgets should reflect this.
- Formal wear as an integral part of a menswear offer needs to be retained, but managed to limit potential influence on gross trading profit.

As an initial approach this sets the scene, but to be accurate the budgeting process needs a context in which it can be undertaken. This context is provided by the other two players in the game – finance and buying. As with merchandising, their defined role within the fashion retail value chain means that as the merchandiser can influence their decisions, so too can they influence the merchandiser. Taking the finance role first, as guardians of the business's finances, it needs a strong influence over the direction of product budgeting. This is done by guiding the shape of the overall strategic direction – without influencing the detailed process – by informing the merchandiser of the financial requirements of the business in the year ahead.

The guidance can cover a wide range of variables. In the case of Prentice Day, the finance team have asked that the following be part of any product budgeting decisions:

- Overall market growth is good, with inflation at 2 per cent. The local market conditions in Oxford Street are excellent.
- A minimum sales turnover budget growth of 10 per cent is needed by the business to support future capital expenditure.
- Markdown spend budgets must be reduced. The company cannot afford the current cost.
- Recognizing the heavy competition, there is no pressure to grow intake margins. However, they must not decline.
- Stock targets can be increased, but to control the impact on the balance sheet, any stock increases must be lower than sales turnover increases.

The second guidance comes from the buyer, who will have been conducting their own research and activities, such as reviewing fashion trends, competitor's ranges, refining customer profiles, sourcing potential suppliers and attending relevant trade shows. They will summarize their research into mood boards, pen portraits and initial product ideas. From there, they identify to the merchandiser their thoughts on upcoming product trends for the new season. For Prentice Day, the buyer concluded that:

- Casual wear is on-trend for the new season and should be grown in the product mix.
- A redefinition of the formal wear range is underway, but to retain credibility as a menswear business it should not be drastically cut back.
- Accessories are an opportunity, but as volumes are low there is no real opportunity to grow intake margin.
- Selling prices cannot go up. The competition is fierce and so to retain existing margin means unit buys need to grow to give suppliers economies of scale and so maintain cost prices.

The valuable context provided by the finance and buying teams, added to the merchandiser's existing analysis, enables the creation of product budgets that will touch the twin roles of product – creative direction and wealth creation. This is a key point to make as the budgeting process is of strategic importance, and as a result, measures not just the economic benefits of trading but also the effectiveness of product management. In recognition of this dual role, product budgets are known as key performance indicators (KPI), in effect meaning that the principle of product budgeting is as much about the attainment and beating of strategic goals for a season as about their financial integrity.

With all the information required in place to allow the budgeting process to commence, the merchandiser will start by creating a KPI budget summary sheet that will be completed with the new season's budgets as they are created. Table 7.2 demonstrates this for Prentice Day.

Table 7.2 *Key performance indicators budget summary*

Product category	Menswear			
	Planning year	Previous year	% Variance	Notes
Sales budget				
Total sales turnover £	0	90,000	0.0	Taken from Chapter 6 Concept to Carrier Bag: Research
Markdown budget				
Markdown %	0%	25%	0.0%	Calculation: (Markdown £ / Sales £)*100
Markdown spend £	0	22,250	0.0%	Taken from Chapter 6 Concept-to-Carrier Bag: Research
Intake margin budget				
Intake margin %	0	62%	0.0%	Taken from Chapter 6 Concept-to-Carrier Bag: Research
Gross profit budget				
Gross trading profit %	0	46.7%	0.0%	Calculation:(((Gross profit £/ (Sales /1.20 VAT))*100)
Gross trading profit £	0	35,005	0.0%	Taken from Chapter 6 Concept-to-Carrier Bag: Research
Stock budget				
Opening stock £	0	50,000	0.0%	Presumed by the author
Closing stock £	0	55,500	0.0%	Taken from Chapter 6 Concept-to-Carrier Bag: Research
Stock turn	0	1.7	0.0%	Calculation: (Sales £/((Opening stock £ + Closing stock £)/2))
VAT: 20%				The prevailing rate of value added (purchase) tax

KPI BUDGETING – SALES TURNOVER BUDGETING

The sales turnover budget holds the key to all of the other KPI budgets and there are various reasons why this is the case. The simplest is that it is logical to do so. If one considers the order of a P&L account, sales turnover is always presented first and the costs that supported its delivery second. Within merchandising, the same rule applies. By defining the sales opportunity first, the remaining budgets can be built up to reflect and support anticipated demand.

The second reason is less logical, but no less important. It is common sense to let the product and its strengths drive the budgeting process. A budget set by connecting customers, demand and translating it into sales opportunity will enable the buyer to have clarity at this early stage of the process as to the probable size and shape of the product range. This lengthens the time available to design and source products to start at the beginning of the budgeting process and not at its end, so affording the buyer the luxury of extra time to work through their ideas. A third – almost flippant – reason is that it is natural to start with sales turnover. When creating a fashion range one thinks of the product, the design and the creativity first. The mechanics of markdown required to clear excess stock or the required intake margin needed to support overheads rarely feature in that early thought process!

To create the sales turnover budget, a merchandiser will use a pyramid approach to take the previous year season's sales data, building onto it a logical approach to creating the budget, resulting in an optimal blue sky budget at the top of the pyramid. The second approach applies commercial judgement and personal gut feel, making allowances for real-life realities that may change expectations (for example – known events which may reduce opportunities or a simple belief that the logical answer is not quite right) (Figure 7.1).

The process of applying logic to create a sales turnover budget begins with taking the previous year actual sales data and applying a like for like (LFL) growth (for example, an allowance for inflation), in this case adding a 2 per cent sales growth provision. This is shown in Table 7.3, while an explanation of the meaning and importance of LFL is provided at the end of this section.

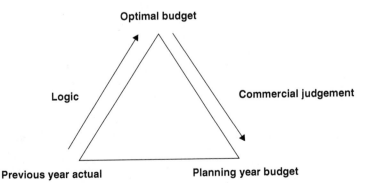

Figure 7.1 The sales planning pyramid

Table 7.3 Adding inflation growth of 2 per cent

	Previous year sales turnover	LFL growth – inflation at 2%	Growth to 10%	Common sense check	Planning sales turnover	Growth versus previous year	Growth versus 2 years ago
Accessories	£10,000	£200					
Casual wear	£40,000	£800					
Formal wear	£40,000	£800					
Sales turnover	£90,000	£1,800					

Note: Data calculation – previous year sales turnover *0.02

This starting point is followed by making an additional sales growth presumption to ensure growth is in line with the guidance form the finance department to budget for at least a 10 per cent growth on the year. The logical product category to grow is casual wear and this is shown in Table 7.4.

Table 7.4 Increasing the total sales turnover budget to 10 per cent growth on the year

	Previous year sales turnover	LFL growth – inflation at 2%	Growth to 10%	Common sense check	Planning sales turnover	Growth versus previous year	Growth versus 2 years ago
Accessories	£10,000	£200	£0				
Casual wear	£40,000	£800	£7,200				
Formal wear	£40,000	£800	£0				
Sales turnover	£90,000	£1,800	£7,200				

Note: Data calculation – previous year sales turnover total *0.08

At this point, as the peak of the sales planning triangle is met, the merchandiser will review the budgets from a commercial aspect. This is done by assessing the evolving budgets against the previous two seasons to identify trends in the shape of the budgets using common sense. Table 7.5 below identifies the current situation if no further thought were given to this budget.

Table 7.5 Common-sense checking of sales budgets

	Previous year sales turnover	LFL growth – inflation at 2%	Growth to 10%	Common- sense check	Planning sales turnover	Growth versus previous year	Growth versus 2 years ago
Accessories	£10,000	£200	£0	£0	£10,200	2%	7%
Casual wear	£40,000	£800	£7,200	£0	£48,000	20%	52%
Formal wear	£40,000	£800	£0	£0	£40,800	2%	-14%
Sales turnover	£90,000	£1,800	£7,200	£0	£99,000	10%	12%

Table 7.5 identifies that if the merchandiser were to finish the sales budgeting process at this point, there might be doubts as to the wisdom of the budgets created. For example:

- Accessories – while there is no compelling reason to significantly grow this category, a growth of just £200 would suggest that there will not be room to make any significant enhancements to the product mix.
- Casual wear – Common sense suggests that the growth focus is correct. The category ran out of stock in the previous year and is now on-trend. There may, however, be a question mark over the large +52 per cent growth compared to two years ago.
- Formal wear – This is difficult to assess. Compared to two years ago, the product category would have a sales turnover budget that is –14 per cent lower and could be in danger of being wound down rather than repositioned.

In a real-life situation, the questions posed above would be answered by discussion, and some 'what-if scenarios' would be worked through to quickly assess alternatives before deciding the correct route to take. The crucial point, though, is to ensure this common sense check is made, as logic and common sense as discussed in Chapter 2 are often not easy bedfellows with fashion and creativity. For the purposes of this case study, we can assume that discussions with the buyer and finance resulted in the following decisions:

- Accessories – a further increase of £300 to the sales turnover budget would be a safe, risk-free approach to help develop the product range.
- Casual wear – while the growths look large, the flexibility within the supplier base, the clear growth potential within the store's location and past sales performance suggest that further growth can be planned.
- Formal wear – The most difficult decision of all. Persuaded by the buyer's strategy, the need to be credible on the high street and the high number of working customers, it was agreed to grow formal wear back to the level of two years ago, adding £6,500 to its sales turnover budget.

These revisions are added to the sales budgeting spreadsheet in Table 7.6.

Table 7.6 Revised sales turnover budgets

	Previous year sales turnover	LFL growth – inflation at 2%	Growth to 10%	Common sense check	Planning sales turnover	Growth versus previous year	Growth versus 2 years ago
Accessories	£10,000	£200	£0	£300	£10,500	5%	10%
Casual wear	£40,000	£800	£7,200	£2,700	£50,700	27%	61%
Formal wear	£40,000	£800	£0	£6,500	£47,300	18%	0%
Sales turnover	£90,000	£1,800	£7,200	£9,500	£108,500	21%	23%

And with that, a sales turnover budget has been created. Table 7.6 identifies that the sales turnover budget for the planning season is £108,500, representing a 21 per cent growth on the previous year. At first glance, this percentage is large and well ahead of the minimum 10 per cent growth guidance from the finance team. The actual cash number growth of £18,500, however, is more modest and has allowed for a reshaping of the product offer towards accessories and casual wear. A bigger concern could be that casual wear has grown too much, and if the trends suddenly change, or the buyer is unable to negotiate an increase in supplier production, then the budgets may prove to be uncommercial.

Thinking this final point through, the overall shape appears to be right, based on the SWOT, product analysis and forecasted trends. The answer must lie instead within risk management and an effective control of the buying budget. A mechanism to limit initial buys to test the water before fully committing the business to the season ahead would be appropriate. The merchandiser will want to use the maximum flexibility of the supplier base identified within the SWOT, so must ensure that such mechanisms are applied further on in the range planning process to come.

FOCUS POINT 7.1: SALES TURNOVER BUDGETS AND LIKE FOR LIKE

Glance through any financial or business press and you will find that when reporting fashion company figures, business journalists always quote their LFL results. For example:

'Department store House of Fraser reported an 11.1 per cent surge in like-for-like sales in the five weeks to New Year's Eve, echoing the similarly strong performance from John Lewis over the period'. (Belfast Telegraph 2012) But what is LFL? And why is it so important?

LFL measures true sales turnover growth as opposed to total growth, and is regarded as a better index to assess business performance. For example, in the table below, a fashion business operates three stores (London, Edinburgh and Cardiff). Of the three stores, Cardiff started trading during the year being reviewed and so has no sales turnover data for the previous year.

Store	Sales turnover this year	Sales turnover previous year
London	£150,000	£150,000
Edinburgh	£150,000	£150,000
Cardiff	£150,000	£0
Total value	£450,000	£300,000

In this example, total sales this year are £450,000, while in the previous year they were £300,000. Using the percentage mix calculation, this represents growth of +50 per cent. However, this impressive growth is in reality the result of opening the new store in Cardiff.

On a LFL basis, the fashion business will strip out any sales turnover performance that is not represented in the previous year figure. And so in this example, to derive the LFL sales turnover performance, the analysis is undertaken exclusive of the Cardiff store.

Store	Sales turnover this year	Sales turnover previous year
London	£150,000	£150,000
Edinburgh	£150,000	£150,000
Total value	£300,000	£300,000

In this case, the LFL sales turnover growth is 0 per cent. This is a very different figure to the +50 per cent shown in the total sales turnover figures.

LFL is valuable as it unmasks the true underlying business performance. If, in the example above, the market as a whole showed sales turnover growth of +10 per cent, then on the total sales turnover measure the business would appear to be doing well. But on the true underlying LFL basis, the performance is poor.

Activity: Review the financial press and build up a table for a collection of retail businesses. Make a note of their reported LFL. Does a pattern emerge linking LFL performance to commentary about their product ranges and competitive position?

KPI BUDGETING – MARKDOWN SPEND BUDGETING

What is the markdown budget? Is it what the customer sees in the form of a percentage off (such as 50 per cent off reduced to clear) or a buy-one-get-one-free offer? Or is it the planning of these offers?

To a merchandiser, markdown is the exact opposite to its meaning to a customer, who sees it as an economic benefit and the opportunity to save a certain amount off an item to buy. This benefit though has to be paid for, and it is the markdown spend budget that covers the cost. Within merchandising, markdown is therefore a:

- cash spend – money spent on promoting or clearing product ranges
- cost – it is a cost item that is a variable within the gross trading profit calculation
- variable cost – markdown spend is directly influenced by the strength of the range and prevailing trading conditions.

The impact of markdown and its cost calculation can be demonstrated below in Table 7.7. It takes an example of a shirt, of which 50 units have been bought in anticipation of selling them for £25, giving a total cash buy value at selling price of £1,250.

Table 7.7 *Relationship between sell-through rate and markdown spend*

Step	Fashion style shirt		
	Units bought of shirt	50	
	Selling price of shirt	£25	
	Total buy value	£1,250	(calculation: 50 units multiplied by £25)
1	Units sold of shirt at £25	25	
2	Sales value at full price	£625	(calculation: 25 units multiplied by £25)
3	Units remaining in stock	25	(calculation: 50 units bought less 25 units sold)
4	Remaining buy value	£625	(calculation: 25 units remaining multiplied by £25)
5	Markdown of 50% on remaining stock	£312.50	(Calculation: £625 remaining stock value multiplied by 50%)
6	Sales value of remaining stock	£312.50	(Calculation: Remaining buy value £625 less markdown value £312.50)
7	Summary		
	Buy value	£1,250	from Step 3
	Sales value	£937.50	(Calculation: sales value at full price plus sales value of remaining stock)
	Markdown value	£312.50	from Step 8
	Markdown expressed as % to sales	33%	(Calculation: markdown value/sales value expressed as a %)

The example demonstrates that the requirement for markdown to clear stocks is related to the full-price sell-through rate achieved prior to the decision to mark down. In the table, a full-price sell-through rate of 50 per cent has resulted in a markdown cost of £312.50. Therefore, the higher the sell-through achieved, the lower the cash value of markdown spent.

A second aspect of the table to note is the markdown percentage to sales, which is shown in the case as being, 33 per cent. This is an important ratio in markdown budgeting, as this figure represents the relationship between markdown costs and sales turnover (in this case, a third of sales potential was lost to markdown). This percentage is a key element in understanding the reliance of markdown in generating sales. The higher it is, the poorer the product range has sold; and in any budgeting process, the eyes of merchandiser, finance team and business owners will fix on this percentage, as it acts as a judgement on the merchandiser's faith in the future product range.

To begin calculating the markdown spend KPI budget, the merchandiser will calculate the markdown percentage to sales for the previous year. The budget analysis showed that markdown cost £22,250 in the previous year, representing a markdown percentage to sales of 25 per cent. The biggest cause of the sales potential loss was formal wear, with a £16,000 spend on sales of £40,000 – a markdown percentage to sales of an unsustainable 40 per cent (Table 7.8).

Table 7.8 *Previous year markdown percentage to sales summary*

| | Previous year analysis | | |
	Sales turnover	Markdown spend	Markdown % to sales
Men's accessories	£10,000	£1,000	10%
Men's casual wear	£40,000	£5,250	13%
Men's formal wear	£40,000	£16,000	40%
Total	£90,000	£22,250	25%

Note: Data calculation – (Markdown spend/Sales turnover) *100

Taking this starting point, the merchandiser is able to make markdown budgeting presumptions.

- Accessories – the stable nature of a product range implies it is safe to presume a similar markdown percentage to sales for the new season.
- Casual wear – being on-trend and despite the large sales turnover growth budgeted, there is no evidence to suggest that a change in markdown dynamic for the new season and a similar markdown percentage would be appropriate.
- Formal wear – A 40 per cent markdown to sales was terrible, implying that markdowns offered to the customer were in excess of 50 per cent. An improved range should imply a lower markdown cost. A markdown percentage to sales of 25 per cent would be a reasonable assumption to allow some scope for the buyer not getting it right!

Taking the markdown percentage to sales presumptions and applying them to the already created sales turnover budgets gives the merchandiser markdown cash spend budget for each product category and for the business as a whole of £20,480.

With this budget created, the merchandiser as a final step will again review its meaning. Table 7.9 shows that the markdown spend budget of £20,480 represents a 19 per cent markdown to sales percentage. This compares to 25 per cent in the previous year and is a big improvement, as the markdown cost to the business is reducing, reflecting a greater emphasis on casual wear and a presumed improvement in the formal wear offer.

Table 7.9 *Markdown spend budgets*

| | Markdown cash spend budget | | |
	Sales turnover budget	Markdown spend budget	Markdown % to sales
Men's accessories	£10,500	£1,050	10%
Men's casual wear	£50,700	£7,605	15%
Men's formal wear	£47,300	£11,825	25%
Total	£108,500	£20,480	19%

FOCUS POINT 7.2: SALES TURNOVER BUDGETS – THE IMPORTANCE OF GETTING THEM RIGHT

Accurate sales turnover budgets are of great importance to a fashion business. By starting the budgeting process, they set the template around which the other budgets will follow. A good demonstration of this comes by reviewing the relationship between sales turnover and markdown spend budgets.

Presume that a business has two product types – core basic and high fashion – and that each one has a sales turnover of £100,000

Product group	Sales turnover
Core basic	£100,000
High fashion	£100,000
Total value	£200,000

Next, presume that each product group requires a markdown spend budget. The core basic product group due to its season less shapes and colours will not require significant markdown to clear stock, as the product can carry through to the following season. The high fashion product, by contrast, will need to be liquated at the end of a fashion season and so inevitably carries greater risk of a higher markdown spend. The table below has a column added, reflecting two differing markdown spends for each product group.

Product group	Sales turnover	Markdown spend
Core basic	£100,000	£5,000
High fashion	£100,000	£30,000
Total value	£200,000	£35,000

Because the markdown spend presumption reflects the type of product, if the £200,000 sales turnover were split differently between the two product groups, then logically the markdown spend budget would have to change, too.

Product group	Sales turnover	Markdown spend
Core basic	£150,000	£7,500
High fashion	£50,000	£15,000
Total value	£200,000	£22,500

With the sales turnover and markdown spend budgets interlinked in this way, a further fact can be acknowledged. The manipulation of product range plans to contain high sales turnover budgets for core basic product enables a fashion business to support profitability. The low markdown spend that comes with this product group type enables fashion styles and high fashion styles to be ranged and the potential markdown spend that comes with them counterbalanced. Brands such as Zara are expert practitioners of this range planning trick – lots of fashion options but with a constant core basic range to offer financial support to them.

Activity: During a main sale period, review the mix of markdown between different fashionabilities. Does it vary by retail business? If so why?

KPI BUDGETING – INTAKE MARGIN BUDGETING

The intake margin budget expressed as a percentage measures the proposed difference between the cost price paid to a supplier for a product and the selling price paid by the retail customer, exclusive of any relevant VAT purchase tax. The higher this percentage is, the bigger the monetary difference within the cost and selling price equation, translating into greater profit potential.

The calculation of any intake margin is very simple and uses just three variables – the selling price/value, the cost price/value and the purchase tax rate. Take as an example the intake margin for a red shirt where the selling price is £75, the cost price is £20 and VAT is presumed at 20 per cent. The intake margin would be would be calculated as follows

- An example of the calculation
    - ((Selling price/1.20 VAT)–Cost price) / (Selling price/1.20 VAT) *100 = intake margin
- Calculation
    - ((£75.00/1.20) – £20)/(£75.00/1.20))*100 = intake margin
    - £62.50-£20/£62.50*100 = 68%

The buyer, being responsible for the negotiation with and management of suppliers, exerts greater influence on the cost price of products sourced, and, at this early stage of the planning process, is unlikely to be in a position to finalize any pricing. Similarly, the finance team exert greater authority than the merchandiser on finalizing a suitable intake margin through their detailed knowledge of the P&L account.

However, the merchandiser must make an assumption on its figure as it is a required component of the gross trading profit calculation. Therefore, at this point, unless there are good reasons not to (the buyer knows of a new cheaper supplier, for example), the merchandiser will take the guidance provided by finance and apply that as an initial budget. In the case of Prentice Day, these 'good reasons' were that there was no pressure to grow intake margins but it was important that they should not reduce. Therefore, the merchandiser applies the intake margins achieved in the previous year as their starting point (Table 7.10).

Table 7.10 *Intake margin percentage by product category*

	Intake margin percentage
Men's accessories	55%
Men's casual wear	65%
Men's formal wear	60%
Total	62%

As the buyer begins the sourcing process and is able to confirm cost prices, the merchandiser will review the actual intake margin achieved against this initial budget. If the actual intake margin falls below the budget figure, there may be a requirement for the buyer to renegotiate with suppliers. If commercial pressures such as rising raw material prices or heavy price competition mean that intake margins cannot be improved, the merchandiser will refer back to the finance team to reassess overhead budgets.

FOCUS POINT 7.3: KPI BUDGETING – THE CAKE AND ITS INGREDIENTS

Look through any business or financial section of a newspaper and invariably there will be a financial update from a fashion retailer. These trading updates give investors and potential investors not just information about the financial strength of the business, but also its prospects in a competitive industry. Such updates, and the audience that they communicate with, seem far removed from the world of B&M, but in reality they are closely related.

Take Next, the enduring middle-market fashion brand which, in 2013, reported that it had earned pre-tax profits of £272m. To record a profit is naturally good, but the sentiments expressed by Lord Wolfson, the chief executive, made a clear connection between the business's financial performance and its B&M teams. He was quoted as saying that 'Next lost out on up to £10m of sales and £2m of profit after the "own goal" of not having enough summer stock during the August heat wave' (Next 2013).

The emphasis placed on sales and stock management can be noted in the above quotation. However, the focus on these two KPI budgets is not the only ingredient within the KPI budgeting cake that can determine if the resulting financial performance will be sweet or not. Consider the role played by the intake margin percentage.

Usually expressed as a percentage, intake margin measures the difference between the cost price paid to a supplier for a product and the selling price paid by the customer exclusive of VAT purchase tax. The higher the percentage, the bigger the monetary gap between cost and selling values to cover the business's cost of goods sold and overheads. The question, though, is what is the right monetary gap?

Different business models will presume a different gap depending on the segment of the market that they operate within. The table below lays out two different business models – the first generates a gross trading profit of £1,900 by selling 10 units of a garment that retails at £250 with an intake margin of 76 per cent.

Units sold	10	Units sold	173
Selling price	£250	Selling price	£25
Cost price	£60	Cost price	£14
Intake margin	76%	Intake margin	44%
Sales turnover	£2,500	Sales turnover	£4,325
Cost of goods sold	£600	Cost of goods sold	£2,422
Gross trading profit	£1,900	Gross trading profit	£1,903

Examples presume 0% VAT

Contrast that table with the second scenario, where a second business also generates a gross trading profit of £1,900, but instead retails its product at £25 at an intake margin of 46 per cent.

The factor that enables the same monetary gross trading profit to be achieved is the number of units sold. Profitability is not the preserve of higher-priced brands, and volume low-price businesses can make as much profit as premium ones if they get the combination of selling price, intake margin and anticipated volume sales ingredients mixed correctly during the KPI budgeting process. Primark is a master at this route to profitability.

Another KPI budget ingredient that can be mixed in different ways is the markdown spend budget. Markdown as a concept implies failure and negativity, and certainly the plethora of ESSs reinforces this viewpoint. However, markdown whilst reducing selling prices need not always reduce profit, too. The table below presents a scenario where a business generates £500 gross trading profit by selling 100 units a week of a £10 garment, which was bought for a £5 cost price.

Sales units per week	100
Original selling price	£10
Cost price	£5
Sales value (sales units*original selling price)	£1,000
Cost value (sales units*cost price)	£500
Profit (sales value-cost value)	£500

The second table presumes that a 10 per cent markdown is applied to the product, reducing the selling price to £9. On the assumption that unit volumes increase by 1.67 times, the business will still generate a gross trading profit of £500.

Sales units per week (100 sales units * 1.67 multiplier)	167
Original selling price	£10
Reduced selling price	£9
Cost price	£5
Sales value (sales units* £9 reduced selling price)	£1,503
Cost value (sales units*cost price)	£835
Markdown cost (sales units * £1 off)	£167
Profit (Sales value-cost value-markdown value)	£501

The markdown spend budget can therefore fulfil two functions within the KPI budgets cake. Its value must be enough to clear budgeted end of season stocks at appropriate markdown depths of 30, 50 or 70 per cent off, but it can also be used a tactical tool to incentivize customers to buy products. If the right mix of percentage of and sales unit multiplier can be found, markdown can also be a source of profitability!

Activity: Review two retailers – a value or supermarket fashion retailer and a luxury or premium one. On average, how many units are on display per option? How great is the difference? What presumptions can you make about their intake margin budgets as a result?

KPI BUDGETING – STOCK TARGET BUDGETING

Correct stock budgeting is vital to any fashion business. Get it right and stock budgeting becomes the lifeblood of a fashion business, while getting it wrong can be its cause of death. The reason for this centres on the impact that the purchase of stock has on debt and cash flow within a balance sheet, meaning the activities of purchasing and management stock levels present a business conundrum. On one hand, it represents the opportunity to convert a buying budget into physical stock for sale to achieve the sales turnover budgets set. However, if the product range is rejected by the customer, stock represents a potentially costly markdown risk that will eat into gross trading profit.

Stock management is of equal importance to the finance team and the balance sheet. The purchase of stock by the buyer requires funds to be available to pay the supplier, and as stock is bought in advance of its sale, the implication is that this is done by taking out loans from a bank. Loans carry a requirement to be paid back with interest, and so the longer a business holds stock the more interest will be paid.

Table 7.11 presumes that a bank loans a fashion business £2,000 at an in interest rate of 10 per cent With this loan, 100 shirts are bought for £20 each, which are supplied and put on sale for £60 each, all of which are sold.

The profit from the trading activity is £4,000; however, the profit will be reduced by the interest required by the bank, which in this example would be £200. If this principle was applied to a business perhaps borrowing £200m, the impact on profits, even if interest rates were just 1 per cent, would add a not insignificant £2m to their costs.

Table 7.11 *An example of the impact of debt on profitability*

Units bought	Units sold	Cost price	Selling price	Profit
100	100	£2,000	£6,000	£4,000
Loan	**Interest**	**Interest cost**	**Profit**	**Profit less interest**
£2,000	10%	£200	£4,000	£3,800

A second consideration is the age of stock held. Fashion is highly cyclical, with new trends and stories emerging throughout a season, meaning that the newest stock is usually the most desirable to customers. Excess stock of dying trends will mean that stock unsold during the season becomes obsolete, no longer a business asset, instead becoming a liability to clear through markdown and significant profit reduction. The turning of a debt into a physical product, to be sold and turned back into money valued at more than the original investment, is at the heart of commercial retail business and requires careful thought in its application.

In deciding the correct stock budget, the merchandiser considers two elements to identify an optimum stock budget. These are the:

- display requirements of the product range
- resupply stock requirement.

Knowing the capacity of stock that the Prentice Day store can display allows the identification of a minimum amount of stock needed to project a credible store environment to the customer. This 'minimum credible offer' (MCO) approach to stock budgeting has three components:

- The linear footage of the store – the total number of shelves or fixture arms available to display stock.
- The number of units to display – the average number of units that all the shelves or fixture arms can accommodate.
- The product range's presumed average selling price – the average selling price of all the options of the range combined.

Through a simple calculation, the merchandiser can work out the value of the stock needed for the display requirements of the range. In the case of Prentice Day, this is £45,000. Table 7.12 below shows its derivation.

Table 7.12 *Minimum credible offer calculation*

Store linear footage	200	Created by the author
Average number of units per linear footage	15	Created by the author
Minimum credible offer – units	3000	(Calculation: store linear footage * units per linear footage)
Average selling price of options	£15	Created by the author
Minimum credible offer – value	£45,000	(calculation: minimum credible offer – units * average selling price)

The MCO approach is of course just that – the minimum stock that a store needs to look filled to a suitable level. It would take just one customer to buy one unit and the store would fall below the minimum stock level needed. Therefore, there needs to be a second element within stock budgeting: an allowance for the length of time that stock replenishment takes to be delivered to store. This second element is calculated using three components:

- number of weeks a supplier would take to fulfil an order for stock
- sales turnover budget for the season
- number of weeks that the season will last.

The manipulation of these components into a stock resupply budget is displayed in Table 7.13. It shows how multiplying an average sales budget by the order fulfilment time identifies the value of stock needed to be available to support the MCO.

The stock target budget is therefore the sum of the two components. In this case a £45,000 display MCO and £10,432 re-supply time totals a stock level budget of £55,432.

Assuming that the merchandiser is happy with the resulting stock budgets, they would move on to the final part of the process: calculating the gross trading profit.

Table 7.13 *Resupply time stock calculation*

Number of weeks to fulfil an order	2.5	Created by the author
Sales budget for the season	£108,500	Sales turnover budget created in third section of this chapter
Weeks in the season	26	Number of weeks being planned
Average sales budget per week	£4,173	(Calculation: sales plan for the season/weeks in the season)
Resupply stock requirement	£10,432	(Calculation: average sales per week * number of weeks supplier takes to fulfil an order)

However, there is one last check on the stock budgets: the calculation of stock turn. Its calculation is explained in Focus Point 7.4, but, in short, stock turn measures the efficiency with which stock is managed. In the case of Prentice Day, the stock turn based on the calculated budget improves from 1.7 to 1.96, adding reassurance to the merchandiser that the stock budgets are in line with product and financial requirements.

FOCUS POINT 7.4: WHAT IS STOCK TURN?

The creation of opening and closing stock budgets enables the merchandiser to calculate stock turn (also known as stock turnover). The calculation for this is quite simple and divides the sales turnover budget by an average stock target budget. Using the KPI summary sheet completed in this chapter, the stock turn for the planning year is:

£108,500/ ((£55,432+£55,432)/2) = 1.96

The £108,500 is the sales turnover budget, while £55,346 represents the opening and closing target budgets. To convert these two stock budgets to an average, they are divided by two.

The previous year stock turn was:

£90,000 / ((50,000+55,500)/2) = 1.71

The question, though, remains what is stock turn and why is its calculation important?

In its simplest terms, stock turn measures the efficiency of a business in the management of its greatest investment: stock. With all investments there are costs, and in the case of stock these costs (debt interest, insurance, storage costs, for example) can weigh heavily on the profitability of a business. To maximize the investment and minimize the cost, good efficient stock management aims to support as high a sales turnover as possible, with the minimum of stock being owned by the business. The more frequently in a season that stock can be purchased, sold and new stocks be purchased is measured by stock turn. The higher the stock turn, the more efficient a business is at managing its flow of products to market and so the lower the cost to the business.

Of course, knowing the rationale of the measure is a good thing, but recognizing what is good and bad is equally important, and not a straightforward answer to provide. Using the same £108,500 sales turnover budget, but in one case changing the stock target budget to £108,500 and in a second to £54,250, the following two stock turns are generated.

£108,500 / ((£108,500+£108,500)/2) = stock turn of 1.00

£108,500 / ((£54,250+£54,250)/2) = stock turn of 2.00

Which is better? Well, a business that can generate the same sales turnover as another – but do so with a lower average stock – must be a more efficient business and carry less cost in the purchase and holding of stock. The aim of all businesses must be to maximize the stock turn, as it facilitates better cost management but also better customer value, as lower average stocks imply more choice as the business is able to refresh product ranges more easily where there is less stock to sell at any one given time.

For the Prentice Day case study, the higher sales turnover budget and lower stock target budget have resulted in an improving stock turn, moving from 1.7 to 1.96. This final analysis tool demonstrates in a single figure the movement of the business into a stronger financial position, and is perhaps the most important of all analyses types as a result.

Activity: Get an idea of stock turns by different retailers. Review their company accounts and divide their gross turnover by their stock position at the end of a financial period. The result will not be 100 per cent accurate but you will get an idea of how efficient they are in their stock management

KPI BUDGETING – GROSS TRADING PROFIT BUDGETING

This final step in the KPI budgeting process relies simply on calculating the gross trading budget. This budget is therefore the profit that results from the KPI budgets created. The gross trading profit calculation has four components. Three are derived from the budgets created during the budget process; the fourth is the purchase tax levy which is set by the government:

- Sales turnover budget
- Markdown spend budget
- Intake margin budget
- Purchase tax (VAT) rate,

The calculation to work out the gross trading profit budget is:

- (sales budget/VAT) * intake margin budget = sales budget at cost price
- (markdown budget/VAT) * intake margin budget = markdown budget at cost price
- Sales budget at cost price – markdown budget at cost price = gross trading profit

Using the calculation, the gross trading profit for the Prentice Day case study is:

- (£108,500/1.20 VAT)*62% = £56,057 sales at cost price
- (£20480/1.20 VAT)*62% = £10,581 markdown at cost price
- £56,057 – £10,581 = £45,476 gross profit

To express this figure as a percentage of sales, the following calculation is used:

- (Gross profit/(sales/VAT))*100
- (£45,476/(£108,500/1.20 VAT))*100 = 50.2% gross profit percentage

With that, the KPI budget summary sheet for the new season can be completed with all the calculated budget information as below in Table 7.14.

Table 7.14 *Completed budget summary sheet*

Product category	Menswear			
	Planning year	Previous year	% Variance	Notes
Sales budget				
Total sales turnover £	108,500	90,000	20.6%	
Markdown budget				
Markdown %	19%	25%	–24.0%	
Markdown spend £	20,480	22,250	–7.9%	
Intake margin budget				
Intake margin %	62%	62%	0.0%	
Gross profit budget				
Gross trading profit %	50.2%	46.7%	7.5%	
Gross trading profit £	45,476	35,005	30%	
Stock budget				
Opening stock £	55,432	50,000	+11%	
Closing stock £	55,432	55,500	–0%	
Stock turn	1.96	1.7	15%	
VAT: 20%				

KPI BUDGETING – KPI BUDGET REVIEW

The review of the budget summary sheet highlights significant changes to each budget compared to the previous year, explaining the collective impact that these have on gross trading profitability and stock turn. KPI budgeting is, in effect, the first factual evidence of the financial impact of the merchandiser's B&M product strategy, meaning the various players can now start to firm up their own budgets and strategies. Finance now has key elements of the P&L balance sheet in place around which overhead budgeting can be completed. The buyer now has information about the financial requirements of the product range, allowing them to begin finalizing their product plans and embarking on supplier negotiations.

A final review of the outputs of the budgeting process discussed between the key players will iron out any concerns or queries, but also lead to the agreement of guidance for the next stage in the process. The simple headline review of the KPI budgets tells the team that:

- Sales turnover growth of 21 per cent is led by an expansion of on-trend casual wear.
- The reduction in markdown spend both in cash and percentage to sales is led by changed product mixes towards on-trend products.
- Intake margin percentage is presumed to be as the previous year. This will need to be monitored during the range planning process.
- Opening stock targets are increased by 11 per cent, but this growth is lower than sales turnover growth, resulting in an improved stock turn.
- The impact on gross trading profit is significant. The KPI budgets combined deliver £45,476 gross trading profit, a 30 per cent increase.

Reviewing the five key messages, all variables are at least level with the previous year, resulting in a larger gross trading profit to cover the overhead and capital expenditure costs of the business. The resultant shape also follows product trends, recognizing that credible ranging is as important as efficiency within product management. These messages will also direct the next actions of both buyer and merchandiser, particularly in the management of the spending of buying budget within the casual wear range. There is both implied opportunity and risk in the budgets, which, if managed correctly through flexibility in the supplier base, will support rather than hinder the B&M team.

Of course, in real life it is not that easy. The KPI budgets may be rejected by the finance team, or the buyer may not be able to deliver product ranges in line with the KPI budget strategy. The truth is that until the product is defined, KPI budgets flex and change to reflect new information, new business needs and the practicalities of life. As a theoretical concept, however, the description of the merchandiser role as being like a bridge between fashion and business, or buying and finance, is clearly demonstrated at the conclusion of the product budgeting process.

FOCUS POINT 7.5: KPI BUDGETING AND RETAIL OPERATIONS

The KPI budgeting process creates the financial ring fence which, once agreed, sets the minimum financial performance that the product range for the season has to deliver to the business. By its nature, KPI budgeting is expressed as numbers, currencies and percentages, and should reflect the concept ideas of both the buyer and the merchandiser, enabling them to progress in tandem through the concept-to-carrier bag process. With KPI budgets in place, there is a further activity that – as a primary function in the value chain – can use the resultant budget shape to ensure that its role in product management can be executed; retail operations.

The sales density calculation, introduced in Chapter 5 as a tool for assessing performance, can also be used to question and make changes to the allocation of space within retail stores. This helps ensure that the visual representation of a product is in line with the financial opportunity identified within the budgeting process. The calculation is used to measure the sales achieved against the amount of store space given over to it, by identifying the projected sales density per distinct section of a store. With this information, the retail operations teams can assess the efficiency of the use of store space and also, if in large stores such as department stores, how best to staff it.

Taking the Prentice Day KPI budgets and applying the sales turnover budget to the existing Prentice Day store layout in the table below identifies that, whilst all product groups have increased sales densities, there is still an imbalance between the three product groups. Casualwear density is far higher than average and is accelerating away from both accessories and formal wear.

Spring/summer season	Actual cash sales turnover	Floor space employed	Sales density this year	Sales density previous year
Men's accessories	£10,500	75 square ft	£140	£133
Men's casual wear	£50,700	325 square ft	£156	£123
Men's formal wear	£47,300	600 square ft	£79	£67
Total sales density	£108,000	1000 square ft	£108	£90

This suggests that it may appropriate to rebalance the floor space in store to make more of the casual wear opportunity and reduce the visual emphasis on the off-trend Formal wear range. The second table below identifies the floor space mix if all product groups were to generate the average £108 density for the season – note that as the density presumption for accessories and casual wear declines, their floor spaces rise, while it is the opposite for formal wear. By applying the average sales density to all product groups, each will be given space in store based on their sales potential. But is that the right approach to take?

Spring/summer season	Actual cash sales turnover	Floor space employed	Sales density this year	Sales density previous year
Men's accessories	£10,500	96 square foot	£108	£133
Men's casual wear	£50,700	468 square ft	£108	£123
Men's formal wear	£47,300	436 square ft	£108	£67
Total sales density	£108,000	1000 square ft	£108	£90

The answer has to be no. The floor space given over to individual product groups should consider more than just a financial element. Different products naturally require different footages; accessories, with its emphasis on wall displays and hung product, can generate very high sales densities. Formal wear, meanwhile, with heavy suits and outerwear, can require to be overspaced relative to sales to accommodate the product range. Casual wear, with its less constructed garments, can be versatile in the way it is displayed and so densities can often vary.

The actual space allocated in store will be dependent on the size of the product range, its display requirements and the financial return that is expected from it. Focusing on one of the three without considering the others would not optimize the visual representation or the financial efficiency of the business.

What should Prentice Day do? Without a discussion on the details of the store, fixtures used or the final product range it is not possible to be totally accurate. However, some broad assumptions can be made. There is no compelling reason to increase the accessories space as it can sweat its space by the use of walls and small fixtures. Casual wear sales density is far higher than the £108 average and will clearly need more space in store to accommodate increased options and buys. Formal wear, on the other hand, can be pruned, as its density is way below the average for the store. The final table below lays out a potential suitable solution for the store.

Spring/Summer season	Actual cash sales turnover	Floor space employed	Sales density this year	Sales density previous year
Men's accessories	£10,500	75 square ft	£140	£133
Men's casual wear	£50,700	410 square ft	£124	£123
Men's formal wear	£47,300	515 square ft	£92	£67
Total sales density	£108,000	1,000 square ft	£108	£90

Activity: Research sales densities for different retailers. What pattern emerges between different sectors of the market?

SUMMARY

At the conclusion of the KPI product budgeting process, a route for using the knowledge and calculated budgets to create the buying budget or OTB is clear, and this is discussed in the next chapter. This chapter has concentrated on presenting the budgeting process in steps, with some flavouring of the process in the form of models to demonstrate the thinking process.

This chapter has not, and cannot, explain a process for all business model types. A fast fashion business would have a different KPI budget shape to a luxury designer brand. The importance of each budget and the best route to its creation will vary by business, too. However, by presenting a process that covers the majority of key decision points, we have demonstrated that the product budgeting process within the context of the fashion merchandiser role is that of a bridge or link connecting the often uncomplementary concepts of fashion and business.

SELF-DIRECTED STUDY

1. Review the financial press for articles about fashion retailers and their trading results. Review how the articles discuss and interrogate product financial data such as sales turnover, markdown spend, stock levels and gross margins.
2. Refer to the companion website for Prentice Day case study exercises.

Further Reading

Goworek, H. (2007) *Fashion Buying*. Oxford: Blackwell

Jackson, T. and Shaw, D. (2001) *Mastering Fashion Buying and Merchandising Management*. Basingstoke: Macmillan

Kunz, G. (2010) *Merchandising – theory, principles and practice 3rd ed*. New York, NY: Fairchild

Bibliography

Belfast Telegraph (2012) *Gloomier outlook on the high street*. [Internet]. Available from http://www.belfasttelegraph.co.uk/news/local-national/uk/gloomier-outlook-on-the-high-street-28702123.html [Accessed 20th January 2014]

House of Fraser (2011) *Annual report* [Internet]. Available from http://www.houseoffraser.co.uk/on/demandware.static/Sites-Site/Sites-hof-Library/default/v1307413182417/PDFS/Highland%20Group%20Holdings%20Limited%2029%20January%202011.pdf [Accessed 20th January 2014]

Next PLC (2013) *Annual report* [Internet]. Available from http://www.nextplc.co.uk/~/media/Files/N/Next-PLC/pdfs/latest-news/2013/ar2013.pdf [Accessed 20th January 2014]

8 Fashion Merchandising: Open to Buy

INTENDED LEARNING OUTCOMES

1. An appreciation of the rationale behind the OTB budget calculation within a fashion business.
2. Understanding the calculation of OTB budgets and their management.
3. Decisions behind the phasing of OTB within a season.
4. An introduction to the WSSI and its uses within stock management.

INTRODUCTION

After the complexities of the budgeting process, this next chapter focuses on the calculation used to derive an open to buy (OTB) buying budget and its use within stock management. The actual practical process to create an OTB budget is surprisingly straightforward; however, its theoretical context is more taxing and this chapter will spend time initially discussing this point. Finally, the chapter will move on to introduce the weekly sales and stock intake report (WSSI) and demonstrate its practical use to phase OTB budgets.

Behind the practicalities and theoretical context of OTB budgeting lies a simple principle; that the derivation of OTB is very much like baking a cake. It comprises different ingredients that, when put together and mixed, create a cake which, once cooked, can be sliced in different sizes and shapes. However, also like a cake, it is not until it is sliced that one knows if the right balance of ingredients and care has gone into its creation and if its intended recipient, the buyer, will like it (Table 8.1).

WHAT IS OPEN TO BUY?

While the calculation and use of OTB may be straightforward, the logic behind its effective budgeting is less clear. The buying of product from a supplier stripped down to its simplest form is a transaction where the buyer gives a sum of money in return for receiving a product, to sell on at a higher price. To facilitate this activity,

Table 8.1 *The concept-to-carrier bag model*

Concept to carrier bag step	Definition
1. Research	Undertaking and collation of relevant fashion research
2. Concept	**Creation of product range concept and direction**
3. Product development	Finalization of concept as a product range
4. Sourcing	Sourcing of suppliers and manufacturers for the range
5. Manufacturing	Manufacture of the product range
6. Shipping	Shipping and delivery of the product range
7. Warehousing	Receipt of the product range, its allocation to store and storage
8. Distribution	Delivering initial store allocations
9. Retail	Display, sale, promotion and stock replenishment
10. Carrier bag	The purchase of the product by a consumer

a fashion business could manage their stock purchases by buying individual products and applying a required mark-up to the cost price to derive a selling value, continuing to do so until a sales turnover requirement is fulfilled. This ad hoc and simple process initially appears a common-sense approach, as it presumes buying the best product available until a defined cash value is spent (Table 8.2).

Table 8.2 *Example of buying, using a mark-up method*

Option	Unit buy	Cost price	Buy cost	Mark up	Selling price	Buy value
Option 1	100	£4.44	£444.00	2.6	£11.54	£1,154.40
Option 2	100	£5.90	£590.00	2.6	£15.34	£1,534.00
Option 3	100	£8.77	£877.00	2.6	£22.80	£2,280.20
Total	**300**		**£1,911.00**			**£4,968.60**

Data calculation
Buy cost   (unit buy * cost price)
Mark-up   required multiplier to derive selling price
Buy value   (unit buy * selling price)

This approach has its merits and focuses purely on matching the best product within a financial parameter. However, the application of a single mark-up is limiting, as its starting point is cost price rather than the selling price. This implies a pushing of prices onto the customer, rather than the retail market demanding appropriate pricing strategies. A second point is that, to a merchandiser, it feels very risky putting so much emphasis on one variable; and taking that point a step further, the competitive pressures facing a modern fashion business suggests that OTB management needs a wider approach, linking buying budgets very firmly within the management of KPI budgets.

If one considers the four scenarios presented below, the rationale for this argument emerges.

Scenario 1
A buyer invests £2,000 by buying 100 units of a pink skirt to sell at £20 each. The option is a success and sells out.

100 units of a pink skirt sold at £20	=	£2,000
Total OTB	=	**£2,000**

Scenario 2
A buyer invests £2,000 by buying 100 units of a pink skirt to sell at £20 each. The option is not liked by customers and only 50 units are sold with 50 units left at the end of the trading period.

50 units of a pink skirt sold at £20	=	£1,000
50 units of a pink skirt closing stock	=	£1,000
Total OTB	=	**£2,000**

Scenario 3
A buyer invests £2,000 by buying 100 units of a pink skirt to sell at £20 each. The option is not liked by customers and only 50 units are sold. To sell the remaining 50 units, the buyer marks down the skirt by £10 to clear and the skirt finally sells out.

50 units of a pink skirt sold at £20	=	£1,000
50 units of a pink skirt markdown cost	=	£500
50 units of a pink skirt sold at £10	=	£500
Total OTB	=	**£2,000**

Scenario 4
A buyer invests £2,000 by buying 100 units of a pink skirt to sell at £20 each. The option is not liked by customers and only 50 units are sold. To sell the remaining 50 units, the buyer marks down the skirt by £10 to clear, but even with markdown, 10 units are left at the end of the trading period.

50 units of a pink skirt sold at £20	=	£1,000
50 units of a pink skirt markdown cost	=	£500
40 units of a pink skirt sold at £10	=	£400
10 units closing stock at £10	=	£100
Total OTB	=	**£2,000**

In each scenario, the value of the total OTB adds up to £2,000 despite comprising different financial components. Of the four, the last is most representative of the competitive landscape facing any fashion retail business, and so implies that calculating OTB is wider in context than simply equalling a sales turnover expectation for a season.

Interrogating all the scenarios also confirms that OTB is derived from the KPI budgeting process. Scenario 4 recognizes the reality that markdown, as well as some element of residue stocks at the end of a season, will occur. The enshrining of the

KPI budgets within OTB places the emphasis on the selling price value of product rather than its cost, and this method of identification of OTB is consistent with the planning process followed so far. It is only once the product development process begins, and the buyer firms up on the options for the product range, that the OTB can be appropriately converted to cost values by using actual rather than presumed cost prices.

There is a second practical reason for valuing OTB at selling value. Chapter 1 identified that the B&M function works alongside others such as design, marketing and retail as part of the product creation and retail process. In their communication with other functions, all decisions need to be valued in a common currency. Targets such as retail bonuses, sales densities and increases in sales turnover on products featured in editorials are all measured at sales value. Within most functions, targets and budgets relate back to the potential sales turnover of a business, and so cross-functional communications are more effective when all activities – including OTB management – reflect sales values as opposed to cost.

There is one further possible addition to the OTB calculation that has not been discussed so far: stock loss. This is the loss to a business from theft, or stock that has got lost in transit through the supply chain. As its measurement applies to stock that has been bought, it is a cost to the business and is budgeted as such by finance. This cost is an inevitable part of the trading process, but businesses place great emphasis on limiting it through rigorous stock management procedures. It can be argued that allowing for inevitable stock loss should be part of the OTB calculation, as stock lost to theft or mishandling cannot be sold. However, in well-run businesses, stock loss as a percentage of sales is low – perhaps 2 per cent as a maximum – and its cost can easily be recouped, perhaps through the re-buy of best sellers once in season, cancelling out its potential part in the OTB calculation.

CREATING AN OPEN TO BUY BUDGET

The review of the budgeting process identified clear parallels between the merchandiser and finance roles, as much of the language used and process followed to date has more in common with accountancy than product. OTB budgeting marks the beginning of the transition in the role away from finance, towards product and range planning. With an OTB budget, the buyer is able to formalize their initial conceptual ideas into a finalized range, while the merchandiser will be in a position to contribute to that final shape and structure of the product range by the creation of its buying budget.

Table 8.3 shows that as the OTB is related to KPI budgets, much of its data can be culled from the budgeting process already undertaken. All that remains is to identify the opening and closing stocks for each product category. This can be done by taking the sales turnover budget for each product group and using the percentage mix calculation to identify each one's mix value. The result is then applied to calculate the opening and closing stock values for each product group (Tables 8.4–8.6).

The calculation of the OTB budget for the three product groups can now be worked out, and, considering the effort to reach this point and the importance

Table 8.3 *Open to buy monitor*

Product	Sales turnover	Markdown spend	Opening stock	Closing stock	OTB budget	OTB spent
Men's accessories	£10,500	£1,050				
Men's casual wear	£50,700	£7,605				
Men's formal wear	£47,300	£11,825				
Menswear total	£108,500	£20,480	£55,432	£55,432		

Table 8.4 *Identify the sales budget percentage mixes*

Product	Sales	% Mix	
Men's accessories	£10,500	9.68%	Calculation:((sales/total menswear sales)*100)
Men's casual wear	£50,700	46.73%	Calculation:((sales/total menswear sales)*100)
Men's formal wear	£47,300	43.59%	Calculation:((sales/total menswear sales)*100)
Menswear total	£108,500	100%	

Table 8.5 *Apply the percentage mixes to the total opening and closing stocks*

Product	% Mix	Stock budgets	
Men's accessories	9.68%	£5,365	Calculation:(total opening stock * accessories sales mix)
Men's casual wear	46.73%	£25,902	Calculation: (total opening stock * casual wear sales mix)
Men's formal wear	43.59%	£24,165	Calculation: (total opening stock * formal wear sales mix)
Menswear total	100%	£55,432	

Table 8.6 *The open to buy monitor updated with opening and closing stock budgets*

Product	Sales turnover	Markdown spend	Opening stock	Closing stock	OTB budget	OTB spent
Men's accessories	£10,500	£1,050	£5,365	£5,365		
Men's casual wear	£50,700	£7,605	£25,902	£25,902		
Men's formal wear	£47,300	£11,825	£24,165	£24,165		
Menswear total	£108,500	£20,480	£55,432	£55,432		

of the OTB budget, its derivation is simplicity itself (Table 8.7). The calculation used is:

- (Sales turnover budget + markdown spend budget + closing stock budget) – opening stock budget = open to buy budget
- (£108,500 + £20,480 + £55,4320) – £55,432 = £128,980

Table 8.7 *Completed open to buy monitor*

Product	Sales turnover	Markdown spend	Opening stock	Closing stock	OTB budget	OTB spent
Men's accessories	£10,500	£1,050	£5,365	£5,365	£11,550	
Men's casual wear	£50,700	£7,605	£25,902	£25,902	£58,305	
Men's formal wear	£47,300	£11,825	£24,165	£24,165	£59,125	
Menswear total	£108,500	£20,480	£55,432	£55,432	£128,980	

The final column on the spreadsheet is at this point blank. This acts as the working element of the spreadsheet and is updated with the value of buys placed by the buyer once the buying process begins.

FOCUS POINT 8.1: OPEN TO BUY – TO RELEASE OR NOT TO RELEASE?

The benefit of having a defined OTB derived from a well-planned, thorough budgeting process is significant. The research and analysis used to create budgets means that the OTB is factually based and objective. A second and perhaps more fundamental benefit is the security afforded to the buyer by knowing that the amount of money they are spending has a sanction behind it, approved by every relevant person within the value chain, who knows not only that the money is being spent, but its total value.

To presume once the budgeting process is complete that the resultant total OTB budget concludes the process would be folly. Fashion buying is in reality a speculative investment made within a highly competitive environment, and the ability to be agile in the spending of OTB is of paramount importance. Agility affords the ability to buy an initial product range offer, to which best-selling options through repeat orders or later-launched products can be bought at a later date.

The sensible approach is to identify the OTB for the season, releasing it in chunks to the buyer to spend. By releasing a certain percentage of the total OTB at a time, there is focus placed on financial and creative control. The business can react to any unforeseen trends or product offers that come to the market, which within a potential year-long life of the season is vital.

The next logical question to ask is: What is the correct percentage of OTB to release at a time? The answer is that the release of OTB must support two elements. First, the customer must be able to have a credible offer to consider, and so the releasing of OTB must be equal to or greater than the value of stock required for a display factor, or fully sized product range. Second, it must be large enough to cover the length of time it will take suppliers to be in a position to manufacture any repeat orders or new phases of products.

Fast fashion brands understand the OTB release concept well. Zara and their supply chain operations at the Cube are able to deliver new product ranges in two weeks and also react to store manager repeat orders. This modern approach to fashion B&M has allowed a reduction in the value of OTB released at the beginning of the season to below 20 per cent of its total. This places a greater emphasis on later elements within the concept-to-carrier bag, such as marketing and retail to ensure small stock holdings in store can be cleared through quickly enough to enable a perpetual OTB release policy to flourish.

Activity: Regularly visit a store known to be fast fashion in its operation over a period of one month. How many new stories are delivered within the period?

A REVIEW OF THE CREATED OTB AND BUDGETING PROCESS

Through the use of models, tables and linked thinking, the budgeting process has reached its conclusion. The OTB budgets created reflect the research, analysis and product budgeting process to date and so offer the roundest commercial view of how each product group within the business will perform.

- The analysis of each product group created a different strategy for each that is reflected in the size of each buying budget created.
- Differing product groups have different financial strengths and weaknesses that have influenced the size of the buying budgets.
- Individual KPI and OTB budgets for product groups allow financial performance to be measured and analysed independently of one another.
- In large complex fashion businesses with different roles and activities, the common language of selling value has been maintained.

By its nature, product budgeting requires a good eye for detail, method and interpretation; but budgets also have to be relevant to both finance and the buyer and their demands. The connection to finance has been emphasized as the KPI budgets feed directly into business accounting. By contrast, the connection to the buyer and the product range to this point have been limited, and it should be recognized that within a real-life scenario, buyer and merchandiser will discuss and feed ideas to each other at all stages of the planning process. This dialogue will directly influence product budgeting as, through the discussion of ideas, the resulting OTB budgets will be more rounded and reflective of three minds rather than one.

A second function of KPI budgets is that as control measures they provide the buyer with a safety net within which to make decisions. The setting of a line beyond which lies a failure to derive an optimized gross trading profit acts as a final arbitrator in decision making. However, the nature of KPI budgets means that they do not inhibit decisions that can lead to profits in excess of budget. A markdown budget need not be spent, and if the buyer finds a supplier willing to take back excess stocks or fund markdown activities, then there is quite rightly no mechanism within KPI budgeting to stop that being agreed.

The most tangible output of the budgeting process is the OTB, which reflects the thoughts, processes and actions of the merchandiser to date. If worked through effectively to the right level within the business hierarchy, an OTB budget acts not just as a control mechanism, but also as a facilitator. Its creation facilitates the buying of stock and the physical realization of the product range within a completed and agreed budgeting process. This caveat is important as, without agreement, the buyer and merchandiser act alone and without recourse should the resulting buy be poor.

Budgets are not a panacea and they do not provide an all-knowing remedy for all the questions posed when planning a product range. The control that they provide is achieved at the beginning of the planning process; as a result, they cannot accurately predict the decisions that will be needed during the later stages of the model. They require constant review and reworking as macro trading realities emerge and the buyer sources product. For the merchandiser, it can be frustrating to return to budgeting on a regular basis, but it is a necessary part of product planning. Too much change can mean that the focus of budgets becomes blurred; and if, ultimately, the biggest cause of change is the product itself, then questions must be raised about the integrity of the planning process overall.

At some point, though, the purchase of product has to be finalized, and whilst the merchandiser has been completing the budgeting process, the buyer will have reached a point where they are able to translate their own ideas into an option detail plan. As this process begins, any potential fallibility of the KPI budgets will emerge as that option detail plan must operate within the confines of the KPI product budgets and resultant OTB.

THE WSSI – OPEN TO BUY PHASING

The rise of the fast fashion concept and its commercial success through regular injections of new ranges throughout a fashion season raises two interesting points about the management of an OTB budget. The ever evolving fashion trends, some of which can be anticipated and some of which cannot, require flexibility in the spending of OTB and the identification of a total budget cannot be enough in itself. Fast fashion business models have also highlighted the importance of managing stock levels to be as low as possible, to increase stock turn achieved over the course of a season. Drip-feeding stock into a business on a weekly basis as opposed to monthly or even just once a season, means that the debt carried by a business at any one time is reduced, as are servicing costs such as interest. Beyond these strategic concepts, there are also good operational reasons for managing OTB into a business; the less stock held at any one given point means there is less space needed to store it and so the overheads on the P&L account can be managed better or reduced.

To keep things simple, it would be very tempting to divide the total OTB by the number of delivery phases that the business felt was right to present enough fashion trends to its customers. However, this would imply that all of the separate phases were of the same value to a business, would all sell at the same rate, and also that trading conditions throughout the season would be the same. These conditions would clearly not be the case, as shown by highly seasonal product categories such as swimwear, lingerie and outerwear. The phasing of OTB is therefore linked to anticipated demand patterns and the factors that influence it such as markdown spend and promotional activities. The management of all these varying factors is worked through by the creation of a WSSI. The WSSI (weekly stock, sales, intake report) is described as an 'unashamedly internal financial control document' (Jackson and Shaw 2001: 110) and is a pivotal document within B&M.

The weekly sales, stock and intake (WSSI) report – or wizzy, at it can affectionately be called – has a frightening reputation preceding it and as a result, on first sight, it is often feared and misunderstood. It can appear intimidating, but is actually very simple in its concept and powerful as a decision-making tool. Once created, it is like a spider's web sitting in the centre of the merchandiser's world, controlling the phasing of product deliveries into a business. It does this by creating weekly sales, markdown and stock budgets which in turn – by using the OTB calculation – create weekly OTB budgets. The WSSI also links other activities within the retail value chain into the product management process, by directly influencing the following:

- The chief executive and board of directors have a snapshot of exactly how the business will deliver its product and financial strategies across a season.
- The buyer will have a weekly OTB budget around which to create different product themes and stories over the course of the season.
- Finance – with weekly budgets in place, cash flow projections can be made to ensure that the optimum management of the P&L and balance sheet is planned;
- Logistics – with weekly OTB budgets, the logistics team can plan the operational requirements of the business such as warehouse capacity management.
- Retail operations – the WSSI and the range plan that follows it identify the size and shape of the product ranges over the course of a season, giving visibility of how store layouts may have to change over time.

In practice, the WSSI is managed in many different ways across fashion businesses, and at its most detailed a WSSI could comprise weekly budgets for a number of product groups and by age of stock within that. The management of a WSSI to this level of detail is of relevance to large complex businesses, where the phasing of KPI budgets into many mini-WSSIs is a necessity to manage millions of pounds' worth of OTB. However, for smaller businesses, a more modest approach to WSSI management would be suitable – if only for one's sanity! Whichever appropriate route to WSSI management is taken requires the document to be created, and Table 8.8 below presents a blank WSSI template.

Reviewing its layout by row and column, the WSSI is shaped as follows.

- Rows
  1. Opening stock – this will be the closing stock budget of the previous season which will become the Week 1 opening stock budget of the new season.
  2. Weeks/months – these are the 26 weeks of the planning season with subtotals for each month.
  3. Closing stock – this will be the opening stock figure of the following season and so is the closing stock budget at Week 26 of this new season.
  4. Season total – this is the bottom line that each budget will add up to and will total the relevant KPI budget for the season.

Table 8.8 The WSSI

2		1	Opening stock					
Weeks/ months	Sales budget	Sales mix	Mark down budget	Mark down mix	Closing stock budget	Open to buy budget	Cover weeks cover	Promotional calendar Planned promotional activities
Week 1	A	0% B	C	0.0% D	E	F	0.0 G	H
Week 2		0%		0.0%			0.0	
Week 3		0%		0.0%			0.0	
Week 4		0%		0.0%			0.0	
Month 1		0%		0.0%				
Week 5		0%		0.0%			0.0	
Week 6		0%		0.0%			0.0	
Week 7		0%		0.0%			0.0	
Week 8		0%		0.0%			0.0	
Month 2		0%		0.0%				
Week 9		0%		0.0%			0.0	
Week 10		0%		0.0%			0.0	
Week 11		0%		0.0%			0.0	
Week 12		0%		0.0%			0.0	
Week 13		0%		0.0%			0.0	
Month 3		0%		0.0%				
Week 14		0%		0.0%			0.0	
Week 15		0%		0.0%			0.0	
Week 16		0%		0.0%			0.0	
Week 17		0%		0.0%			0.0	
Month 4		0%		0.0%				
Week 18		0%		0.0%			0.0	
Week 19		0%		0.0%			0.0	
Week 20		0%		0.0%			0.0	
Week 21		0%		0.0%			0.0	
Month 5		0%		0.0%				
Week 22		0%		0.0%			0.0	
Week 23		0%		0.0%			0.0	
Week 24		0%		0.0%			0.0	
Week 25		0%		0.0%			0.0	
Week 26		0%		0.0%			0.0	
Month 6		0%		0.0%				
		3	Closing stock					
4 Season Total		100.0%		100.0%				

- Columns
  A. Sales budget – the calculated weekly sales budget.
  B. Sales mix – the historic sales mix by week used to calculate the sales budget.
  C. Markdown budget – the calculated weekly markdown budget.
  D. Markdown mix – the historic markdown mix by week used to calculate the markdown budget.
  E. Closing stock – the required closing stock budget at the end of each week.
  F. OTB – the calculated OTB for each week.
  G. Cover – the weeks cover generated by the sales and stocks budgets.
  H. Promotional calendar – a diary of planned promotional activities related to sales and markdown budget mixes.

THE PRENTICE DAY CASUAL WEAR WSSI

Using the KPI budget data summarized in Table 8.7 and applying them to historic weekly sales and markdown mixes, the merchandiser can create the WSSI. For simplicity and to avoid repetition, the WSSI used to demonstrate the process will be that of casual wear only.

Referring back to the completed OTB monitor in Table 8.7:

- The sales budgets by week add up to £50,700.
- The markdown budgets by week add up to £7,605.
- The closing stocks for each week are the derived stock budget of £25,902.
- The cover for each week is the sum of the calculation:
  - Closing stock/sales
    o For example, in Week 1, £25,902/£1,014 = 25.5 weeks cover.

With the weekly shape of the WSSI established, all that remains is for the OTB budget for the season to be phased by week. This is done using the OTB calculation introduced earlier in this chapter.

- (Sales turnover budget + markdown spend budget + closing stock budget) – opening stock budget = open to buy budget
- For Week 1 this would be:
  - (Week 1 sales + Week 1 markdown + Week 1 closing stock) – Week 1 opening stock = OTB for Week 1
  - (£1,014 + £0 + £25,902) – £25,902 = £1,014 OTB
- For Week 2 this would be:
  - (Week 2 sales + Week 2 markdown + Week 2 closing stock) – Week 2 opening stock = OTB for Week 2
  - (£1,167 + £0 + £25,902) – £25,902 = £1,167 OTB

The WSSI, having identified a weekly OTB budget, ensures that there is now a mechanism to value each different product phase into the business over the course of the season ahead. The next step is to use this phasing to identify the number

Table 8.9 The final WSSI for Prentice Day casual wear

| Weeks/ months | Sales budget | Week 52 | | | | £25,902 | | | |
		Sales mix	Markdown budget	Markdown mix	Closing stock budget	Open to buy budget	Cover weeks cover	Promotional calendar planned promotional activities
Week 1	£1,014	2.00%	£0	0.00%	£25,902	£1,014	25.5	
Week 2	£1,167	2.30%	£0	0.00%	£25,902	£1,167	22.2	
Week 3	£1,318	2.60%	£0	0.00%	£25,902	£1,318	19.7	
Week 4	£1,413	2.80%	£0	0.00%	£25,902	£1,413	18.3	
January	£4,912	9.70%	£0	0.00%				
Week 5	£1,413	2.80%	£0	0.00%	£25,902	£1,413	18.3	
Week 6	£2,028	4.00%	£0	0.00%	£25,902	£2,028	12.8	Loyalty event
Week 7	£1,471	2.90%	£0	0.00%	£25,902	£1,471	17.6	
Week 8	£1,471	2.90%	£0	0.00%	£25,902	£1,471	17.6	
February	£6,383	12.60%	£0	0.00%				
Week 9	£1,521	3.00%	£0	0.00%	£25,902	£1,521	17.0	
Week 10	£1,521	3.00%	£0	0.00%	£25,902	£1,521	17.0	
Week 11	£3,550	7.00%	£690	9.10%	£25,902	£4,240	7.3	Mid-season sale
Week 12	£2,282	4.50%	£460	6.00%	£25,902	£2,742	11.4	Mid-season sale
Week 13	£2,028	4.00%	£460	6.00%	£25,902	£2,488	12.8	Mid-season sale – final offers
March	£10,902	21.50%	£1,610	21.20%				

Week 14	£1,522	3.00%	£0	0.00%	£25,902	£1,522	17.0	
Week 15	£1,572	3.10%	£0	0.00%	£25,902	£1,572	16.5	
Week 16	£1,623	3.20%	£0	0.00%	£25,902	£1,623	16.0	
Week 17	£1,623	3.20%	£0	0.00%	£25,902	£1,623	16.0	
April	£6,340	12.50%	£0	0.00%				
Week 18	£1,623	3.20%	£0	0.00%	£25,902	£1,623	16.0	
Week 19	£1,623	3.20%	£0	0.00%	£25,902	£1,623	16.0	
Week 20	£1,623	3.20%	£0	0.00%	£25,902	£1,623	16.0	
Week 21	£1,572	3.10%	£0	0.00%	£25,902	£1,572	16.5	
May	£6,441	12.70%	£0	0.00%				
Week 22	£1,522	3.00%	£0	0.00%	£25,902	£1,522	17.0	
Week 23	£6,085	12.00%	£2,873	37.80%	£25,902	£8,958	4.3	Summer sale launch
Week 24	£3,045	6.00%	£1,398	18.40%	£25,902	£4,443	8.5	Summer sale
Week 25	£2,535	5.00%	£766	10.10%	£25,902	£3,301	10.2	Summer sale
Week 26	£2,535	5.00%	£958	12.60%	£25,902	£3,493	10.2	Summer sale last week
June	£15,722	31.00%	£5,995	78.80%	£25,902			
			Week 27					
Spring Total	£50,700	100.00%	£7,605	100.00%	£25,902	£58,305		

of options that can be bought within each phase, which will be the subject of Chapter 9 – range planning.

In the meantime, what else can be learnt from the WSSI? One final thought about product budgeting and OTB management comes out of it. Table 8.9 presents a phased OTB, the commercial strength of which would depend on the business model concerned and its supply chain capabilities. It does, however, present an interesting mix of OTB phasing which is worthy of attention. Table 8.10 simplifies the OTB phasing into monthly chunks and calculates the percentage mix for each. The first observation is that each month has a different OTB percentage mix, justifying the earlier discussion about needing OTB phases dictated by sales, markdown and stock phasing. A second observation is that the OTB mix also shows the impact of markdown periods on stock phasing. The months where there is markdown spend (April and June) also carry the highest OTB phasing, which is required to provide fresh, new collections to replace the discontinued ones.

Table 8.10 *Open to buy phasing by month*

Month	OTB	Mix
January	£4,912	8.4%
February	£6,383	10.9%
March	£12,512	21.5%
April	£6,340	10.9%
May	£6,441	11.1%
June	£21,717	37.2%
Total	£58,305	100.0%

One can also see from the OTB mixes a clear product planning strategy – regular phases of new ranges in January and February, with a larger more authoritative injection of product as mid-season sales activity clears out fragmented earlier deliveries. These are followed by further regular intake in time for the summer sale and the large early deliveries of new transitional autumn ranges in July.

So what is the moral of this chapter and the OTB story? Effective OTB management is more than just about achieving a sales turnover budget. Where commercial awareness of budgets and fashion trends can merge together, the delivery of new product can be as profitable as it is creative, so overcoming the natural paradox between the definitions of fashion and business.

FOCUS POINT 8.2: THE WSSI – THE WHOLE STORY

The WSSI is often seen as a key training tool for assistant merchandisers before being promoted to merchandisers. This policy is well founded, as the WSSI is in many ways the glue that holds the entire merchandising function together and appreciating its depth and relevance is vital for the planning process to be effective.

The WSSI report's great strength lies in its versatility. The principles that shape it can be applied with varying degrees of complexity that are suitable to the size and shape of the business concerned. The WSSI at its simplest is a tool that is used as a control document to manage stocks – by defining the weekly value of stock intake required based on agreed KPI budgets. Retail processes and fashion retail in particular are unfortunately not quite as simple as that, meaning that the actual WSSI standard used within the industry is more complex than one might think initially.

The first WSSI principle to note is its use of time. The KPI budgets that create a WSSI also form part of businesses' P&L and balance sheet ledgers, and so WSSI conforms to accounting norms of 52-week financial years divided into discrete halves: the first half (Weeks 1–26) and the second half (Weeks 27–52). The start and end date of these discrete accounting periods is determined by the start and end of the business financial year and *not* the start and end of a fashion season. For example, the explanation of the concept-to-carrier bag process in Chapter 2 used January as an example start month for a spring season (Weeks 1–26) and July for the start of an autumn season (Weeks 27–52). However, if a business's financial year started say in April, then the first half of the WSSI would run between April and October with the second half reflecting the November to March period. So what is the result? Over the season, the OTB phased in through the WSSI must comprise different season's collections, in turn meaning the WSSI must be made up of layers of different budgets set for different seasonality of stock.

The second complicating factor is the product itself. If one considers a 26-week timeframe, the amount of product bought will vary in its creative direction; heavy winter coats would be relevant for only part of a winter period, while core basic product such as white T-shirts would be relevant throughout the year. A single top line WSSI, therefore, is not an appropriate tool to manage OTB and so it must be subdivided into individual product WSSIs that reflect the product hierarchy of the business.

The third and final complication refers to the size and complexity of the business being planned. The bigger and more complex the product range, the more B&M teams and so the more WSSIs being used. In a department store, for example, individual WSSIs must number in the hundreds and so will require co-ordination and strict management.

Beyond these three factors there lies of course the little responsibility for the merchandisers to budget at many levels, all of which must add up to the overall business budgets on the P&L and balance sheet.

So how complex could a WSSI be?

Well, using a premium high-street womenswear retail brand with four product groups, there could be 16 seasonal WSSIs that need to be phased across 26 weeks which would give 416 individually phased OTB budgets to be worked out just for one financial half.

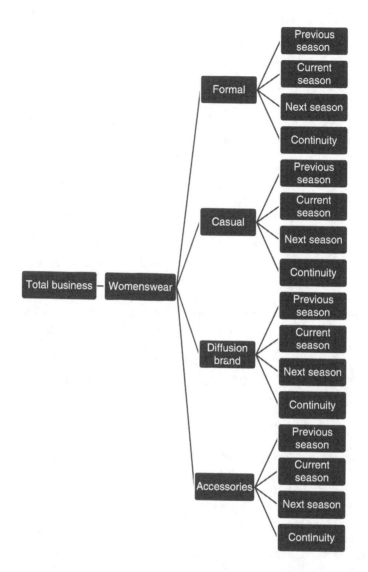

If that brand also ranged menswear and childrenswear, then that number could increase to 1,248 seasonal WSSIs. Across a full year of two financial halves, the number would increase to 2,496.

The scope of the WSSI is mind-blowing, but luckily it is such an important document that all B&M software systems that have been developed to help the planning process include a program that lets the computer take the strain out of WSSI planning.

Activity: Visit a department store and review the menswear section. How many disticnt product groups are there? Work out, using the model above, how many individual WSSIs exist for the menswear department.

SUMMARY

This chapter has identified the open to buy components components and how they work together to identify the amount of money available to buyers to spend on product. This has been done with one important qualification: that OTB is planned and calculated at selling value. This is important, because it is consistent with all of the analysis and budgeting completed to date and is the common language that unites all activities within the retail value chain. The relevance of OTB at selling value was also highlighted in the creation of a WSSI, where OTB is phased in over the course of season relative to the sales, markdown and stock budgets that have already been identified as part of the product budgeting process.

At this point, the buyer and merchandiser are now ready to move forward to the process of putting products into the range. To do this, the focus of the merchandiser role begins to change towards that of product, creativity and range planning. This will mean the buyer and merchandiser will work more closely together to articulate, using their own knowledge and plans, the creation of the product range for the new season.

SELF-DIRECTED STUDY

1. Review the Prentice Day case study exercises on the companion website

Further Reading

Goworek, H. (2007) *Fashion Buying*. Oxford: Blackwell

Jackson, T. and Shaw, D. (2001) *Mastering Fashion Buying and Merchandising Management*. Basingstoke: Macmillan

Kunz, G. (2010) *Merchandising – Theory, Principles and Practice, 3rd ed*. New York: Fairchild

Bibliography

Jackson, T. and Shaw, D. (2001) *Mastering Fashion Buying and Merchandising Management*. Basingstoke: Macmillan

9 Fashion Merchandising: Range Planning

INTENDED LEARNING OUTCOMES

1. An introduction to the range-planning concept and its value within B&M.
2. A review of the inputs into the range-planning process and the creation of a range plan.
3. Finalizing the product range through the use of an option detail plan.
4. Understanding the benefits of range planning to buyer and merchandiser

INTRODUCTION

The creation of a product range and the styles, colours and prices chosen to be within it is a significant part of the role of the fashion buyer, who creates their product range by merging customer, cultural and fashion trends into product ranges. Once completed, their next step would be to source these products, buying in quantities that match the products' potential and the OTB budget available.

In a small-scale business with limited product ranges, buying product and creating supplier orders within an OTB is easily manageable. The greater the size and scale of the product ranges, option plans and number of stores to stock, the more complex this becomes and the easier it is to lose sight of an overall size and shape of the range. Following a process where each option is bought one after the other without an overall target number of options could result in the buyer finding they have run out of OTB before all their desired range has been bought. Alternatively, if at the end of the buying process, there is OTB remaining, then the business may be at risk of not having enough stock to support the sales turnover and other budget presumptions. To prevent these possible imbalances, the merchandiser can offer a link between budgeting and option planning, that link being the range-planning process. This determines firstly how many options can be bought with the available budget; and then ensures secondly that each option is bought to the correct demand level.

The chapter will review this link and demonstrate the relevance of the range-planning process by using the Prentice Day casual wear OTB budget and applying it in this chapter, to create firstly a range plan and secondly an option detail which is used to finalize the unit buy quantities for a product range (Table 9.1).

Table 9.1 *The concept-to-carrier bag model*

Concept-to-carrier bag step	Definition
1. Research	Undertaking and collation of relevant fashion research
2. Concept	Creation of product range concept and direction
3. Product development	**Finalization of concept as a product range**
4. Sourcing	Sourcing of suppliers and manufacturers for the range
5. Manufacturing	Manufacture of the product range
6. Shipping	Shipping and delivery of the product range
7. Warehousing	Receipt of the product range and its allocation to store and storage
8. Distribution	Delivering initial store allocations
9. Retail	Display, sale, promotion and stock replenishment
10. Carrier bag	Purchase of the product by a consumer

AN INTRODUCTION TO RANGE PLANNING

Up until this point, the merchandiser role has been rooted very firmly in financial planning. Range planning finally sees the merchandiser link firmly with the buyer to develop the OTB budget into the language of product. This is done through both roles engaging together to create the season's product ranges, which can represent the most exciting and nerve-racking aspects of the planning process. It is exciting as the work already completed begins to turn into a physical range, but nerve-racking as any significant gaps in thinking will start to show from this point onwards.

These potential gaps in thinking are easy to spot by customers in store. Product ranges that are imbalanced between differing product types – too many dresses and not enough blouses for example – or are short of stock on offer, particularly by size, are signs of this. These imbalances can be caused by a poor working relationship between buyer and merchandiser, with differing strategies and interpretation of previous research leading to mismatches in the resulting product range. If one considers the complexities of both the buyer and merchandiser roles, it easy to understand how potential gaps in thinking could occur. To have reached this point, the buyer will have been working with abstract ideas based primarily, though not exclusively, on prediction and feeling. Merging these ideas with the logical thinking of KPI budgeting does not come easily, requiring work to weld the two approaches together to ensure balance within a product range.

Rather like a glove fitting a hand, range planning is the mechanism to check that the buyer's proposed product range fits the calculated KPI budget shape and vice versa. The creation by the merchandiser of a range plan that identifies an ideal number of options that fits within the OTB fulfils this task; naturally, it is rare for an immediate fit between the two. Often there follows a further period of discussion, negotiation and trading of ideas between buyer and merchandiser to reach a mutually agreeable course of action before moving on to finalize the range plan. A more worrying situation is where the gap between the two is too large for a simple resolution, and this is usually the result of failures to interpret and understand the potential impact of each other's activities, in turn meaning that the OTB budget presumptions could be invalid. If the buyer proposes to buy more options than the range plan has identified, then to fit within OTB budgets they would have to reduce the unit buy of each, putting availability of peripheral sizes and replenishment allocations at risk. Alternatively, if the merchandiser has overbudgeted for a product group, then to fill the OTB, the buyer may over-option (buy too many products) leading to confused product ranges in store and poor sell-through rates.

THE RANGE PLAN

The importance attached to range planning can be intimidating, certainly it has the power to act as a snake would in a game of snakes and ladders: to send both buyer and merchandiser back to the beginning of the planning process. This need not be the case, as by the time the merchandiser will have reached this point, they should have collated, reviewed and accurately interpreted a large volume of relevant data. Table 9.2 below is an example range plan populated with data from the research and budgeting process to date.

Reviewing the table, it comprises the following columns:

Table 9.2 The casual wear range plan

1	2	3	4	5	6	7	8	9
Product group	OTB budget	Average selling price	OTB units	Rate of sale	Life cycle	Sell-through rate	Average unit buy	Ideal option plan
Trousers	£19,824	£0	0	5	0	80%	0	0
Shirts	£12,244	£0	0	5	0	80%	0	0
T Shirts	£26,237	£0	0	8	0	80%	0	0
Total	£58,305	£0	0	6	0	80%	0	0

1. The casual wear product groups.
2. The OTB budget for casual wear for the season – taken from the completed OTB monitor from Chapter 8.
3. The presumed average selling prices for the new range.
4. OTB units – the cash budget converted to units.
5. The rate of sale presumptions – analysis in Chapter 6 identified that the average rate of sale was 4.4 units. For this season, a raised average of six units will allow volume growth to help prevent selling out.

6. Life cycle – the number of weeks each product range is planned to be prime on the shop floor. This will be dictated by the flexibility within the supply chain: the lower the life cycle, the greater the number of product ranges that can be bought.
7. The sell-through rate presumptions – analysis in Chapter 6 identified that the average full-price sell-through rate was 86 per cent. To further prevent selling out, the presumption for the new season has been planned at 80 per cent.
8. Average unit buy – the average number of units to be bought of each option.
9. Ideal option plan – the total options that can be ranged within the OTB budget.

Table 9.2 amplifies the point that good range planning is reliant on information gained through good research and budgeting, as, with the exception of the average selling price and life cycle, all of the decision levers for the process are already in place. Following on, all future decisions about sourcing, manufacturing and delivery will therefore be in line with the requirements of not just fashion trend but also sound business finance. Tables 9.3 and 9.4 complete the range plan by adding the average selling prices and life cycle data to then calculate the average unit buy and ideal option plan.

Table 9.3 The casual wear range plan

		1				2		
Product group	OTB budget	Average selling price	OTB units	Rate of sale	Life cycle	Sell-through rate	Average unit buy	Ideal option plan
Trousers	£19,824	£50	0	5	8	80%	0	0
Shirts	£12,244	£35	0	5	8	80%	0	0
T Shirts	£26,237	£16	0	8	8	80%	0	0
Total	£58,305	£0	0	6	8	80%	0	0

The sources of the average selling price and life cycle decision points are:

1. Average selling price – Historic average selling prices of previous ranges could be used, or the buyer could advise of changes to average selling prices based on competitor comparative shops. In this example, the merchandiser has applied historic average selling prices based on the product analysis from Chapter 6.
2. Life cycle – Prentice Day has a flexible supplier base and can plan to have multi-product ranges to be phased into the store throughout the season. By choosing an eight-week life cycle, each product range will have a two-month selling period.

With a range plan complete, the obvious question is: What is it telling the merchandiser? Followed by: Is it the right answer? Taking the first point, Table 9.4 identifies that:

Table 9.4 *The calculated casual wear range plan*

		2	1				3	4
Product group	OTB budget	Average selling price	OTB units	Rate of sale	Life cycle	Sell-through rate	Average unit buy	Ideal option plan
Trousers	£19,824	£50	396	5	8	80%	50 units	8 options
Shirts	£12,244	£35	350	5	8	80%	50 units	7 options
T Shirts	£26,237	£16	1,640	8	8	80%	80 units	21 options
Total	£58,305	£24.44	2,386	6	8	80%	60 units	36 options

Data calculations
1. OTB units – OTB budget/Average selling price
2. Casual wear average selling price – Total OTB/total OTB units
3. Average unit buy – (rate of sale * lifecycle)/sell through rate
4. Ideal option plan – OTB units/average unit buy.

- the buyer should range 36 options in total for casual wear in the season, of which 21 options should be T-shirts
- the average unit buy placed be 60 units of each option
- bigger buy depths of 80 units for T-shirts should be placed and lower than average buys should be made for trousers and shirts.

Compared to the previous year there has been a significant strategic change within the casual wear offer. Review the product analysis in Chapter 6 to see that:

- 36 options compares to 17 options in the previous year
- 21 T- shirt options compares to eight in the previous year
- A 1,640 total unit buy for T-shirts compares to 992 units last year.

The completed range plan has fulfilled two functions. It has identified to the buyer the required option information to allow them to create a total product range, in line with the planning strategy set at the beginning of the planning process. Further to this, the range plan has identified a shape within which it is unlikely that the buyer will overspend against the OTB and KPI budgets set for the season. However, range plans do have their flaws, the most fundamental being that it is a generic snapshot that takes an average set of presumptions to generate its results. Fashion of course is anything but generic, and the individual options that comprise a product range will have different characteristics that affect their value and importance to a business. To be effective, the range plan should have these individualities recognized within their individual buy quantities.

A second limitation with the range plan is that it does rely heavily on presumption, taking historical product analysis, such as rate of sale, and applying its findings to future presumed values in its working. Good range plans therefore rely somewhat on commercial gut feel, and for a merchandiser with much experience this commercial approach is eagerly anticipated and well liked. For the inexperienced, though, this can compromise the range-planning process if the merchandiser has not had the time to develop this important skill.

These limitations help to answer the second question: Is it the right answer? The glib response to this is that in fashion there is no right answer, and that the qualitative aspects of fashion buying are based on subjectivity and creativity. However, fashion is also a business and while the range plan may be a generic average, it is the right starting point. It establishes the right shape but not the right detail. That comes with the second stage of range planning – the creation of the option detail which uses the range-plan shape and moulds it into a unique option plan for the season ahead.

FOCUS POINT 9.1: THE INITIAL OPTION PLAN AND BRAND PERSONALITY

Walk into any good fashion store and the image that the business conveys will be articulate and well executed. The image is tied into the personality of the brand and can be conveyed in numerous ways. Brands such as Desigual promote quirky, non-conformist approaches to fashion, underscored by the inverted s that screams unconventional, spontaneity and unstructured to the customer. Of course, this brand personality is nurtured and reflected in all that the brand does, including the presentation of its product offer within stores.

The matching of the brand, its personality and associated characteristics within the product range is a key weapon in the armoury of a fashion business, and much thought goes into matching the two together. Take Gant UK as an example.

The preppy fashion business has particular challenges in ensuring that the product bought for its stores can present a unified brand image to its customers. With differing genders, capsule ranges, product groups and trends, the ranges offered need cohesion to present a unified image to its customers, putting its brand image and visual presentation at the forefront of its planning process.

The differing primary and secondary value chain activities of B&M and store design worked together to create a unified approach to laying out its stores. Optimized store layouts that were designed around fixture planning identified the stock capacity that stores could hold. With a layout identified, the business used the MCO concept (minimum credible offer) to match store layout to the product range's average rate-of-sale characteristics to determine how many options could be displayed within the agreed store layout.

With a comprehensive MCO in place, the range-planning process not only considered fashion trends, product and OTB budgets in its calculations, but it also added maximum display requirements into the mix. Completed range plans could then be compared to the MCO, allowing buyers and merchandisers to ensure that their product ranges did not just support their research and product concepts, but could also support the image presented to the customer.

Activity: Review different retailers across all levels of the market. How does each one project its image through it range planning and clarity of product offer?

THE OPTION DETAIL – QUALITATIVE AND QUANTITATIVE ASPECTS

The generic nature of the range plan means that the core limitation of the process is that the options that the buyer will have developed will be anything but generic. All options in a product range will have a number of qualitative characteristics, such as colour, fabrication and shape, and the differing combinations of these will generate differing levels of value to a business. The option detail focus is to understand the qualitative character of each option, to then apply suitable quantitative characteristics (rates of sale, life cycles and sell-through rates) that reflect the combined character of the product.

For example, the qualitative characteristics of a navy cotton T-shirt compared to a salmon-red raw silk print shirt imply differing quantitative characteristics (Table 9.5).

Table 9.5 *Cotton T-shirt and raw silk print shirt product characteristics*

	Navy cotton t shirt	Raw silk print shirt
Qualitative	Core colour, simple shape, easy fabric	Trend colour, specific shape, exclusive fabric
Quantitative	Higher demand, large value to business	Lower demand, less financial value to business

In effect, the option detail is the summary of the actual options to be ranged. As each one's qualitative characteristics is revealed, the merchandiser will flex the quantitative assumptions from the range plan to best reflect their character. The navy cotton T-shirt example in Table 9.5 would be likely to have the characteristics of greater commercial strength and high demand, so needing stronger quantitative characteristics such as higher rates of sale and sell-through rate applied to it, compared to the raw silk shirt.

Like most things in life, product characteristics can be overemphasized, and the more variations used to review options the more obscure the information generated becomes. Terry Green, the then Chief Executive of Debenhams, made a good point when he stated that the dynamics of a best seller in the range will always be the same; it is just the shape and colour of products that change each season, and that over-analysis can lead to paralysis in decision making! The trick is to use and interpret the right characteristic types to direct the quantitative decisions within the option detail. The best way to do this is to think as a customer, and determine what product characteristics would most influence their purchase decisions.

The navy T-shirt has multiple end uses from nightwear to casual wear through to sportswear. It is a simple easy piece that will appeal to a wide range of customers, and will require no deep intellectual thought in its purchase. Its potential usage is so broad that demand will be constant throughout the season. To be relevant to the customer, the navy T-shirt needs simple basic fabrications and styling to fulfil its role in a wardrobe, and to be consistent it must have a simple easy price; it is, in effect, core to any menswear range.

The salmon-red raw silk shirt has a different set of characteristics. Its uses are more limited and it is clearly suited to be a smart casual look that co-ordinates with other pieces in the range. The salmon-red colour will not appeal to all customers, and some may even feel intimidated by its tone. The raw silk fabrication will require care in wearing, cleaning and storage and that will further put off some potential customers. The price of the garment will be higher than a simple cotton shirt, so it will have to have other attributes – such as being on-trend – to convince the customer to buy it. By ranging this product, the buyer would know that it is a key fashion style for the season, but once trends change its place within the range will come to an end.

The simple review of the two options highlights key qualitative characteristics that could influence the correct unit buys for each.

- Style description – the type of product and its potential problem-solving capabilities.
- Fabrication type – the versatility of the fabric used.
- Colour – the type of colours that have been ranged.
- Price – a selling price that is consistent with the style/colours.
- Fashionability – the influence of fashion trend on the product.

Mixing these differing characteristics to create individual unit buys is perhaps the most contentious of all buyer/merchandiser discussions. There is a high degree of subjectivity and personal choice which could influence either player, but ultimately the decision should rest with the buyer, rather than the merchandiser acting in the role of frustrated buyer!

FOCUS POINT 9.2: MULTI-STORE RANGE PLANNING

Range planning for a single retail outlet such as Prentice Day is relatively simple, assuming that the research and product concept are reflected within the range-planning process. However, there are many retail businesses that have more than one store, with differing demographics, physical sizes and local competition. The question that comes to mind when considering this is: How does range planning support such diversity within retail store estates?

One route could be to dismiss the question and operate all stores independently and so range plan each store separately. A good, highly successful example of this in the UK is Fenwick, the largest independent department store group that operates 11 stores across the country. Being decentralized, the business is able to plan each store as if it were a single business, and product ranges are bought within a store OTB budget. This has brought the business great success, but is enabled by the relatively small number of stores operated and by its concentration on buying wholesale brands, rather than being an own label business.

For a national or international chain with a large store estate and a significant own-label operation, the question still remains as to how they accommodate a multi-operation within the range-planning process. The answer lies – as do most things within fashion merchandising – in defined product hierarchies. By creating a store-grading structure, the merchandiser is able to apply a ranking of stores based on the most suitable criterion that fits the brand and its operation. A first possible route is to rank stores by sales turnover as shown in the example below, with stores ranked by turnover highest to lowest and a defined OTB being split by each store's percentage mix of turnover.

Stores	Sales turnover	% Mix	OTB	Av selling price	Unit buy	Life cycle	Rate of sale	Sell-through rate	Average unit buy	Ideal option plan
Store 1	£25,000	31.3%	£34,375	£25	1,375	6	5	70%	43	32
Store 2	£20,000	25.0%	£27,500	£25	1,100	6	4	70%	34	32
Store 3	£20,000	25.0%	£27,500	£25	1,100	6	4	70%	34	32
Store 4	£10,000	12.5%	£13,750	£25	550	6	2	70%	17	32
Store 5	£5,000	6.3%	£6,875	£25	275	6	1	70%	9	32
Total	£80,000	100.0%	£110,000	£25	4,400	6	3	70%	27	32

With this ranking, the normal range-planning process can identify the appropriate unit buy and option plan for each store in the estate. In this example, each store can range the same number of options but will need differing buy quantities.

The greater the number of stores in the estate, the less uniform they will be – physical size and the number of options able to be displayed will differ. A more suitable approach would be to rank stores firstly by size and then by sales turnover within that. The table below is a re-presented range plan, in which the store estate is sorted by size of store and then adjusted by rate of sale to reflect a reduction in ideal options to mirror the decline in size of store.

Stores	Size	Sales turnover	% Mix	OTB	Av selling price	Unit buy	Life cycle	Rate of sale	Sell-through rate	Average unit buy	Ideal option plan
Store 1	500 square ft	£25,000	31.3%	£34,375	£25	1,375	6	5	70%	43	32
Store 4	500 square ft	£10,000	12.5%	£13,750	£25	550	6	2	70%	17	32
Store 2	300 square ft	£20,000	25.0%	£27,500	£25	1,100	6	7	70%	60	18
Store 3	200 square ft	£20,000	25.0%	£27,500	£25	1,100	6	11	70%	94	12
Store 5	100 square ft	£5,000	6.3%	£6,875	£25	275	6	5	70%	43	6
Total		£80,000	100.0%	£110,000	£25	4,400	6	3	70%	27	20

In reviewing the table, some key points emerge. Store 4, despite being a low turnover store, is now ranked with Store 1 as they are both the same physical size. Stores 2, 3 and 4 have seen their option plans reduce significantly to reflect their smaller sizes, but –to ensure their OTB can be filled – have had a corresponding increase in their average unit buy.

This poses a further dilemma, look at Store 5 as an example. Due to its size and lower turnover, it has been ranked lowest in the store ranking, giving it the lowest number of options. However, what if this store –despite being small – is located in the most prestigious of locations and should as a result carry the widest product range to make a statement to the world? Increasingly, retail brands are developing their range planning by setting a third planning criteria; that of demographic to store rankings. The third table below elevates Store 5 to the top of the range plan to enable the range plan to be ranked first by demographic, then by size and finally by turnover.

Stores	Size	Sales turnover	% Mix	OTB	Av selling price	Unit buy	Life cycle	Rate of sale	Sell-through rate	Average unit buy	ideal option plan
Store 5	100 square ft	£5,000	6.3%	£6,875	£25	275	6	0.8	70%	6	43
Store 1	500 square ft	£25,000	31.3%	£34,375	£25	1,375	6	5.0	70%	43	32
Store 4	500 square ft	£10,000	12.5%	£13,750	£25	550	6	2.0	70%	17	32
Store 2	300 square ft	£20,000	25.0%	£27,500	£25	1,100	6	7.0	70%	60	18
Store 3	200 square ft	£20,000	25.0%	£27,500	£25	1,100	6	11.0	70%	94	12
Total		£75,000	93.8%	£110,000	£25	4,400	6	3.0	70%	27	19

Again the rate of sale presumption has been manipulated to increase its option count, but in doing so its unit volumes have declined to allow more options to be displayed, but at a lower display factor.

This final hierarchical ranking, whilst complex, enables product ranges to be better targeted and so more financially sound. The question though is: Does it work? Within the UK, a good example of this approach to range planning is House of Fraser, whose most premium and directional stores are also some of their smallest. The City and Westfield Shepherd's Bush stores have a distinctly different ranging approach than their larger flagship store on Oxford Street.

On a practical level, hierarchical range planning requires very full research and an appreciation of range-planning assumptions such as rate of sale and sell-through rates at store level. For businesses that have hundreds or thousands of stores, that level of research is a Herculean task. Thank goodness for ICT and the many data-mining software packages available to retailers today!

Activity: Count the number of options within a distinct product group (e.g. dresses, skirts or blouses) that are on display in differing stores. Which has the most options and which the least? Is there a link between number of options displayed and the average number of units available per option?

CREATING THE OPTION DETAIL

Having created a range plan, this section presumes that the buyer has decided to create an option detail for the T-shirt product group. This is shown in the option detail in Table 9.6, and in this case the buyer has proposed to buy five options – three core basic, two fashion styles and no high fashion options.

Prior to completing the option detail, the merchandiser must consider and understand the following points:

1. The descriptions, fashionabilities and selling prices of the options ensure that the right quantitative characteristics are applied to the option detail.
2. The life cycle used should match the range plan to ensure the option detail is in line with strategy.
3. The appropriate rate of sale and sell-through rates are used to reflect each option's characteristics.
4. The option detail buy at selling value must not add up to more than the OTB budget for the phase that the range is planned for.

The solutions to Points 1 and 2 are provided, in the case of Point 1 by the buyer, and Point 2 from the range plan. The average rate of sale and sell-through rate presumption can be taken from the range plan, but then flexed depending on the implied qualitative strengths of each option. A good approach to helping with this is to use the fashionabilities to make the appropriate decision.

- Core basic options – all quantitative characteristics must be well above the averages of the initial option plan as this fashionability sold out in the history year.
- Fashion style options – the product analysis in Chapter 6 showed these as being generally below-average performers in the business and so should have quantitative characteristics just below average.

Finally, the WSSI identifies the maximum amount of the OTB budget that can be applied to this option detail. Being the first range of the season, with a planned life cycle of eight weeks, the maximum selling value that the option detail must add up to will be the OTB budget for Weeks 1–8 combined: £11,295 (see Table 9.7).

Taking all the new details into account, the merchandiser will complete the option detail by applying the known facts and mixing them with commercial gut feel. These second points are reflected in the applied rate of sale and sell-through presumptions where the core basic options have been given higher than the averages

Table 9.6 The option detail

Option	Description	Colour	Fashionability	Cost price	Selling price	Weeks life cycle	Rate of sale	Sell-through rate	Unit buy	Buy cost value	Buy selling value
1	Basic T-shirt	White	Core basic	£4.00	£15.00	8					
2	Basic T-shirt	Black	Core basic	£4.00	£15.00	8					
3	Basic T-shirt	Navy	Core basic	£4.00	£15.00	8					
4	Polo T-shirt	Blue	Fashion style	£7.70	£25.00	8					
5	Polo T-shirt	Red	Fashion style	£7.70	£25.00	8					

Table 9.7 Identifying the OTB value from the WSSI

Weeks/ months	Sales budget	Sales mix	Week 52 Markdown budget	Markdown mix	£25,902 Closing stock budget	Open to buy budget	Cover weeks cover	Promotional calendar planned promotional activities
Week 1	£1,014	2.00%	£0	0.00%	£25,902	£1,014	25.5	
Week 2	£1,167	2.30%	£0	0.00%	£25,902	£1,167	22.2	
Week 3	£1,318	2.60%	£0	0.00%	£25,902	£1,318	19.7	
Week 4	£1,413	2.80%	£0	0.00%	£25,902	£1,413	18.3	
January	£4,912	9.70%	£0	0.00%				
Week 5	£1,413	2.80%	£0	0.00%	£25,902	£1,413	18.3	
Week 6	£2,028	4.00%	£0	0.00%	£25,902	£2,028	12.8	Cardholder event
Week 7	£1,471	2.90%	£0	0.00%	£25,902	£1,471	17.6	
Week 8	£1,471	2.90%	£0	0.00%	£25,902	£1,471	17.6	

applied to the range plan. Table 9.8 presents a completed option detail, using the following calculations to identify the unit buy and its cost and selling values.

- (Rate of sale * life cycle)/sell-through rate % = unit buy;
- Unit buy * cost price = buy cost value
- Unit buy * selling price = buy selling value.

FOCUS POINT 9.3: THE INTAKE MARGIN PERCENTAGE CHECK

The achieved intake margin percentage of the option detail must be reviewed to ensure margin budgets are being adhered to. During the KPI budgeting process, an intake margin budget of 65 per cent was set to be achieved by the casual wear product category. This product range's actual intake margin is 65.9 per cent.

Calculation

((Selling price/1.20 VAT) – Cost price) / (Selling price/1.20 VAT) * 100
((£9,400/1.20) – £2,672) / (£9,400/1.20) * 100
(£5,161) / (£7,833) * 100 = 65.9%

This means that this range plan's intake margin is 64 per cent, revealing a bigger gap between cost and selling prices than was presumed within the KPI budgeting process.

With a completed option detail, the die has been cast for this product range, allowing the next steps in the concept-to-carrier bag process to begin: sourcing, manufacturing and delivery. Retailing by its nature is full of risk. The simple concept of taking a pot of money, turning it into a product to sell and doing so at a profit is in theory straightforward. In the realities of highly competitive global markets, however, the actual truth lies in the territory of risk, uncertainty and difficulty. Analysing the completed option detail, its shape and direction is vital to assess if it is in line with the planning strategy and reflects evolution in target customer demand and the businesses financial requirements.

In the case of Prentice Day the casualwear research identified:

- Overall, the strong casual wear product category performance was the result of excellent trading of core basic options
  - There was consistency in the performance of each product group.
  - Core basic options performed best, achieving the highest rates of sale and sell-through as well as the lowest average covers.
  - Fashion styles within the range did not stand out as being of note and could be described as being of average performance.
  - Meanwhile, high fashion styles across all measures performed poorly.
  - Casual wear KPI budgets needed to reflect its strength but required a controlled approach to prevent the business being exposed to undue risk.

Table 9.8 The completed option detail for casual wear T-shirts

Option	Description	Colour	Fashionability	Cost price	Selling price	Weeks life cycle	Rate of sale	Sell-through rate	Unit buy	Buy cost value	Buy selling value
1	Basic T shirt	White	Core basic	£4.00	£15.00	8	12	80%	120	£480.00	£1,800.00
2	Basic T shirt	Black	Core basic	£4.00	£15.00	8	12	80%	120	£480.00	£1,800.00
3	Basic T shirt	Navy	Core basic	£4.00	£15.00	8	12	80%	120	£480.00	£1,800.00
4	Polo T shirt	Blue	Fashion style	£7.70	£25.00	8	8	80%	80	£616.00	£2,000.00
5	Polo T shirt	Red	Fashion style	£7.70	£25.00	8	8	80%	80	£616.00	£2,000.00
							12	80%	520	£2,672.00	£9,400.00

The four tables which follow summarize and review the option detail to assess its adherence to what was set out to be achieved at the start of the planning process.

- Fashionability analysis
  - Core basics have increased within the mix versus the previous year across both metrics.
  - An interesting point to note is the different mix percentages between unit and buying selling value. Core basics, for example, represent 69 per cent of the units bought but only 57 per cent of the selling value to the business, caused by the lower selling prices of this basic product (see Table 9.9).

Table 9.9 Fashionability analysis

Fashionability	Units bought	% Mix	Previous year mix	Buy selling value	% Mix	Previous year mix
Core basic	360	69%	67%	£5,400	57%	53%
Fashion	160	31%	26%	£4000	43%	34%
High fashion	0	0%	7%	0	0%	13%
Total	520	100%	100%	£9,400	100%	100%

- Unit buy analysis
  - Table 9.10 summarizes the unit buys by fashionability and then reinterprets these into a unit buy per week. This is done by applying the life cycle presumed on the range plan (eight weeks) and for last year, the actual life cycle at the point of the initial analysis (20 weeks).
  - The analysis shows that unit buy volumes per week have increased and that over the course of the season, it is likely that, once all buys have been complete, unit buys will have raised further.

Table 9.10 Unit buy analysis

Unit buys	Unit buys	Buy per week	Unit buys previous year	Buy per week previous year
Core basic	120	15	221	11
Fashion	80	10	86	4
High fashion	0	0	36	2
Average	104	13	124	6

- Price analysis
  - Price analysis allows the buyer and merchandiser to assess the product range's price positioning relative to last year.
  - The analysis indicates that the price architecture for this range has moved decisively towards opening price points. This is in line with the SWOT and 4P analysis conducted by Prentice Day's owners (see Table 9.11).

Table 9.11 *Price analysis*

Price	Options	Mix %	Previous year	Mix %
£15	3	60%	3	38%
£25	2	40%	3	38%
£35	0	0%	2	25%
Total	5	100%	8	100%

- Colour analysis
  - A final analysis is a review of colour mixes to assess the impact that the range will have in store. There is a danger that the scale of core basics in any fashion business could swamp the excitement and interest provided by fashion and high fashion options.
  - The colour analysis suggests that the range plan, while delivering the unit buy growth and price realignment, has been at the expense of 'excitement' in the range. This must be corrected in future T-shirt ranges (see Table 9.12).

Table 9.12 *Colour analysis*

Colour	Options	Mix %	Previous year	Mix %
White/black/ navy	3	60%	4	50%
Blue	1	20%	1	13%
Red	1	20%	1	13%
Green	0	0%	1	13%
Yellow	0	0%	1	13%
Total	5	100%	8	100%

Summarizing the option detail is useful for checking the validity of the product range compared to the initial planning strategy, but also for identifying any unintended consequences that may have occurred as a result. The move towards core basics was certainly the correct one and has been delivered through the KPI budgeting and range-planning process, but it has been at the expense of excitement and individuality. Further to this, the beauty of being able to identify OTB phasing through the WSSI is that with a flexible supplier base not all the OTB budget has yet been spent. The buyer and merchandiser still have the opportunity to reflect on the range plan analysis and make any adjustments to the next option details that they feel are suitable.

A SUMMARY OF THE RANGE-PLANNING PROCESS

The range plan and its associated activities are probably the most enjoyable part of the planning process for both buyer and merchandiser. The supreme effort by both roles to reach this point is rewarded by seeing the product range come alive in front of their eyes. Options that existed in a nebulous format become tangible, are given names and assume personalities. Personal favourites begin to emerge and, by making targeted decisions, accurate and realistic unit buys are created. There is of course plenty of room for dissent and, for example, if at the end of the process the OTB budget has not been met or if the range appears imbalanced towards one particular fashionability, then revisions will of course need to be made.

By this point the scale of any revision should be minor – the range plan should have ironed out significant discrepancies and the process should be amenable and fun. The working on the option detail plan together brings other benefits to buyer and merchandiser beyond that of enjoyment. The working on the final range together allows them to understand better each one's thinking and expectations for the range. This has multiple benefits as it adds knowledge to the future steps in the planning process – the sizing and allocation of the options. It also allows time to discuss how the product range should be promoted, and which options are priorities for delivery, promotion and replenishment.

Another impact of the range plan is that it reinforces the relationship of buyer and merchandiser as being a team. The product range becomes a joint effort that they both support and develop. To emphasize this point, in large fashion businesses, once the option range plan is finalized, the buyer and merchandiser will present their product ranges and the research and concepts that stand behind it to the chief executive and the senior management team, in a final range review for their sign-off and approval. This review is of great importance as it offers a chance for the range not just to be approved, but also reviewed against the original planning strategy. Range planning also acts as an enabler of the supply chain activities, meaning that final supplier negotiations can commence, orders be placed and contracts raised. The product range is no longer an idea but a reality. Its sourcing, manufacture, delivery and distribution to retail channels can begin in earnest.

FOCUS POINT 9.4: THE 80/20 RULE

The Pareto principle is useful within range planning as it acts as a reminder of the imbalances in the relationship between effort and reward. Named after the economist Vilfredo Pareto, the principle asserts that 20 per cent of an input investment generates 80 per cent of reward. Pareto first developed the idea in 1906 by discovering a correlation between an input value and its output value. As an example, he noted that 80 per cent of land in Italy was owned by 20 per cent of the population. with similar relationships in other countries too.

The 80/20 rule has become a general measure within business and is particularly relevant within B&M. If one considers a product range of two options; a navy T-shirt and a salmon-red raw silk shirt, then each one represents 50 per cent of options available. However, the commercial strength of the navy T-shirt is far greater and will generate a far larger value return to a business.

A commercial fashion option range plan will naturally reflect the 80/20 rule. In a product range that comprises two core basic, five fashion style and three high fashion options, the input investment into the product range by option would be:

Core basic	2 options	= 20% of the option range plan
Fashion style	5 options	= 50% of the option range plan
High fashion	3 options	= 30% of the option range plan
Total	10 options	

However, the sales potential of the fashionability types would be very different and would be likely to carry the following unit buy mix.

Core basic	700 unit buy	= 70% of the unit buys
Fashion style	250 unit buy	= 25% of the unit buys
High fashion	50 unit buy	= 5% of the unit buys
Total	1,000 unit buys	

Good effective range planning inevitably has parallels to the Pareto principle, it is common sense and commercially astute. The skill within B&M is to recognize the validity of the model, to replicate it within option range planning but not on the shop floor.

Fast fashion brands are experts at applying the Pareto principle. Zara is well renowned for translating trends throughout a fashion season and presenting a fresh updated collection every two weeks. These numerous options are displayed effectively, but alongside the ever present small-option, big-business core basic options in store.

Activity: Research further the 80/20 rule. What influence does it have in fashion and the wider world?

SUMMARY

This chapter has focused on the relationship between creativity and numbers with the focal point of this being the range plan. The introduction of the range and option detail plans has shown how those two opposing definitions of fashion and business can be finally reconciled.

The numbers presented have relied upon previous chapters, with the fundamental point that this chapter has attempted to convey that if a merchandiser has good thorough product research, then range planning will be the application of known data and so should not be feared. The key, though, is in the depth of knowledge possessed about one's business and product. One extra point that should be made is that the right quantitative assumptions to apply within the process vary, with no standard correct answer. The examples used in this chapter are just that, open to be challenged, but that in some ways is the fun of a range review; a good debate and discussion to fully interrogate the merchandiser's mind and commercial awareness.

SELF-DIRECTED STUDY

1. Undertake a comparative shop of an own-label and brand retailer. Create a mix analysis of product type, price point, colour and country of origin to understand how their product ranges are constructed.
2. Refer to the companion website for Prentice Day case study exercises.

Further Reading

Goworek, H. (2007) *Fashion Buying*. Oxford: Blackwell

Jackson, T. and Shaw, D. (2001) *Mastering Fashion Buying and Merchandising Management*. Basingstoke: Macmillan

Kunz, G. (2010) *Merchandising – Theory, Principles and Practice, 3rd ed.* New York: Fairchild

10 Fashion Merchandising: Sizing, Deliveries and Allocation

INTENDED LEARNING OUTCOMES

1. A discussion of the buyer–merchandiser–supplier relationship.
2. Key concepts in size curve management.
3. Initial allocation and its role in supporting brand personalities.
4. Delivery management and its dynamics.

INTRODUCTION

The practical creation of size curves, allocation plans and identification of delivery requirements is undertaken once the option detail has finalized the product range and the unit buy of each option. However, the thinking and collation of the data required for each of these later activities occur much earlier within the planning process. This chapter will demonstrate why this is the case, and also offer practical evidence to complete these final steps within the planning process.

Table 10.1 shows where the sizing, delivery management and allocation activities lie within the concept-to-carrier bag model, and that while this chapter focuses on the final planning activities of the merchandiser, there is still plenty more to the role that occurs after this point. Planning a range is one side of the coin, the other is its trading – the active process of creating a product range, driving its performance as hard as is commercially possible, making sure every effort is made to achieve or exceed the KPI budgets set for the product earlier in the planning process.

However, for trading to commence the product has to be manufactured and delivered. The merchandiser contributes to this by providing suppliers with several pieces of information that are crucial to their efficient supply of product; the size curves and delivery requirements for each option. With these two activities complete, the merchandiser can then identify the initial allocations for each option that will be delivered to stores, once the product has been received from the supplier.

To demonstrate these activities, the chapter will take product information from the Prentice Day T-shirt range plan, created in Chapter 9, to offer insights into the role of the merchandiser at this point in the concept-to-carrier bag model.

Table 10.1 *The concept-to-carrier bag model*

Concept to carrier bag step	Definition
1. Research	Undertaking and collation of relevant fashion research
2. Concept	Creation of product range concept and direction
3. Product development	Finalization of concept as a product range
4. Sourcing	**Sourcing of suppliers and manufacturers for the range**
5. Manufacturing	**Manufacture of the product range**
6. Shipping	**Shipping and delivery of the product range**
7. Warehousing	**Receipt of the product range and its allocation to store and storage**
8. Distribution	Delivering initial store allocations
9. Retail	Display, sale, promotion and stock replenishment
10. Carrier bag	Purchase of the product by a consumer

THE MERCHANDISER–SUPPLIER RELATIONSHIP

Before moving on to the main topics of this chapter, it is worth spending some time considering the relationship between the merchandiser and their suppliers. Usually, the key relationship between retailer and manufacturer lies with the buyer, rather than the merchandiser, with this reflected throughout the concept-to-carrier bag process. The buyer – with their skill set lying very firmly in creativity and product development – naturally leads the sourcing of suppliers, products and their components. This developmental process will mean that the buyer will both source new suppliers and develop relationships with existing ones in line with market and product trends, best matching supply of product to potential customer demand. However, this does not preclude the merchandiser from developing contacts with suppliers and being involved in the retailer/supplier working relationship. The exact nature of this varies depending on the complexity and size of the retail business, but it is possible to make some broad assumptions.

At its simplest, the relationship between a retailer and supplier pivots on reaching a point where the retailer commits to buying product from the supplier. From the retailer's perspective, the decision to place an order will depend on the product fulfilling a number of criteria such as:

- fulfilling an identified customer need (for example, appropriate fashionability, design)
- being at an appropriate quality level
- being at a cost that will allow a suitable intake margin percentage to be achieved

- available and delivered at a time that suits the retailer
- being manufactured in line with the retailer's ethical trading standards.

Reviewing the list, there will be decision points which the buyer will negotiate with the supplier, but these will depend on the merchandiser providing the negotiation detail – KPI budgeting to derive intake margin, buying budgets and OTB phasing plans for example. To do this effectively, it has to be implied that the merchandiser – while not managing the supplier relationship process – will influence its direction.

As product development proceeds to range planning, explicitly requiring the buyer and merchandiser to work more closely together, decisions such as size curves, confirmed delivery dates, purchase order management, sealing and delivery tracking begin to take precedence within the B&M function. Decisions made by both roles at this point will directly influence each other. For example, a merchandiser's decision to delay deliveries would change the production priorities of a supplier, so changing the sealing process of the buyer. The triumvirate will therefore need to have regular contact with one other, bringing the merchandiser firmly into the retailer/supplier relationship.

In practical terms, many retail fashion businesses split the physical decision-making process between buyer and merchandiser at the point of raising confirmed purchase orders, which act as legally binding agreements to buy product. An approved purchase order allows the management of remaining product development decisions to rest with the buyer, whilst the orderly delivery of stock and authorities to ship can rest with the merchandiser. The finalized purchase order that facilitates this role demarcation contains relevant details, the origins of which will come from both buyer and merchandiser:

- purchase order number – the unique reference for the order
- buying terms – the agreed financial terms agreed between retailer and supplier
- shipping details – the agreed process to deliver stock
- product details – the agreed product descriptions, cost prices and unit buy quantities by size
- the value of the order
- signatures – signed by an authorized signatory of the retail business.

The creation of an approved purchase order still needs some final detail from the merchandiser to allow the manufacturing process to begin; unit buys require size curves applied to them, initial allocations decided and finally delivery phasing to be worked out.

SIZE CURVES

The creation of accurate size curves relies on effective analysis to guide the process of deciding the correct balance of size availability for each option. A first danger point within this is that reliance on past sales history is as good as any other starting point; if it is solely relied upon, then size curves created may not be relevant.

As silhouettes differ year on year, the historic sales by size may not always translate easily season to season. The size analysis undertaken must be as individual as possible to the new product range – a simple generic size analysis to cover as many products as possible is not appropriate. A second point is that, by reviewing previous season sales by size, one can assess what has been sold but not necessarily what could have been sold had the size curve been different. If a size consistently sells out early in a season, its true potential has not been realized, and so in any sizing activities an element of speculation is required concerning what 'might have been'.

However, despite these two dangers, it should also be recognized that, without an average size curve, manufacturing garments would be more expensive and take longer as each option would need to be production-planned individually. The innate skill within size curve planning is to negate the dangers within the analysis, rather than simply being aware of how to calculate the curve. If executed well, size curves can overcome their inherent weakness to be a valuable source of driving multi-sales across options, enabling them to be mixed and matched by customers to their own individual size preferences.

In practical terms, knowing the right point within an options life cycle at which to analyse size curve data eliminates much of the identified weaknesses. To highlight this, Tables 10.2–10.5 below follow the sales and stock history of a past Prentice Day white basic T-shirt for a 12-week life cycle. Table 10.2, for example, shows:

- the sizes ranged (sizes XS to XL)
- cumulative sales achieved up to Week 3 by size (total 64 units)
- the percentage mix of sales to Week 3 by size
- the stock remaining at the end of Week 3 (total 156 units)
- the percentage mix of stock remaining at the end of Week 3 by size
- the total unit buy by size (total 220 units)
- the percentage mix by size of the buy.

By plotting the changes in the T-shirts sales and stock ratio at Weeks 3, 6, 9 and 12 it is possible to see changes in the size curves relative to the availability of stock. Over the next four tables, review in particular the sales and stock ratios for sizes XSmall and XLarge.

Table 10.2 *Size curves at Week 3*

White T-shirt: sales Weeks 1–3

Size	XS	S	M	L	XL	Total
Sales	11	17	19	12	5	64
% Mix	17%	26%	30%	19%	8%	100%
Stock	13	18	38	45	42	156
% Mix	8%	12%	24%	29%	27%	100%
Total buy	24	35	57	57	47	220
% Mix	11%	16%	26%	26%	21%	100%

At Week 3, sizes XS and XL sales mixes differ to both the stock and buy mixes, suggesting that size XS sales are stronger than the buy size curve predicted (17 per cent sales mix versus 11 per cent buy mix), while size XL sales are weaker than the buy size curve (8 per cent versus 21 per cent).

Table 10.3 *Size curves at Week 6*

White T-shirt: Sales Weeks 1–6						
Size	XS	S	M	L	XL	Total
Sales	22	34	38	24	10	128
% Mix	17%	26%	30%	19%	8%	100%
Stock	2	1	19	33	37	92
% Mix	2%	1%	21%	36%	40%	100%
Total buy	24	35	57	57	47	220
% Mix	11%	16%	26%	26%	21%	100%

Size XS sales mixes are maintained at 17 per cent; however, only has two units are left in stock so future potential is limited. Size XL, meanwhile, still has healthy stocks and will be able to continue to sell at its current rate, so maintaining its sales potential.

Table 10.4 *Size curves at Week 9*

White T-shirt: sales Weeks 1–9						
Size	XS	S	M	L	XL	Total
Sales	24	35	57	36	15	167
% Mix	14%	21%	34%	22%	9%	100%
Stock	0	0	0	21	32	53
% Mix	0%	0%	0%	40%	60%	100%
Total buy	24	35	57	57	47	220
% Mix	11%	16%	26%	26%	21%	100%

By Week 9, size XS is out of stock and so its cumulative sales mix is beginning to decline, whilst size XL is able to continue selling as stocks remain high. As a result, its cumulative sales mix begins to increase.

Table 10.5 *Size curves at Week 12*

White T-shirt: sales Weeks 1–12						
Size	XS	S	M	L	XL	Total
Sales	24	35	57	48	20	184
% Mix	13%	19%	31%	26%	11%	100%
Stock	0	0	0	9	27	36
% Mix	0%	0%	0%	25%	75%	100%
Total buy	24	35	57	57	47	220
% Mix	11%	16%	26%	26%	21%	100%

By 12 weeks, the sales mix of size XSmall has reduced from its initial 17 per cent to 13 per cent of total sales. As sizes Small and Medium have also sold out, their sales mixes too have reduced compared to the initial analysis in Week 3. At the other end of the scale, the sales mixes of sizes Large and XLarge have increased between Weeks 3 and 12 as these have remained in stock, meaning actual sales have been recorded throughout the twelve-week life cycle.

There is therefore, a correlation between life cycle, sales and stock mixes, making it key to review these at the point in time when all sizes ranged are holding an optimum number of units. In the example above, this would be at Week 3, as this is the period when all sizes reflect accurate sales to stock mix, so best reflecting true opportunity.

Referring again to the Prentice Day case study and the option detail created in Chapter 9, shown below in Table 10.6, the final step in the sizing process is to work out the unit buys for each size.

This final step is straightforward! Using the basic white T-shirt unit buy from the above range plan and using the following calculation identifies that the XSmall unit buy is:

- Unit buy * XSmall mix = XSmall unit buy
  o 120 units * 17% = 20 units

Table 10.7 identifies the size curve for all sizes ranged of the white basic T-shirt.

FOCUS POINT 10.1: THE IMPORTANCE OF SIZING WITHIN FASHION

It can be very frustrating for a retailer's customer to find the perfect product only to discover that their size is not available. What can be more frustrating is then to find particular sizes left over on the sale rail at the end of the season. The simple question of why a retailer cannot pay as much attention to sizing as they do to the design and creative elements within the products is one that seems to never end. Making sure that size curve analysis is undertaken at the correct time within the life cycle of the product is an important step in resolving the issue; however, it is not the only one.

First, the sizes themselves may be incorrect. 'Size UK' – a 2002 national survey, the first since 1951 – was undertaken by a number of stakeholders including the London College of Fashion, Marks and Spencer, Arcadia group and House of Fraser. Its aim was to provide an up-to-date review of the actual size and shape of the UK population that would enable retailers to update their size charts to better reflect body and shape. As part of the survey, 5,000 men and 5,000 women were measured in electronic booths that took about 150 measurements on each body. The people were active: measurements took place in colleges and in retail stores, while inactive members of the population were not measured. The results showed that waist sizes had expanded 6 inches, and that body shape and so product blocks required updating, which meant a realignment of sizing as its historic sales patterns were being skewed by customers having to size up or down to find product to fit. (Size UK 2002)

A second issue is the temptation for buyers and merchandisers to try to squeeze more options into a product range than the range plan allows. Take the example of the Prentice Day range plan calculated in Chapter 9 and replicated below.

Product group	OTB budget	Average selling price	OTB units	Rate of sale	Life cycle	Sell-through rate	Average unit buy	Ideal option plan
Trousers	£19,824	£50	396	5	8	85%	47	8
Shirts	£12,244	£35	350	5	8	85%	47	7
T-shirts	£26,237	£16	1,640	8	8	85%	75	22
TOTAL	£58,305	£24.44	2,386	6	8	85%	56	37

If, for example, the buyer and merchandiser decided that the ideal option plan was too low and they wanted to treble the options without changing the OTB budget, the effect on the average unit buys would be to reduce them as shown below.

Product group	OTB budget	Average selling price	OTB units	Rate of sale	Life cycle	Sell-through rate	Average unit buy	Ideal option plan
Trousers	£19,824	£50	396	1.7	8	85%	17	23
Shirts	£12,244	£35	350	1.7	8	85%	17	21
T-shirts	£26,237	£16	1,640	2.7	8	85%	25	66
TOTAL	£58,305	£24.44	2,386	2.3	8	85%	22	110

As each extra option is added, the unit line buy reduces and so fewer units are available by size, and at some point size curves will fragment even before they reach stores.

Activity: Review size curves available in a number of different stores. Which retailer offers the best size curve and which has run out of certain sizes? What does that tell you about their sizing analysis?

Table 10.6 *The completed range plan for casual wear T-shirts*

Option	Description	Colour	Fashionability	Cost price	Selling price	Weeks life cycle	Rate of sale	Sell-through rate	Unit buy	Buy cost value	Buy selling value
1	Basic T-shirt	White	Core basic	£4.00	£15.00	8	12	80%	120	£480.00	£1,800.00
2	Basic T-shirt	Black	Core basic	£4.00	£15.00	8	12	80%	120	£480.00	£1,800.00
3	Basic T-shirt	Navy	Core basic	£4.00	£15.00	8	12	80%	120	£480.00	£1,800.00
4	Polo T-shirt	Blue	Fashion style	£7.70	£25.00	8	8	80%	80	£616.00	£2,000.00
5	Polo T-shirt	Red	Fashion style	£7.70	£25.00	8	8	80%	80	£616.00	£2,000.00
							12	80%	520	£2,672.00	£9,400.00

Table 10.7 *Size curve for the white basic T-shirt*

White T-shirt: size ratio

Size	XS	S	M	L	XL	Total
Total buy	20	31	36	23	10	120
% Mix	17%	26%	30%	19%	8%	100%

INITIAL ALLOCATIONS

Jackson and Shaw state that the range-planning process means that 'the range plan is the main source document for planning what lines options and how many of them will go to each individual branch' (Jackson and Shaw 2001: 140). Having presented the range plan at work in Chapter 9, the sense in this assertion is clear. The initial allocation process does, however, have its roots much further back in the planning process, with the decisions made prior to range planning, ultimately shaping the intellectual direction of physical stock management. Elements of the concept-to-carrier bag model and the decisions made throughout it must all be considered, so ensuring that the business's image is reflected in how it presents its stock, as well as supporting the financial requirements of efficient stock management.

From a quantitative perspective, the range plan coupled with the defined size curves provides the following components that are relevant to the allocation process:

- the options that require to be allocated
- the stores to be ranged with the options
- unit buys from which the allocation quantity is derived
- the sizes available and the curve shape required.

Taking this starting point, the merchandiser can begin to build the allocation plan by collating all the available data from the planning process into an allocation table, as shown in Table 10.8 below. The following example presumes that the merchandiser is allocating the white basic T-shirt from the completed option detail.

Table 10.8 *Draft allocation plan*

Fashion brand	Prentice Day
Style	Basic T-shirt
Colour	White
Fashionability	Core basic
Total unit buy	120
Stores ranged	1
Size ratio	17%/26%/30%/19%/8%
Display factor	
Rate of sale	
Resupply time	
Allocation calculation	
Total initial allocation	
Allocation % of buy	

The derivation and the subsequent allocation decisions will, however, come from a wider source of data and business strategies which will influence allocation decisions. The addition of qualitative elements to supplement the quantitative process helps influence judgements about whether the decisions look and feel right commercially.

Mixed together, these twin elements include:

- the business model and the personality of the brand
- the product type, fashionability and the options role within the range plan
- visual merchandising strategies that reflect the brand personality
- the rates of sale and sell-through rate assumptions of the product
- the supplier location and flexibility within the supply chain
- the phasing of stock intake requirements through the WSSI.

Taking each in turn, it then becomes possible to assess the impact of qualitative influences on a quantitative process.

- The business model and the personality of the brand

For Prentice Day, the original SWOT and 4P marketing analysis identified very clearly that the business was focused on mid-market, core basic product ranges, with loyal regular customers. Ensuring the allocation reflects this model will require a focus on volume opportunities through simple standardized approaches to store layouts and large allocation quantities, to ensure option and size availability at all times.

- The product type, fashionability and the options role within the range plan

Taking the overall business model requirements into consideration requires further refinement by taking time to assess the role of each product in the range, to understand what its problem-solving characteristics are. Each product has a distinct reason for being in a range, but labouring for hours over how each one will answer the problems of the businesses customers will be an unnecessary waste of time. However, some broad conclusions can be made. Core basics, as volume sellers, will need a differently sized allocation quantity to a fashion option, which will have more specific and so more limited volume potential. High fashion options which will have very limited buy quantities will tend to be allocated on more of a case-by-case basis.

- Visual merchandising strategies that reflect the brand personality

While visual merchandising (VM) strategies are beyond the remit of the merchandiser, there is a requirement to understand how allocated product will look in store. An eclectic, bespoke product offer will need to look and feel very different to one that is core basic in focus. The merchandiser will need to know the number units of an option type that retail operations consider to be a credible statement for display, and to ensure that this display factor is built into the allocation plan.

- The rates of sale and sell-through rate assumptions of the product

These considerations are very much the domain of the merchandiser and will have been carefully considered throughout the range-planning process. These assumptions – which drove the range planning process and the resultant unit buys for each option – must be carried through into the allocation plan.

- The supplier location and flexibility within the supply chain

This point is possibly the most important of all. At the heart of good allocation planning lies stock management; ensuring that stock levels in store are optimum. Too much stock and the shop floor becomes clogged, whereas too little will mean that volume potential is lost by out of stocks and size fragmentation. Referring to the SWOT complied in Chapter 5, the Prentice Day business benefits from a flexible supply chain which can support short lead-time orders. Knowing the lead time in conjunction with the display factor and rate of sale assumptions will enable optimum allocation quantities to be planned.

- The phasing of stock intake requirements through the WSSI

The final consideration is more of an output of the process. Assuming the relevant depth of thought has been applied to the allocation plan, stocks in store for each option will correct. This should mean that any differences between the allocation and unit buy quantities will not need to be allocated at this point. Where this is the case, it allows the merchandiser to split the unit buy into different delivery phases, allowing the supplier to better manage their production capacity. The retail business too can benefit from improved cash flow within their balance sheet;

Taking these qualitative and quantitative considerations into account for Prentice Day, Table 10.9 builds an allocation plan for the white basic T-shirt.

The example in Table 10.9 shows a process and train of thought integral to the planning process undertaken – and this is common across all retail businesses, with the obvious exception of pure play-online retailers.

With an allocation in place, there is a further final decision to make about whether the merchandiser should decide to phase the option into more than delivery? There are two ways to decide this. First, in the example shown, the allocation of 68 units represents 57 per cent of the total unit buy – just over half of the total. Holding the balance of the order (in this case, 52 units) means that the retailer will have to find storage space for unallocated stock, and will be paying interest on the debt that it would have taken out to pay for the product. In this case, it makes perfect sense to split the order in two, delivering 68 units initially, with the remaining 52 units delivered a few weeks later.

To identify when the second delivery should be made, the cover calculation can be used to divide the proposed initial 68-unit order by the planned rate of sale, to identify the weeks cover at which the stock will turn and at which point stocks will be lower than the display factor. Table 10.10 shows this cover check in action.

Working through the calculation, as sales each week reduce the stock holding and the cover reduces in line with reducing stocks, it identifies that by the end of Week 4

Table 10.9 *Final allocation plan*

Fashion brand	Prentice Day
Style	Basic T-shirt
Colour	White
Fashionability	Core basic
Total unit buy	120
This delivery	120
Stores ranged	1
Size ratio	17%/26%/30%/19%/8%
Display factor	4 units per size = 20 units total
Rate of sale	16 units per week
Resupply time	3 weeks from placing order to delivery
Allocation calculation	Display factor+(Rate of sale * resupply time)
Total initial allocation	20 units+(16 units * 3) = 68 units
Allocation by size	11/17/20/12/5 = 68 units
Allocation % of buy	57%

Note: Data sources
Display factor – presumed by the author.
Rate of sale – taken from the option detail plan (see Chapter 9).
Resupply time – presumed by the author.

Table 10.10 *Delivery-phasing cover check*

	Week 1	Week 2	Week 3	Week 4
Opening stock	68	52	36	20
Rate of sale	16	16	16	16
Closing stock	52	36	20	4
Cover	3	2	1	0
Display factor	20	20	20	20

Note: Data calculation – Cover calculation: closing stock/sales

stocks will be below the store's display factor. The cover check analysis has therefore identified that to maintain the store's VM requirements, it would be prudent to take delivery of the balance of the buy early in Week 4.

FOCUS POINT 10.2: ALLOCATION PLANNING – THE OOS PERCENTAGE

Fashion retailing is not a linear industry, and while the components in allocation may be broadly similar in all business model types, what constitutes the right answer will vary considerably. Beyond the example given in this chapter, there could be many kinks and curves that change the allocation-planning process. Probably the most common decision that is included within the process concerns how much should be allocated as a percentage of a delivery?

That question is like asking how long a piece of string is, as the dynamics that went into the planning process up to this point are likely to vary not just from business to business but by individual product type, too. A better question to ask addresses how a merchandiser can optimize stock management within the requirements of the business model.

Different businesses will operate their value chain to best fit the demands of product management, and a starting point to decide how to optimize stock management would be to identify some influences on the topic:

- The frequency of change within the product mix – brands such as Zara will inject new options into their business more frequently than a brand such as Gant. Therefore, the pressure to deliver, allocate and sell out of an option is more immediate and so there may be no time built into the value chain for regular stock replenishment.
- Use of promotional strategies – some brands will hold regular promotions, such as one-day and mid-season sales, whereas others may only discount at end-of-season sales. The type and regularity of promotions changes the pace of replenishment, with rates of sale achieved varying significantly in differing weeks of a fashion season, so changing the amount of reserve stock needed at any one time.
- Different budget requirements – the emphasis placed by luxury and premium brands on design, fabrication and embellishment naturally places their product into a smaller and more elite customer segment, in which scarcity of product is valued, with buy quantities smaller, possibly bespoke. This will mean that allocation quantities may equal as much as 100 per cent of the buy. By contrast, businesses that work on volume and efficiency of scale will expect to hold reserve stock to infill size or colour shortages while the product life cycle is active.
- The capabilities of the supply chain will influence allocation plans. The resupply time is a component of identifying the initial allocation quantity, but for some suppliers and product types that could be zero. Where there is no practical ability for the supply chain to resupply product if it sells well, then the only other route to maintaining reserve stocks is to deliver all buy units together and use warehouses to hold potentially large quantities of stock to replenish stores.
- The product itself will determine replenishment criteria. Like the example above discussing different budget requirements, different fashionability attributes will require different replenishment strategies and so different quantities of reserve stock.

The important point in stock management is to understand the impact of these influences and measure the efficiency with which decisions about allocation and reserve quantities are decided. This measurement tool is known as the out of stock percentage (OOS). In short, OOS identifies the unavailability of a style/colour/size (a unit buy for each size, also known as a sku – stock keeping unit) for retail sale at the time of measurement. A study commissioned in 2008 identified that direct potential sales loss due to out of stocks measured 4 per cent (Gruen and Corsten 2008), which, whilst small as a percentage, is large as a potential shortfall in cash sales. To remedy this, attention is needed not just to supply chain initiatives such as cross-dock distribution and other pre-retail activities, but also aligning rate of sale demand forecasting with accurate stock management to identify optimum allocation and replenishment strategies.

Activity: Research the concept of cross-dock and distribution centre operations within fashion businesses.

UPDATING THE WSSI, MANAGING PURCHASE ORDERS AND DELIVERIES

As discussed in Chapter 8, the phasing of OTB through the WSSI allows a retail business to manage the flow of new products over the course of a season. The benefits of improvements to cash flow, freshness in product in store and a better managed supply chain process that the WSSI provides should be matched by the by the practical process of deciding delivery phasing. The creation of a delivery schedule, as an extension of the option detail, is used to provide a single source summary of the finalized product deliveries by date, units and value over the course of a season. The value of the delivery schedule lies in its relevance throughout the value chain, so facilitating a smooth delivery process as well as providing vital financially relevant information to the merchandiser and finance team. Its creation means:

- The merchandiser can plot range plans to allocation plans to delivery phasing and from there compare actual delivery requirements against the presumed OTB phasing on the planned WSSI.
- The finance team can use actual delivery requirements and apply them to the cash flow presumptions on the balance sheet to assess actual debt requirements over the course of the season.
- The B&M team can use the delivery schedule to raise purchase orders in a timely, ordered process.
- The logistics team can plan warehouse capacity and the flow of goods in, deliveries of stocks to stores and the efficient storage of put-away stock.
- Retail operations can, like the logistics teams, plan the management of retail stores to assess when and how to relay store layouts as new seasons begin. As the season develops, they can also make changes as new deliveries and products arrive over its course.

For Prentice Day, and its small case study example, this may all seem unnecessary. However, in large retail chains where product ranges may be measured in hundreds of options and millions of pounds' value, with thousands of staff in the value chain, a well-managed and accurate delivery schedule is vital. Table 10.11 presents an

Table 10.11 Delivery schedule for casual wear

Option	Description	Colour	Cost price	Selling price	Unit buy	Buy cost value	Buy selling value	1 January (Week 1)	22 January (Week 4)
1	Basic T-shirt	White	£4.00	£15.00	120	£480.00	£1,800.00	68/£1,020	52/£780
2	Basic T-shirt	Black	£4.00	£15.00	120	£480.00	£1,800.00	68/£1,020	52/£780
3	Basic T-shirt	Navy	£400	£15.00	120	£480.00	£1,800.00	68/£1,020	52/£780
4	Polo T-shirt	Blue	£7.70	£25.00	80	£616.00	£2,000.00	45/£1,125	35/£875
5	Polo T-shirt	Red	£7.70	£25.00	80	£616.00	£2,000.00	45/£1,125	35/£875
					520			294/£5,310	226/£4,090

example of a delivery schedule for the product range created in Chapter 9, reflecting the delivery-phasing requirements identified in Table 10.10.

Identifying all intake information through the delivery schedule also allows the merchandiser to assess the impact of the delivery phasing of finalized purchase orders on the WSSI. The role of the WSSI is to make sure that the principles of good stock management are adhered to, so updating it constantly as new orders are placed enables the merchandiser to keep an eye on the flow of stock into the business.

Table 10.12 demonstrates the impact of the allocation and delivery schedule decisions on the casual wear WSSI. It has been updated with the finalized order phasing from the delivery schedule and then, by using the flowing OTB calculation, assessed the impact on the closing stock budget.

- (opening stock + orders placed) – (sales + markdown) = closing stock

For Week 1, this would be:

- (Week 52 closing stock + 1 January delivery) – (Week 1 sales + Week 1 markdown) = Week 1 closing stock

Or in numbers:

- (£25,902 + £5,310) – (£1,014 + £0) = £30,198

The new closing stock is higher than the budgeted closing stock for Week 1 of £25,902, and as the WSSI is worked through further, there is a regular small overstock until Week 7 when OTB of £424 becomes available. Small over- or understocks by week are quite normal at this stage of the planning process; it would be unrealistic to expect a perfect matching of KPI budgets, WSSI phasing, range plans and allocation phasing. The scale of these discrepancies can be quantified through the cover calculation shown below:

- closing stock/sales = cover

For Week 1 this would be:

- closing stock Week 1/ sales Week 1 = Week 1 cover

Or in numbers:

- £30,198/£1,014 = 29.8 weeks cover

And that is it! The planning process for this phase of the casual wear range for Prentice Day is complete. The suppliers will create the physical product and deliver the first of the orders on 1 January. However, this is just one phase of the Prentice Day product range; the same process will need to be followed for the remaining casual wear OTB, as well as those for the accessories and formal wear product categories.

Table 10.12 Updated WSSI, reflecting the impact of the orders placed on closing stocks

	Week 52			£25,902				
Weeks / months	Sales budget	Markdown budget	Closing stock forecast	Closing stock budget	OTB	Cover forecast	Cover budget	Promotional calendar – planned promotional activities
Week 1	£1,014	£0	£30,198	£25,902	£5,310	29.8	25.5	
Week 2	£1,167	£0	£29,031	£25,902	£0	24.9	22.2	
Week 3	£1,318	£0	£27,713	£25,902	£0	21.0	19.7	
Week 4	£1,413	£0	£30,390	£25,902	£4,090	21.5	18.3	
January	£4,912	£0						
Week 5	£1,413	£0	£28,977	£25,902	£0	20.5	18.3	
Week 6	£2,028	£0	£26,949	£25,902	£0	13.3	12.8	Cardholder event
Week 7	£1,471	£0	£25,902	£25,902	£424	17.6	17.6	
Week 8	£1,471	£0	£25,902	£25,902	£1,471	17.6	17.6	
February	£6,383	£0						
Week 9	£1,521	£0	£25,902	£25,902	£1,521	17.0	17.0	
Week 10	£1,521	£0	£25,902	£25,902	£1,521	17.0	17.0	
Week 11	£3,550	£690	£25,902	£25,902	£4,240	7.3	7.3	Mid-season sale
Week 12	£2,282	£460	£25,902	£25,902	£2,742	11.4	11.4	Mid-season sale
Week 13	£2,028	£460	£25,902	£25,902	£2,488	12.8	12.8	Mid-season sale – final offers
March	£10,902	£1,610						
Week 14	£1,522	£0	£25,902	£25,902	£1,522	17.0	17.0	

(continued)

Table 10.12 Continued

Weeks / months	Sales budget	Week 52 Markdown budget	Closing stock forecast	£25,902 Closing stock budget	OTB	Cover forecast	Cover budget	Promotional calendar – planned promotional activities
Week 15	£1,572	£0	£25,902	£25,902	£1,572	16.5	16.5	
Week 16	£1,623	£0	£25,902	£25,902	£1,623	16.0	16.0	
Week 17	£1,623	£0	£25,902	£25,902	£1,623	16.0	16.0	
April	£6,340	£0						
Week 18	£1,623	£0	£25,902	£25,902	£1,623	16.0	16.0	
Week 19	£1,623	£0	£25,902	£25,902	£1,623	16.0	16.0	
Week 20	£1,623	£0	£25,902	£25,902	£1,623	16.0	16.0	
Week 21	£1,572	£0	£25,902	£25,902	£1,572	16.5	16.5	
May	£6,441	£0						
Week 22	£1,522	£0	£25,902	£25,902	£1,522	17.0	17.0	
Week 23	£6,085	£2,873	£25,902	£25,902	£8,958	4.3	4.3	Summer sale launch
Week 24	£3,045	£1,398	£25,902	£25,902	£4,443	8.5	8.5	Summer sale
Week 25	£2,535	£766	£25,902	£25,902	£3,301	10.2	10.2	Summer sale
Week 26	£2,535	£958	£25,902	£25,902	£3,493	10.2	10.2	Summer sale last week
June	£15,722	£5,995	£25,902	£25,902				
		Week 27						
		£7,605						
Spring total	£50,700				£58,305		13.2	

A SUMMARY OF THE PLANNING PROCESS

As Part Two draws to a close, it is worth spending a short time reflecting on its contents. Over the course of six chapters, the process demonstrated has taken an initial product concept and built that into a researched, budgeted product range, which at its end reflects the original strategy objectives. The process is not a definitive one; there are too many different business models, organizational hierarchies and product types within the world of fashion for one to exist. Instead, it is a process that captures the nuances and discipline required by the fashion merchandiser to be effective in their role. What the process described has not done, apart from not being definitive, is show the potential totality of the role and how modern commercial pressures – such as multichannel strategies, issues such as corporate social responsibility, or in-season flexible trading – are delivered.

Leaving aside what Part Two has not done and instead concentrating on what it has, some key messages can be discerned. First, the quantitative elements of any product range are relevant throughout the planning process, carrying equal weight to those issues judged to be qualitative. The size, shape and characteristics that a product range offers to a retailer's customers owes as much to the fashion merchandiser as the buyer. The context of the merchandiser role established in Part One – to act as a bridge between the conflicting demands of fashion and business, or buyer and finance – allows product ranges to be balanced, as well as made relevant by the buyers' creative skill.

A second point is that in the modern, complex and competitive world it is unrealistic to expect a single role, the buyer, to be able to possess either the time or the skill set to juggle both the qualitative and quantitative requirements of the product management process. There are many talented buyers creating wonderful ranges, but the competitive landscape, increasingly sophisticated consumers and supply chain capabilities mean that the activities undertaken by a fashion merchandiser are more than just desirable, they are vital. This point is highlighted by the number of merchandising rather than buying jobs that are regularly on offer at the back of trade journals. For example *Drapers*, the UK trade journal, advertised 574 merchandising jobs versus 266 buying jobs on its website whilst this chapter was being written (Drapersjobs.com 2013).

A further point is that the merchandiser activities have been shown to be both logical in operation and commercial in approach. This is an important point, as the rise of business to customer relationships, social media, brand management and their personalities requires an awareness of product, its market and the customer attitudes within to make effective quantitative decisions. By appreciating the languages of product and finance, the merchandiser role has become more commercially astute and the planning process has benefited from that.

With the context of the role established in Part One and then demonstrated through Part Two, it is right to consider what has yet to be discussed. The modern world of retail fashion is full of competing ideas and business approaches. The development of models such as fast fashion, off price, online and others means that a one-size-fits-all planning process does not exist. Thought needs to be given to the broad reshaping of the merchandiser role to fit new ways of operation. Thought needs to be given also to the immediate pressures facing retail businesses, such as ethical trading, globalization and supply chain capability. These will be discussed in Part Three, along with the biggest missing part of the discussion so far – trading.

The problem with planning a product range is that it is, at best, a justified guess about what will be needed to maximize wealth creation in the season ahead. There is no crystal ball to predict the weather, economic trends, the ability of all activities in the value chain to work harmoniously together. Worst of all, there is no way of knowing what the competition is planning to try to snatch market share. The effectiveness of a retailer to navigate these uncertainties and react to the challenges thrown at them in season requires the product range to be traded once it has been delivered. Trading is of the moment, exciting and dynamic, with the merchandiser role pivotal in this process. They must keep an eye on trading performance, understand the implications of it, and then act upon that understanding to maximize opportunities as they arise and negate weaknesses before they become problems. How this is done will open the next and last part of this book, and also lead to the final discussion concerning the merchandiser and their role within a fashion retail business.

CHAPTER AND PART II SUMMARY

This chapter has acted as the finishing point for the planning processes of the fashion merchandiser and also this second part of the book. It has presented the links between the finalized option detail, size curves and allocation of stock to stores by again taking the Prentice Day case study and breaking it down further into phased deliveries of the basic white T-shirt. With that, the planning process is complete and one is left with the impression that for the merchandiser, the planning process is shaped like an inverted triangle – at its beginning, there is the widest amount of data to sort through, while at its end one is left with a sku in the product range, beyond which there is no further layer of product to plan.

SELF-DIRECTED STUDY

1. Refer to the companion website for Prentice Day case study exercises.
2. Understand a chosen retailer's allocation approaches by reviewing the units on display and size curves of different options. Is there a relationship between amount on display and selling price?

Further Reading

Goworek, H. (2007) *Fashion Buying*. Oxford: Blackwell

Jackson, T. and Shaw, D. (2001) *Mastering Fashion Buying and Merchandising Management*. Basingstoke: Macmillan

Kunz, G. (2010) *Merchandising – Theory, Principles and Practice, 3rd ed.* New York: Fairchild

Bibliography

Drapers. (2013) *Live fashion jobs*, [Internet]. Available from http://www.drapersjobs.com/ [Accessed 19th October 2013]

Gruen, T. and Corsten, D. (2008) *A comprehensive guide to retail out of Stock Reduction*, [Internet]. Available from http://www.nacds.org/pdfs/membership/out_of_stock.pdf [Accessed 20th January 2014]

Size UK (2002) *Results from the UK national sizing survey*, [Internet]. Available from http://www.arts.ac.uk/research/research-projects/completed-projects/sizeuk-results-from-the-uk-national-sizing-survey/ [Accessed 20th January 2014]

An Introduction to Part Three

This final part moves on to discuss the merchandiser role within the context of a modern business environment. There is a greater emphasis, as in Part One, on discussing ideas and issues, but references where relevant will be made to the practical application presented in Part Two. References will therefore be made again to the Prentice Day case study, supported by reliance on various tables and examples taken from Part Two.

The flexibility afforded by the advances made in technology, changed demand patterns and supply chain capabilities means that rigid planning following a linear path is no longer the norm. While the strategic planning process remains the same, there is a greater focus on trading to ensure that the product range's potential is worked to its maximum. This 'of the moment' aspect of buying and merchandising is discussed in Chapter 11. Part Three then moves on to discuss the emergence of e-retailing and corporate social responsibility, their effects on the merchandiser role, and how they can reshape their decisions

Finally, to pull the strands of all three parts together, a final chapter will, with a supply chain management focus, discuss the relationships within the fashion retail value chain, and how their common working and goals together contribute to the complex but highly addictive product management process.

11 Trading

INTENDED LEARNING OUTCOMES

1. The limitations of the planning process and the need to trade the proposition.
2. Re-forecasting the KPI budgets and understanding in-season product analysis.
3. Deciding on repeats, cancellations and OTB management.
4. Promotional and end-of-season sale planning activities.

INTRODUCTION

The reality of the planning process beyond the pages of this text is naturally more complex than the linear model presented in Part Two. Changes of mind are common, as are problems with OTB budgets and option details not matching, product designs requiring changes due to intake margin pressures or even just because better ideas come along. The greatest complexity is within the process itself, its potential timeline is long – up to a year from the initial research to the sale of the final unit of the range at the end of the season. This prompts two observations; first, the integrity of the process must carry limitations because of this length of time; and second, these become more pronounced the longer the timeframe is, because assumptions made towards the beginning of the planning process lose relevance as time goes on.

The expectation of a perfect matching of supply and demand within product management is therefore unrealistic, particularly if one considers the uncertainties of day-to-day life. The unpredictable weather, competitors launching surprise promotions or macro shocks such as in 2008, when retailers bought their autumn/winter collections in advance of the collapse of Lehman Brothers, and 'then had to trade in the "post-Lehman Armageddon"' (Financial Times 2013). In fact, it seems miraculous at times that any product range or business is successful at all.

In reality there are too many variables at play, many of which are out of the control of the B&M function, to prevent errors or oversights in the planning process being made. This means that retailers have to understand how to overcome these uncertainties and limitations, build further processes to identify any overlooked opportunities and risks in season, and from there, define the action that is needed to maximize its true potential. This maximization process is known as trading the season or trading the proposition, and this chapter will review the tools at the disposal of the fashion merchandiser to deal with the realities of trading a product range (Table 11.1).

Table 11.1 *The concept-to-carrier bag model*

Concept to carrier bag step	Definition
1. Research	Undertaking and collation of relevant fashion research
2. Concept	Creation of product range concept and direction
3. Product development	Finalization of concept as a product range
4. Sourcing	Sourcing of suppliers and manufacturers for the range
5. Manufacturing	Manufacture of the product range
6. Shipping	Shipping and delivery of the product range
7. Warehousing	Receipt of the product range, and its allocation to store and storage
8. Distribution	**Delivering initial store allocations**
9. Retail	**Display, sale, promotion and stock replenishment**
10. Carrier bag	**The purchase of the product by a consumer**

PLANNING VERSUS TRADING

While planning activities define a product range, it is the trading activities that make it work to the best of its ability, making the two very different in their timing and application. Planning by its nature is very precise, accurate and shaping, while trading is exciting and fluid with ever changing demands and reactions to trading patterns designed to maximize the range's financial contribution. The two activities do, however, correlate very strongly and the trading strategy follows closely that of planning, as it utilizes outputs such as the KPI budgets, the WSSI and OTB phasing. These tools are reinterpreted continuously throughout the season to reflect the latest trading conditions facing the business. Trading is not therefore about complete change (unless the season is a complete disaster), but refinement and adjustment, and its effectiveness relies upon the following tools to guide its decisions:

- KPI budgets
  - Assessed to compare actual trading data against the budgeted expectation. Financial trends are reflected by reforecasting the WSSI to determine the impact on available OTB for any remaining weeks of the season.
- OTB budgets
  - Where the result of trading is that OTB is higher than budget, there is the opportunity to buy more product and grow the business. Where it is lower, the business needs to be retrenched and buys reduced.
- Product range research, analysis and adjustment
  - The product analysis identifies which options are selling well and which are not, and reviews opportunities to adjust future buy quantities or make cancellations to outstanding orders.
  - Where new product ranges are required, the buyer and merchandiser will identify within the re-forecasted OTB a buy value and create new option details.
- Allocation and replenishment
  - Adjustments are made to allocation quantities based on revised rates of sale, store ranging or buy quantities.

- Promotional planning
  - Thought is given to the spending of the markdown budget through the planning of promotions to either reduce stocks of poorly selling options, or to further drive up volumes of strongly selling ones.
- ESS planning
  - The ESS will be planned to best liquidate residue stocks of the season's ranges and to make way for the first intake of the following season's product ranges.

Trading the proposition therefore follows the same logic of budgetary and stock management; it differs though in the speed at which it is completed. Trading is a continuous cycle and has the effect of compressing much of the planning disciplines into one week or less, every week, for the duration of the season. This makes it highly complex to manage within the tight deadlines of quickly reacting to trade to constantly reshape the product range so that it improves as the season progresses. This places importance on the efficiency of the value chain and the activities within it become paramount as it waxes and wanes in line with the demands emanating from the B&M team.

A final thought, prior to moving on to looking at the trading process in depth, concerns the relationship between business logic and commercial acumen. Whilst there will always be a logical way to approach trading and prompt decision making, there is also a lot of guesswork and presumption. Apart from judging if an option is performing well, the merchandiser will also need to assess if it has reached its full potential or there is more to be exploited from it. Commercial acumen and good old-fashioned gut feeling are the most effective tools that a merchandiser can bring to trading activities, and making room for them in the decision-making process is as important as following a logical approach.

REVIEWING KPI BUDGET PERFORMANCE IN SEASON

The creation of product KPI budgets being the core element of the merchandiser role not surprisingly means that their review is also central to the trading process. Understanding a product's actual financial performance is clearly important, but knowing how best to react to that performance is more complicated. The understanding of financial performance must be a regular and thorough activity, reliant upon the WSSI being updated weekly for comparisons to be made against budgetary planning presumptions. As an example, Table 11.2 replicates an eight-week snapshot of the casual wear WSSI, calculated in Chapter 10, that enables trading performance versus budget to be assessed. To facilitate this, additional sales turnover, markdown spend, closing stock and cover forecast columns have been added to the table.

The table presumes that the first four weeks of the season are complete, which is reflected in the forecast columns having been updated on the WSSI to show that:

- Sales turnover was strong throughout January and cumulatively by the end of the month was £5,403.
- This represents a 10 per cent (£491) overperformance to budget.

Table 11.2 Casual wear WSSI budget plans for Weeks 1–8

| | | | Week 52 | | £25,798 | £25,798 | | | |
Weeks/ months	Sales forecast	Sales budget	Markdown forecast	Markdown budget	Closing stock forecast	Closing stock budget	Open to buy	Cover forecast	Cover budget
Week 1	£1,115	£1,014	£0	£0	£29,993	£25,798	£5,310	26.9	25.4
Week 2	£1,284	£1,167	£0	£0	£28,709	£25,798	£0	22.4	22.1
Week 3	£1,450	£1,318	£0	£0	£27,259	£25,798	£0	18.8	19.6
Week 4	£1,554	£1,413	£0	£0	£29,795	£25,798	£4,090	19.2	18.3
January	£5,403	£4,912	£0				£9,400		
Week 5		£1,413				£25,798			18.3
Week 6		£2,028				£25,798			12.7
Week 7		£1,471				£25,798			17.5
Week 8		£1,471				£25,798			17.5
February		£6,383		£0					

- Both planned stock deliveries were delivered as planned in Weeks 1 and 4.
- Closing stocks were above budget, but the sales turnover overperformance has meant that weekly covers were in line with budget, and that stock turn targets are in line to be met.

This is clearly a good position to be in, but by itself, beyond some relief that the product strategy is working, what can the merchandiser do with the information to make it more dynamic?

A quick and effective tool to make sense of this overperformance is the balance-to-achieve (BTA) analysis, which summarizes cumulative sales turnover data relative to its budget and then identifies if the original seasonal total sales turnover budget is still realistic. Table 11.3 is a BTA summary analysis, showing that, in this case, if sales turnover presumptions are not increased at least in line with the 10 per cent growth experienced to date, then by Week 26 sales turnover growth to budget will have declined to just 1 per cent.

Table 11.3 Casual wear BTA at Week 4

	Actual	Budget	% Variance
Actual sales Weeks 1–4	£5,403	£4,912	10%
Unchanged sales forecast Weeks 5–26	£45,788	£45,788	0%
Total sales forecast Weeks 1–26	£51,191	£50,700	1%

In effect, the BTA analysis has identified the scale of difference between actual trading results and the original budget presumptions made earlier in the planning process. It highlights that it would be nonsensical not to react to current performance. If the first four weeks of the season can be 10 per cent higher than budget, then there is no logic in not increasing the sales turnover forecast for the remaining weeks of the season by at least 10 per cent, perhaps more.

Judging an exact percentage by which to increase future sales forecasts relies upon a subjective attitude to the analysis of available data and commercial gut feeling. The historic strength of casual wear within Prentice Day suggests that there may be further sales turnover growth to be had, and that the forecast for the remainder of the season should be higher than the current 10 per cent overperformance. In practice, the best way to decide what a suitable growth rate to apply would be worked through using various scenarios, which would then be sanity-checked by reviewing the resultant covers and stock turn.

Tables 11.4 and 11.5 reflect a decision by the merchandiser to apply a sales turnover forecast of +15 per cent to remaining weeks on the WSSI, which then identifies associated knock-on effects to the markdown spend and OTB forecasts:

- No changes have been made to Weeks 1–4 as these are now in the past.
- The +15 per cent sales forecast growth has been applied to Weeks 5 through to 26.

Table 11.4 Reforecast casual wear WSSI

Weeks/ months	Sales forecast	Sales budget	Markdown forecast	Markdown budget	Week 52 Closing stock forecast	£25,798 Closing stock budget	£25,798 Open to buy forecast	£25,798 Cover forecast	Cover budget
Week 1	£1,115	£1,014	£0	£0	£29,993	£25,798	£5,310	26.9	25.4
Week 2	£1,284	£1,167	£0	£0	£28,709	£25,798	£0	22.4	22.1
Week 3	£1,450	£1,318	£0	£0	£27,259	£25,798	£0	18.8	19.6
Week 4	£1,554	£1,413	£0	£0	£29,795	£25,798	£4,090	19.2	18.3
January	£5,403	£4,912	£0	£0			£9,400		
Week 5	£1,555	£1,413	£0	£0	£28,240	£25,798	£0	18.2	18.3
Week 6	£2,230	£2,028	£0	£0	£26,010	£25,798	£0	11.7	12.7
Week 7	£1,620	£1,471	£0	£0	£25,798	£25,798	£1,408	15.9	17.5
Week 8	£1,620	£1,471	£0	£0	£25,798	£25,798	£1,620	15.9	17.5
February	£7,025	£6,383	£0	£0			£3,028		
Week 9	£1,750	£1,521	£0	£0	£25,798	£25,798	£1,750	14.7	17
Week 10	£1,750	£1,521	£0	£0	£25,798	£25,798	£1,750	14.7	17
Week 11	£4,085	£3,550	£0	£690	£25,798	£25,798	£4,085	6.3	7.3
Week 12	£2,625	£2,282	£0	£460	£25,798	£25,798	£2,625	9.8	11.3
Week 13	£2,330	£2,028	£0	£460	£25,798	£25,798	£2,330	11.1	12.7
March	£12,540	£10,902	£0	£1,609	£0		£12,540		
Week 14	£1,750	£1,522	£0	£0	£25,798	£25,798	£1,750	14.7	17
Week 15	£1,810	£1,572	£0	£0	£25,798	£25,798	£1,810	14.3	16.4
Week 16	£1,810	£1,623	£0	£0	£25,798	£25,798	£1,810	14.3	15.9
Week 17	£1,865	£1,623	£0	£0	£25,798	£25,798	£1,865	13.8	15.9
April	£7,235	£6,340	£0	£0	£0		£7,235		
Week 18	£1,820	£1,623	£0	£0	£25,798	£25,798	£1,820	14.2	15.9
Week 19	£1,820	£1,623	£0	£0	£25,798	£25,798	£1,820	14.2	15.9

Week 20	£1,820	£1,623	£0	£0	£25,798	£1,820	14.2	15.9
Week 21	£1,760	£1,572	£0	£0	£25,798	£1,760	14.7	16.4
May	£7,220	£6,441	£0	£0	£0	£7,220		17
Week 22	£1,675	£1,522	£0	£0	£25,798	£1,675	15.4	4.2
Week 23	£6,500	£6,085	£3,450	£2,873	£25,798	£9,950	4	8.5
Week 24	£3,300	£3,045	£1,300	£1,398	£25,798	£4,600	7.8	10.2
Week 25	£2,550	£2,535	£1,650	£766	£25,798	£4,200	10.1	10.2
Week 26	£3,100	£2,535	£2,000	£958	£25,798	£5,100	8.3	
June	£17,125	£15,722	£8,400	£5,996	£25,798	£25,525		
				Week 27				
				£7,605				
Spring Total	£56,548	£50,700	£8,400		£25,798	£64,9481	2.9	13.2

- The small markdown budget in March is no longer needed as the product category is strong and price reductions can be delayed to the end of the season.
- There is a need for an increased markdown spend in the ESS, and the forecast for June reflects a bigger ESS caused by increases in OTB.
- Closing stock forecasts have not been changed from the budget.
- The OTB calculation has been used to identify changes to OTB phasing and the total OTB for the season.

Table 11.5 *Reforecast casual wear WSSI summary*

	Forecast	Budget	Increase
Sales turnover	£56,548	£50,700	12%
Average cover	12.9 weeks	13.2 weeks	– 3 days
Stock turn	1.99	1.96	level
Markdown spend	£8,400	£7,605	10%
Markdown % to sales	14.9%	15%	Level
Total orders placed and OTB	£64,948	£58,305	11%

The summary of the changes made to the WSSI in Table 11.4 highlights that all budget variables reviewed have either improved or are level with the planning presumptions. A possible exception could be that of the markdown spend, which is 10 per cent higher than budget. It may be surprising to see this growth; however, the dynamic that most products will not sell-through fully still applies and with increased OTB will come some additional build-up of residue stocks requiring clearance at the end of the season. The key to the impact of the increased markdown spend can be seen in the markdown percentage to sales which has reduced, albeit slightly, meaning that the new forecast has reduced the influence of markdown within the season overall, helping to strengthen overall profitability. The ultimate impact of the reforecast, however, is that a new higher OTB has been identified, and this early warning prompts the next trading activity, the identification of the products that are driving the overachievement, and ensures they are re-bought.

REPEATS AND CANCELLATIONS

With the reforecast WSSI identifying that OTB is growing, a next logical step is to spend it as quickly as possible. Matching exactly increased buying budgets to individual product performance is challenging as often good trading performance masks significant divergence in option reaction. Understanding achieved rates of sale and sell-through rate percentage compared to the planning assumptions is a good way to unmask this scale of difference between good and bad sales trends. Re-using the two retail calculations that helped shape the product analysis and the option detail also ensures there is consistency of thought as if one matches actual to presumed performance a sense of scale of difference emerges between the two.

Table 11.6 presents trading data for the T-shirt product range, and uses the white basic T-shirt to exemplify the performance analysis:

Table 11.6 T-shirt unit sales and stock analysis at Week 4

Option	Description	Colour	Fashionability	Selling price	Stores	Sales 1–4	Stock units remaining	Rate of sale	Sell through rate
1	Basic T-shirt	White	Core basic	£15	1	72	48	18	60%
2	Basic T-shirt	Black	Core basic	£15	1	72	48	18	60%
3	Basic T-shirt	Navy	Core basic	£15	1	28	92	7	23%
4	Polo T-shirt	Blue	Fashion style	£25	1	40	40	10	50%
5	Polo T-shirt	Red	Fashion style	£35	1	10	70	2.5	13%
	T-shirt total					222	298	11.1	43%

- Between Weeks 1 and 4, 72 units have been sold generating an average rate of sale per week of 18 units
  - (sales/lifecycle) = rate of sale
  - (72/4) = 18 units
- The sell-through rate based on actual sales and delivered stock is at 60%
  - (sales/units delivered) * 100 = sell-through rate %
  - (72/120) * 100 = 60%

Reviewing the options together indicates a mixed trading performance; three are outperforming their range assumptions and are on course to overachieve on the sell-through rate assumption by Week *, as shown in Table 11.7. A further two are underperforming and are unlikely to achieve their planned sell-through rates.

The combination of research into actual performance, which is then anchored in an original option detail, gives a holistic review that is objective and factually based. Clear extremes opportunity can be gleaned from Table 11.7 in the form of the basic T-shirt in white and black along with the blue polo shirt. The analysis also acts as a warning sign to poor performance. The navy basic T-shirt and red polo shirt rates of sale are well short of the range-planning assumptions, so carrying markdown risk; this needs to acknowledged and actions proposed to negate their poor performance.

Taking first the opportunity, decisions on how to react centre on the point that the option is at within its planned lifecycle. At four weeks, the range is halfway through its life cycle and a first question should be whether to extend its place within the range beyond the planned eight weeks? The answer to the first question lies depends upon each option's role within the product range. Core basics, for example, provide easy, price-efficient, reliable product to the customer, while for the business they generate safe, relatively risk-free volume sales and so cash flow. It would therefore be a nonsense to discontinue the excellently core basic options and deprive an easy purchase to the customer and further financial safety to the business.

Deciding what to do with the blue style polo T-shirt is more difficult. Fashion styles represent for the business a commercial route to the interpretation of trend and the opportunity to attract the interest of customers on a regular basis. The danger with extending the blue polo shirt is that it may not respect that inevitable need for freshness throughout the season as new fashion trends emerge. Fast fashion brands such as Zara and H&M demonstrate this so well by emphasizing choice and width of range, over more limited collections and depth of buy. In the case of Prentice Day, however, the blue polo shirt has a compelling reason to be re-bought: it is highly likely to sell out!

Table 11.8 takes the repeats process to its next step by presuming to extend the three options' life cycles to a total of sixteen weeks. It works through re-buy quantities, the calculations for which are exemplified using the white basic T-shirt.

- White basic T-shirt
  - Rate of sale * 12 weeks (Weeks 5–16) = 216 forecast unit sales
  - Forecast sales – stock remaining units = 168 unit re-buy
  - Unit re-buy * selling price = value of OTB spent = £2,250.

Table 11.7 Actual rate of sale and sell-through rate percentage compared to option detail

Option	Description	Colour	Fashionability	Rate of sale actual	Rate of sale range assumption	Sell- through rate at 4 weeks	Sell- through rate assumption at 8 weeks
1	Basic T-shirt	White	Core basic	18	12	60%	80%
2	Basic T-shirt	Black	Core basic	18	12	60%	80%
3	Basic T-shirt	Navy	Core basic	7	12	23%	80%
4	Polo T-shirt	Blue	Fashion style	10	8	50%	80%
5	Polo T-shirt	Red	Fashion style	2.5	8	13%	80%
	T-shirt total			11.1	12	43%	80%

Table 11.8 Calculated re-buys

Option	Description	Colour	Fashionability	Selling price	Stores	Sales units 1 to 4	Stock units remaining	Rate of sale	Forecast sales 5–16	Re-order
1	Basic T-shirt	White	Core basic	£15	1	72	48	18	216	168
2	Basic T-shirt	Black	Core basic	£15	1	72	48	18	216	168
4	Polo T-shirt	Blue	Fashion style	£25	1	40	40	10	120	80

The total value of the identified re-buys is £7,040, and with these calculated the process of applying size curves raising purchase orders and recording the orders placed on the WSSI can commence. Attention can now turn to the two options that are not performing and decisions made about what to do with them. Table 11.9 demonstrates the impact of a poor reaction by forecasting sell-through rates forward to the end of Week 8 and then identifies any resulting overstock.

- Navy basic T-shirt
  - Unit buy = 120 unit buy
  - Forecast sales Weeks 1–8 = 56 units
  - Stock remaining = 64 units
  - Sell-through rate % = 47%

High residue stocks will exist at the end of Week 8 caused by the low rates of sale. The optimum solution for the retailer would be to negotiate to return the stock balances to the supplier using the repeat buys as a negotiating tool. However, if the supplier has fulfilled all the contractual obligations of the original purchase order, and unless the supplier agreed to a deal, it would be ethically wrong to attempt to penalize the supplier for the poor performance of the buyer and merchandiser's chosen range. In reality, deals are often done and the supplier may offer solutions such as stock returns, the sharing of markdown costs or a reworking of the excess stock into another shape or colour. Whatever the outcome, the options will weigh down in some form on the business's P&L and balance sheets, emphasizing the pressure on the buyer to get it right first time!

PROMOTIONAL PLANNING

It is a law of nature that markdown will be required to manage stock levels within a fashion business. No buyer or merchandiser can predict with 100 per cent certainty every potential transaction within a season, and so the spending of markdown is a necessity whose use and cost can be managed. If one considers a typical high street, the regularity of the use of markdown is quickly apparent, whether it be in the expected mid-season sale and ESS or the unexpected promotion that fashion businesses adopt from time to time. This seeming reliance placed on markdown to promote a business presents something of a paradox for the merchandiser.

To the customer, the marking down of the selling price of a product to a lower one is a benefit, and one that can be made use of with alacrity. In 2012, for example, the website of the London department store Selfridges crashed under the weight of online users wanting to snap up the post-Christmas bargains (Daily Mail 2012), while Next is known to open its doors early on the first day of their sales to capture the maximum sales opportunity. For the merchandiser, markdown being a cash cost is one that logically should be minimized and where possible avoided. Markdown, though, does not always need to be a burden and can be used not as a distress tool but as a profit-generating one. Whereas the customer sees a universal benefit in price discounting, for a fashion business, markdown has two uses; one being beneficial and one negative.

Table 11.9 Calculated sell-through rates and overstocks

Option	Description	Colour	Fashionability	Selling price	Stores	Unit buy	Rate of sale	Forecast sales 1 to 8	Stock remaining	Sell-through rate
1	Basic T-shirt	Navy	Core basic	£15	1	120	7	56	64	47%
4	Polo T-shirt	Red	Fashion style	£25	1	80	2.5	20	60	25%

Looking at its beneficial properties, the application of a point of sale (POS) markdown can be used to tactically increase market share, overcome short-term stock problems or to increase cash profit. POS markdown is used within a short limited timeframe (for example, a one-day sale, or a week-long promotion) and markdown cost is only incurred on the sales achieved within that period. At the end of it, selling prices revert back to their original levels and no further markdown costs are taken. POS markdown is widely used across all sectors of the retail industry, and within fashion is applicable where products are ranged to be promoted in this way (multi-purchase offers) or where the supply chain can turn stock deliveries on and off at short notice if trading requires a temporary boost (core basics).

Tables 11.10 and 11.11 demonstrate the impact of POS markdown and how it can be used profitably to drive sales increases. The tables presume that a navy basic T-shirt priced at £10 sells 100 units a week, generating a gross trading profit of £500 as a result.

Table 11.10 *Basic navy T-shirt sales and gross trading profit analysis pre-markdown*

Basic T-shirt – navy	
Sales units per week	100
Original selling price	£10
Cost price	£5
Sales value (sales units * original selling price)	£1,000
Cost value (sales units * cost price)	£500
Profit (sales value – cost value)	£500

Note: VAT presumed at 0%

Table 11.11 *Basic navy T-shirt sales and gross trading profit analysis post-markdown*

Basic T-shirt – navy	
Sales units per week (100 sales units * 1.67 multiplier)	167
Original selling price	£10
Reduced selling price (Original selling price less 10% POS)	£9
Cost price	£5
Sales value (sales units * £9 reduced selling price)	£1,503
Cost value (sales units * cost price)	£835
Markdown cost (sales units * £1 off)	£167
Profit (sales value-cost value-markdown value)	£501

Note: VAT presumed at 0%

Table 11.11 meanwhile presumes that a short one-week promotion is required to increase volume sales to capture market share from a rival, in this case in the form of a 10 per cent reduction in selling prices. By accurately predicting the amount that unit volumes will raise, the merchandiser is able to assess if the promotion will be profit negative, neutral or incremental. This sales multiplier can be seen at work in

Table 11.11 where the effect of reducing selling prices by 10 per cent in combination with a sales multiplier of 1.67 times maintains gross trading profit at £500.

The regular use of POS markdown on the high street is testament to its versatility and effectiveness. It is a good way to generate cash flow, gain or protect market share and supplement main sale-period offers. POS markdown can, though, be like a drug; many retailers have found themselves reliant upon it to paper over short-term trading problems. Over the long term, however, this is hugely damaging to their credibility and brand personality.

The second and more obvious use of markdown is to permanently reduce selling prices to liquidate stocks of an option, and this approach is known as clearance markdown. Clearance markdown is expensive, with the power to wipe out any profits generated during the full-price selling season. Its use is therefore limited to main sale periods, or where an option is no longer in line with trend, requiring it to be withdrawn from the range.

Tables 11.12 and 11.13 shows its calculation, by presuming that an option that sells for £15 has come to the end of its life cycle, having sold 350 of a 700 unit buy (50 per cent sell-through rate). Table 11.12 demonstrates the impact on gross trading profit, presuming a 50 per cent clearance markdown is applied, while Table 11.13 presumes a 33 per cent markdown is taken.

Table 11.12 *Example of the cost of permanently reducing selling prices by 50 per cent*

Units bought	700
Buy selling value (700 units * £15 selling price)	£10,500
Buy cost value (700 units * £8 cost price)	£5,600
Sales value at full price (50% sell through rate)	£5,250
Stock value to be marked down(buy selling value – sales value at full price)	£5,250
Markdown cost (Stock value remaining * 50% off selling price)	£2,625
Sales value reduced price (stock value to be marked down – markdown cost)	£2,625
Profit (full price sales value + reduced price sales value – markdown cost – buy cost value)	–£350

Note: VAT presumed at 0%

Table 11.13 *Example of the cost of permanently reducing selling prices by 33 per cent*

Unit bought	700
Buy selling value (700 units * £15 selling price)	£10,500
Buy cost value (700 units * £8 cost price)	£5,600
Sales value at full price	£5,250
Stock value to be marked down(buy selling value – sales value at full price)	£5,250
Markdown cost (Stock value remaining * 33%)	£1,732
Sales value reduced price(stock value to be marked down – markdown cost)	£3,518
Profit (full price sales value + reduced price sales value – markdown cost – buy cost value)	£1,436

Note: VAT presumed at 0%

The two differing gross trading profits are stark, and while the actual impact on profits is influenced by intake margin, the better the planning and trading, the lesser the need to rely on expensive clearance markdown. Its use is as a result strictly controlled: only to liquidate failed product ranges or overcome poorly designed quantitative assumptions that led to imbalances in unit buy quantities.

CASE STUDY 11.1: MARKDOWN AS A DRUG FOR FASHION BUSINESSES

'The refusal by many retailers to resort to price-discounting kept high street sales in positive territory last month despite unhelpful weather, according to the latest figures. Don Williams, national head of retail and wholesale at BDO, said fashion stores had learnt from previous years and were not panicking in the face of poor weather and consumers who were still reluctant to spend' (The Scotsman 2013).

Planning a season's product range is one thing, but delivering all of the assumptions and budgets that went into its creation is another. Unfortunately, the trading environment is uncertain and no buyer or merchandiser has the power to stop a variable such as the weather from ruining a well-thought-out product range. When things do start to go wrong, it is a temptation to use markdown to overcome the challenges presented, and many businesses have resorted to such a use. Markdown can, however, turn from being a saviour to an enemy, as many businesses have found to their cost.

Fat face is a British brand that retails fashion ranges appealing to customers who need clothing to support their outdoors active lives, and in less than 30 years the business has grown to an estate of over 200 stores and a sales turnover in excess of £100m (Fat Face 2013). This growth, while impressive, had come at a cost. In 2010, it was estimated that the brand was on sale for 48 weeks of the year and that half of its product ranges were sold at a discount (Drapers 2013). Anthony Thompson commented that 'coming off the discounting "drug" does take time,' and admitted 'you have to take a deep breath and keep your eye on the medium-to-long-term especially as there will be points in the financial year where you are facing a tough comparable' (Drapers 2013).

So how can a fashion business get itself into this situation? There are many reasons – overambitious planning, lack of control mechanisms within the value chain to question decisions, poor economic conditions, rabid competition on the high street and the pursuit of market share can all contribute. So too can panic, leading to ill-thought-through reactive trading in season to the many bumps in the road. To avoid these pitfalls requires not just planning and trading discipline but flexibility. The more flexibility within the supply chain, the more routes to overcoming the bumps; branch transfers of stock from one location to another to ease stock problems, minimal spending of OTB in advance of the season, the use of postponement strategies to spend OTB in season, and positive promotions such as relationship-building activities to win customer trust and loyalty are but a few.

For Fat Face it worked. The brand revealed that Earnings Before Interest, Tax, Depreciation, Amortization (EBITDA) had soared by 29 per cent for the 53 weeks to June 2013 on turnover up by 8 per cent – record results for Fat Face and a strong performance by anyone's standards (Drapers 2013).

Activity: Research articles that discuss the use of markdown by retailers. Look out for commentary about reliance on markdown, full-price trading strategies or the impact of markdown on gross margins.

END-OF-SEASON SALE

As time moves on and the next season approaches, the closure of the current one and its ESS will be planned. The planning of this vital trading period can often be seen in a distress context, with an emphasis on reducing prices to clear residue stocks of current product to make way for the next. However, it can also be viewed as an opportunity that can deliver benefit to a fashion business by delivering cash flow and an effective route to transition from one season to the next.

The timing of an ESS is often the cause of debate and speculation. Their usual timings – December/January for winter sales and June/July for summer sales, oddly seem to be launched midway through a season. If one plots generic high street sale timings against a simple delivery phasing model, a clear pattern and rationale for this emerges. Table 11.14 shows a six-month season that has two delivery phases – the first in January and the second in April. In general, retailers can have up to three months to pay their suppliers, delaying payment for deliveries in this case until March and June, just at the time of sale periods on the high street. The effect on cash flow of having to pay suppliers can be hugely draining and the one thing that a fashion business needs at this time is cash inflows, which the timing of ESSs facilitates.

Table 11.14 Phasing of delivery, supplier payment and sale periods

	January	February	March	April	May	June
Phase 1 delivery	X					
Phase 2 delivery				X		
Phase 1 supplier payment			X			
Phase 2 supplier payment						X
Sale activity			Mid-season sale			End of season sale

The second facilitative aspect of the ESS is that it allows for the orderly conversion of a product offer from one season to the next, within a short defined period of time. A fundamental element within fashion is time – trends and fashion seasons are time-limited, and so using sale to ensure the conversion of the shop floor or online site to a full-price representation of the upcoming trends can be managed – as stock levels of one season decline, so the levels of the next can rise until the process is completed and the customer sees only prime full-price seasonal product. Without an ESS to force the pace into a matter of weeks, product range launches can become fragmented and lack a competitive edge.

Taking these two outputs of ESS activity as desirable outcomes creates a strategic vision for the planning of the period. The vision must include an attitude of first price right price, meaning that appropriate markdowns should be applied to ensure that stocks are reduced to the appropriate budgeted level and that as much cash is generated within the period. A second element should be to focus not just on sale reductions but also on delivery management of new season stock to be phased in manageable quantities, allowing the business to trade prime immediately as the sale ends (Table 11.15).

To do this, the merchandiser will turn once again to the latest reforecast WSSI which will dictate:

- The required sales turnover for the sale period
  - The cash sales inflow to the business
- The available markdown spend for the sale period
  - The cost to the business of reducing selling prices
- The required stock targets for the sale period
  - Derived in the planning process as being the sum of display factor and resupply time.

Table 11.15 Forecast casual wear WSSI for Weeks 22–26

	Sales forecast	Markdown forecast	Closing stock forecast	OTB forecast	Cover forecast
Week 22	£1,675	£0	£25,798	£1,675	15.4
Week 23	£6,500	£3,450	£25,798	£9,950	4.0
Week 24	£3,300	£1,300	£25,798	£4,600	7.8
Week 25	£2,550	£1,650	£25,798	£4,200	10.1
Week 26	£3,100	£2,000	£25,798	£5,100	8.3
June	£17,125	£8,400		£25,525	

The ESS aim to clear stocks inevitably means that the price reductions required to do this will be large to attract customers and offer them a good. The suitable level of markdown percentage that will be relevant will vary depending on the product type or levels of competition. Despite this, there are some general considerations that help the merchandiser decide upon a suitable markdown offer:

- 10–20 per cent off
  - Reductions of this level will not clear stocks within a short time frame and are more appropriate as POS promotional markdowns.
  - Some fashion retailers may offer this type of promotion during a main sale to drive volume sales of ongoing continuity products such as underwear.

- 30-40 per cent off
  - This is a useful first markdown offer for options that have performed better than average, and has a lower impact on gross trading profitability than deeper markdown offers.
  - As the sale moves on, the effectiveness of this level of markdown wears off and it is unlikely to clear stocks over the period of the whole sale.
- 50 per cent off and above
  - This depth of markdown is very expensive, but its use is unavoidable where the range has poor sellers, or the competition moves to this level.
  - Its use tends to be limited in the early weeks of sale periods and then all products are consolidated to this level midway through the sale.

The first step in planning a sale will be to identify which products are to be cleared, at what initial markdown depth and in what time frame. The WSSI will guide this thinking:

- The sale period starts in Week 23 and ends in Week 26 – giving a four-week window to clear current season's stocks.
- The WSSI identifies the forecast stocks, sales turnover, markdown spend and OTB for each week of the sale period within which the sale must be structured.

In addition to this, the merchandiser also knows that the shape of the re-forecast WSSI was guided by:

- the casual wear product range trading above budget, implying that it is 'safe' to use the 30 per cent markdown depth at the start of the sale
- the fact that, despite the overperformance, there have been poor sellers, and so there will need to be some representation of a 50 per cent offer.

The melding of this existing knowledge into a sale offer is done through the creation of a sale planning sheet, as shown in Table 11.16. Important elements of this example document to note are:

- It covers the entire sale period and starts by identifying the split of stocks between 30 per cent and 50 per cent off. In this case, as casual wear is performing well, the emphasis at the beginning of the sale will be to mark down the majority of stock by 30 per cent and have a small 50 per cent offer to clear the very worst performing options.
- Commercial cover presumptions, guided by the WSSI cover budget, can be applied to each markdown offer to identify a likely sales turnover by offer type.
- The sales turnover will in turn identify the required markdown spend for each week.
- Halfway through the sale as stocks fragment, and to speed up the conversion of the shop floor to new season stock, all sale product will be offered at 50 per cent off.

- New season full-price product will be phased in as reflected in the last forecast WSSI; by the end of the ESS period, the store should be as close to 100 per cent prime as possible.

Table 11.16 *Sale-planning spreadsheet*

Week 23	Opening stock	Sales turnover	Markdown spend	OTB	Closing stock	Cover
30% off	£20,638	£4,500	£1,929	£0	£14,209	3
50% off	£5,160	£1,500	£1,500	£0	£2,160	1
New season	£0	£500	£0	£9,929	£9,429	19
Total	£25,798	£6,500	£3,429	£9,929	£25,798	4

Week 24	Opening stock	Sales turnover	Markdown spend	OTB	Closing stock	Cover
30% off	£14,209	£2,200	£943	£0	£11,066	5
50% off	£2,160	£400	£400	£0	£1,360	3
New season	£9,429	£700	£0	£4,643	£13,372	19
Total	£25,798	£3,300	£1,343	£4,643	£25,798	8

Week 25	Opening stock	Sales turnover	Markdown spend	OTB	Closing stock	Cover
30% off	£0	£0	£0	£0	£0	0
50% off	£12,426	£1,650	£1,650	£0	£9,126	6
New season	£13,372	£900	£0	£4,200	£16,672	19
Total 638	£25,798	£2,550	£1,650	£4,200	£25,798	10

Week 26	Opening stock	Sales turnover	Markdown spend	OTB	Closing stock	Cover
30% off	£0	£0	£0	£0	£0	0
50% off	£9,126	£2,000	£2,000	£0	£5,126	3
New season	£16,672	£1,100	£0	£5,100	£20,672	19
Total	£25,798	£3,100	£2,000	£5,100	£25,798	8

The strength of the sale-planning document and thought process lies within is its ability to interrogate the commercial aptitude of the sale offer to clear down within a specified sale period. In the example above, the stock and cover presumptions have resulted in a sales turnover and markdown spend forecast that is in line with the WSSI, meaning that sale period will deliver the forecast gross trading profit expectations. Further to this, if one reviews the closing stock figures in Week 26, 80 per cent of stock in the business at the end of the sale will be of the new season, delivering the other role of a sale: to facilitate a smooth transition to the new season and the resumption of a prime offer to the consumer.

FOCUS POINT 11.1: ALTERNATIVES TO THE USE OF MARKDOWN

The spending of markdown to either promote or clear stocks at the end of a season is a powerful tool with which to overcome trading issues. For the customer, there is the benefit of buying product at a price that is lower than the original, while for the merchandiser, it allows the reduction of total stock holding to budgeted levels. However, it can be hugely damaging to gross trading profits and have the effect of dragging businesses that would rather trade at full price into the discounting arena. In December 2013, Marks and Spencer was 'hit by a 'highly promotional market' and 'exceptionally unseasonal' weather in October, which left fashion retailers with unsold winter coats and jumpers' (Daily Telegraph 2014). The highly promotional market meant that as the stock levels of winter clothes did not decline as budgeted, weaker retailers began to discount, leading to a knock-on effect of discounting as competitors reacted to their actions.

The use of markdown is highly volatile, and it is easy to be dragged into a trading situation where to remain competitive a retailer has to discount. It is not surprising that retailers have sought alternatives to negate this trading risk. One common route is to engage in the purchase of special buys. These are managed by holding back a proportion of a season's OTB during the planning and trading of a season, to be spent on products bought especially for the sale period. Due to the high unit volumes that can be driven in sale periods, the retailer can negotiate to buy large volumes of stock from a supplier and, in turn, be offered lower cost prices which are duly passed on to their customers. The advantages of special buys are felt by all players in the transaction. The supplier ensures that their factories are kept busy and achieves economy of scale, so reducing their costs; the retailer can offer discounted product without incurring excessive markdown costs; while the customer gets a bargain!

There are some brands for whom being seen to discount is not appropriate. They prefer to negotiate a sale or return agreement with their suppliers. SORs are in effect a process by which the supplier agrees to take back any unsold stock at the end of a season. This benefits the retail brand as its brand equity is maintained and it is able to clear stocks without the use of markdown. It also gets a cash flow boost once the supplier has credited it with the value of stock returned. For the supplier, the use of SOR is often a route into a prestigious retailer, and if they are a wholesale supplier, then they can limit the damage done by the retailer having to use markdown to clear stocks. A final route to negating the cost of markdown is to pass out the begging bowl. The request by retailers to suppliers to contribute to the cost of markdown is common, and its effectiveness is dependent on the buyer–supplier relationship and the balance of power between their two businesses.

Activity: During a sale period, look out for the prevalence of special buys or products marked as sale or return. Which product category do you find them in the most?

SUMMARY

Whilst the tools and process of trading have their origins within the planning process, the dynamics of trading are very different. The examples contained within this chapter are not exhaustive, but they do show possible routes to tempering the inherent weaknesses of the planning process. Reviewing them, one is struck with the thought of vagueness still: What is the right answer? What is the right cover to use when planning the first week of a sale? What happens if the reforecast WSSI turns out to be inaccurate? Unfortunately, those questions cannot be answered: each business and its market will differ, and what is right for one may be wrong for the next. What is important is to always question and make judgements at a practical level. At a more theoretical level, it can be recognized that differing business models will use data in different ways, attaching differing levels of importance to each. The following chapters will discuss these final considerations and review e-retailing, corporate social responsibility and the supply chain within the context of the fashion merchandiser role.

SELF-DIRECTED STUDY

1. Refer to the companion website for Prentice Day formal wear case study exercises.

Further Reading

Jackson, T. and Shaw, D. (2001) *Mastering Fashion Buying and Merchandising Management*. Basingstoke: Macmillan

Kunz, G. (2010) *Merchandising – Theory, Principles and Practice, 3rd ed.* New York: Fairchild

Varley, R. (2001) *Retail Product Management*. London: Routledge

Bibliography

Felsted, A. (2013) *Markdowns level out in discount Britain*. Financial Times [Internet] Available from http://www.ft.com/cms/s/0/9b30cadc-31d5-11e3-817c-00144fe-ab7de.html [Accessed 20th January 2014]

Nolan, S. (2012) *Selfridges website crashes as hunt for a Boxing Day bargain hits fever-pitch while online shoppers are set to boost economy by £1billion by end of tonight*. Daily Mail [Internet]. Available from http://www.dailymail.co.uk/news/article-2253318/Boxing-Day-sales-Selfridges-website-crashes-bargain-hunters-buy-sale-items-web.html [Accessed 20th January 2014]

Jeff, D. (2013) *Retailers benefit from avoiding price discounting*. The Scotsman [Internet] Available from http://www.scotsman.com/business/scottish-business-briefing-monday-june-3rd-2013-1-2952581 [Accessed 20th January 2014]

Fat Face (2013) *The Fat Face story*, [Internet]. Available from http://www.fatface.com/corporate/our-story/page/corpffstory [Accessed 20th January 2014]

Parry, C. (2013) *Facing forward: How Fat Face's bid to reduce discounting has paid off*, [Internet blog]. Available from http://www.drapersonline.com/blogs/the-drapers-daily/facing-forward-how-fat-faces-bid-to-reduce-discounting-has-paid-off/5051426.article [Accessed 20th January 2014]

Ruddick, G. (2014) *Marks and Spencer suffers again as Christmas sales fall*. Daily Telegraph, [Internet]. Available from http://www.telegraph.co.uk/finance/newsbysector/retailandconsumer/10559733/Marks-and-Spencer-suffers-again-as-Christmas-sales-fall.html [Accessed 20th January 2014]

12 E-Retailing

INTENDED LEARNING OUTCOMES

1. E-retailing defined and reviewed within the context of buying and merchandising.
2. A discussion of the impact of e-retailing on the product management process.
3. Issues in stock management within the e-retailing environment.
4. The relevance and benefits of drop shipping within e-retailing.

INTRODUCTION

The development of the e-retailing business model has had a profound effect on commerce and the way fashion product is bought by consumers. The ability to shop 24 hours a day, via an electronic device whether at home, in the office or whilst mobile was beyond the wildest imagination of those who can remember 20th-century shopping characteristics. The scale of product that can be accessed is incredible, and the fact that choices need not be limited to a local high street but can be broadened to other towns, counties and countries means that the opportunity to be truly unique in what we wear is upon us.

The business benefits of e-retailing are easy to imagine. The move to trading online via either a pure play or a multi-channel operation enables a business to have exposure to a wider potential market than its local one. A bigger business implies greater economy of scale in a cut-throat industry, enabling the risks of trading to be balanced across a wider operational portfolio of distribution channels. In addition to the wider trading opportunity, the mixing of service standards such as free delivery and customer relationship management (CRM) activities that pivot around the brand, the impact on business size and shape by e-retailing is widespread.

Buying and merchandising is not immune to this, and this chapter will concentrate on this aspect of e-retailing only, to demonstrate practical differences between the processes laid out in Part Two and the e-retailing impact on the role of the fashion merchandiser. This chapter will not act as a holistic summary of differing distribution channels, marketing approaches or a detailed technological discussion; rather it will pose relevant questions about this new route to market for a retail business.

E-RETAILING REVIEW

E-retailing is defined as being 'online and other electronic transactions involving goods and services' (Gamans-Poloian 2009: 3), and by its nature it is part of the B2C (business to customer) business model, where a retailer transacts with a customer. E-retailing has developed its place within commerce today; in December 2013, for example, Mintel reported that online retail sales in Europe had grown to a value of £33b and that it now represented over 10 per cent of all retail sales (Mintel 2013). As the penetration of e-retailing grows, statistics within this already impressive number can be astounding. Pure play businesses, whose business models are to trade solely through an online presence, such as asos and Amazon, continue to record sales growth rates of 20 and 30 per cent or higher year on year. Similarly, multichannel retailers, those who trade across more than one channel, have found success. John Lewis has developed a successful approach to e-retailing and its online store already represents 25 per cent of its gross sales. (John Lewis 2013). Mintel meanwhile reported that within the 16–24-year age group, consumers are now more likely to purchase fashion product online and that successful e-retailers such as asos heavily use CRM tools such as social media, blogs and interactive events to capture this potential demand (Mintel 2013).

The final point above is interesting, it emphasizes the role of the consumer and their attitudes within the B2C e-retailing relationship. As e-retailing developed in the late 20th century and on into the 21st, the rate of take-up of the opportunity varied between differing business models. Luxury brands were known for their reluctance to move away from the bricks and mortar model for fear that the luxurious and exclusive value of their businesses would be diluted. Today, though, luxury brands have vigorously engaged with all aspects of technology. At Burberry, for example, has integrated its online customer experience into its bricks and mortar stores, as seen when it launched its branch on Regent Street in London.

Despite these statistics, not all fashion businesses have adopted the e-retailing model. Chanel is famous for not trading online, preferring to emphasize differentiation through its tailoring, perfectly fitting products and range exclusiveness. Primark, at the other end of the high street, does not trade online at all. It states that its low selling prices posed profitability challenges online because of associated costs such as order fulfilment and delivery (Coen 2013). What e-retailing, where relevant, can provide is a route to expand trading opportunities that requires as a starting point, like other distribution channels, an approach that is correct for the brand, its personality and of course its target customers.

THE IMPACT OF E-RETAILING ON B&M ACTIVITIES

The rationale of an e-retailing operation has similarities with the discussion in Chapter 1 which reviewed the size and scale of the retail industry, and the developments over the post-war period that have led it to its current position.

- The consumer – Despite the sophistication of brands and their emphasis on defined personalities and building relationships with consumers, the premium that an individual business holds over the consumer purse is under constant threat. The mid-1990s Easy Jet campaign that advertised its flights as being the same price as a pair of jeans articulated a growing understanding by consumers of the price and value relationship. Within fashion e-retailing this relationship has been broadened into width of product range and on demand availability.

- Technology – The sheer scope of technological routes to purchase online has made it easier for businesses to develop an e-retail offering. Desktops, tablets and mobile telephones can act as digital stores, while Wi-Fi and superfast broadband have facilitated their usage and e-retailers businesses have been quick to utilize available technology.
- Business reach – An online presence allows a business to widen its reach beyond its local market as markets are no longer bound by national or geographic borders. A reflection of the importance of wider market opportunities can be seen in the development of systems to facilitate overseas shipments. Neiman Marcus teamed up with 51 Global Ecommerce to expand the markets within which it operates to 100. This collaboration will enable the brand to retail abroad, relying on their partner software to convert currencies, calculate sales taxes and custom duties and handle customs paperwork (Multi-Channel Merchant 2012).
- Customer relationship management (CRM) – This enables businesses by mapping the consumer journey to start and maintain a relationship with their customer. CRM tools can include loyalty cards and personalized marketing shots, but, as technology has developed and e-retailing has grown, these tools have become fully integrated with the retail process. Asos customers for example can upload a free in-house magazine encouraging product awareness and discretionary spend.

The summary above gives insights into the business opportunity afforded by e-retailing, but it would be wrong, however, to automatically assume that strong demand will always equal easy sales turnover and gross trading profit. Boo.com in 2000, and more recently the troubles of the off-price Cocosa brand, are examples of failure within the e-retailing model. When, in 2011, the Duchess of Cambridge wore a shift dress from the Reiss, its website crashed due to the sudden rush to buy the dress online, and waiting lists had to be created whilst a repeat buy was hastily organized. An alternative experience of the Internet's power was experienced by Claire's Accessories in 2012, when an independent jewellery designer, Tatty Devine, posted evidence on a blog that suggested their designs had been copied. Customer reaction through social media was to condemn Claire's Accessories not just for copying another's designs, but also for the brand's reaction in blocking users and deleting negative comments from their social networking sites.

The Reiss and Clare's Accessories examples are of particular relevance to the B&M function, underlining that there are fundamental implications on product management if one is to trade online. Referring again to the concept-to-carrier bag model, examples of these implications can be identified.

- Research and analysis – Assessing the success or failure of a product range requires a changed mix of analyses tools. Not having a physical store presence changes analysis tools such as density analysis, store performance and range-planning decisions. Extra analysis is needed to identify which products have good or bad returns rates, the cost of those returns, and the impact of returns on average stock levels and stock turn, all of which have the power to impact an e-retailer's P&L or balance sheet.

- Concept – The changed research impacts the product concept with additional KPI budgets (for example returns management, stock management). Similarly search engine rankings, average basket size and values are important measures to assess efficiency of the product range. For the buyer, the wide potential customer base extends the trends and product types that are relevant, significantly impacting their ability to present a cohesive targeted offer. Asos, for example, ranged 65,000 options to 7.1m active customers with an average 2.74 visit frequency in 2013 (asos 2013), a far bigger option choice and customer demographic than an average high street shop.

- Product development and sourcing – With a large multimarket consumer base, the relevance of a single range plan for a season or OTB budget becomes questionable. A business could sell to hot or cold climates at the same time, or offer a bespoke ordering service (for example, the customized Timberland boot). The role of products within a range changes as does its qualitative characteristics – it no longer requires hanger appeal but instead needs to be modelled or presented to accentuate styling, fabrics, shape and versatility.

- Manufacturing, shipping and warehousing – Stock availability, speed of purchase and an efficient order delivery and returns process, at customer convenience, are the hallmarks of a good e-retailing operation. Once sold, a product can embark on a worldwide journey that needs to be managed and be visible at all times. Once delivered to the customer, it could be returned, require reprocessing and be put back into free stock in a central warehouse. Stock management in effect becomes central to the service standard of the e-retailer and so plays a greater role within product management.

- Distribution and retail – Hand in hand with a different structure to stock management comes a different distribution process and management of stock and sales turnover once launched on an online store. Sales trend complexity is heightened by exposure to different markets, potentially in different time zones and seasons happening at the same time. Good trading research to support this complexity requires a changed set of analysis tools. Rates of sale and sell through remain important, but search engine optimization and regional analysis of trends become relevant.

- The carrier bag – The ability of consumers to browse numerous online sites whether they are e-retail, social media or personal sites puts an increased emphasis on product and stock management to contribute to brand trust and loyalty. The Reiss and Claire's Accessories examples demonstrate this point well. Modcloth, a US independent online retailer, emphasizes this further through their 'be the buyer' strategy which enables customers to vote on which samples should be ranged, adding a further dimension to ensuring that a retail business captures its customers' disposable income.

Picking up the key messages from this section, there are many potential implications on the role of B&M, and the merchandiser in particular, within the e-retailing arena. Whilst the aim of e-retailing is the same as that of a traditional bricks and mortar one, the emphasis placed on elements within each one's approach to product management differs. To demonstrate such differences, the next three sections will offer examples of the potential impact on the merchandiser role under the following headings:

- E-retailing and product management activities
- E-retailing and stock management activities
- E-retailing and drop shipping activities

E-RETAILING AND PRODUCT MANAGEMENT

Retail businesses emphasize developing their brands, personalities and marketing communications and weaving product management into this, enables a cohesive image to be communicated to their customers and the wider world. Referring back to Chapter 2, one of the activities of the buyer is to liaise with the retail operations and marketing teams to contribute to visual merchandising and marketing strategies. This activity helps ensure that this cohesiveness is delivered, as in practical terms, the customer sees this in the form of well-laid-out stores, stock levels appropriate to the size of store, with consistency in display factors and sizes available. This traditional bricks and mortar approach has over time produced some visionary approaches to brand management and, as supply chain capabilities have improved, much greater clarity in product display and stock management. By contrast, e-retailing changes the focus, web pages and e-stores still require thought and application in their use, but the loss of a physical store in which to display stock has fundamental consequences for the B&M planning process.

First, the dynamic of a good product range can change. To entice customers, retailers have always ensured that the options ranged will create meaningful stories and themes that will sit well together with store. This has had the effect of creating an artificial limit on the number and type of options that could be ranged. For example, a product story that was allocated to a single four-arm fixture logically would have a predetermined finite number of options that could be displayed, or that were appropriate to that fixture. Supplementary to this, options have always had hanger appeal meaning that their display in store was taken into consideration when being designed (for example embellishments). E-retailing challenges these conventions, as gone are the finite limitations on product range size, and the restrictions on product design.

The quest for originality within product ranges, coupled with the desire of the buyer to express their ideas through as many options as possible, has often been denied by the immoveable demands of the merchandiser to buy within the shape of the range plan and the OTB budget, acting as a break on wide shallow product ranges. These two blocking factors lose their potency within the e-retailing arena, as the potential customer base is broadened beyond a local market, and stock budgets are no longer constrained by display factors or other artificial components of a physical brand image.

The 65,000 options ranged by asos discussed earlier in the chapter, and the reported 426 units sold per second by Amazon in the peak cyber Monday Christmas selling period in 2013 (BCGR 2013), go some way to demonstrating that width of range within e-retailing appears paramount. An article by Jack Jia asserted that the result of increased market segmentation and niche lifestyle consumers has led to the Pareto Principle approach to product management being replaced by 'long tailing' (Jia 2007). Long tailing, also known as the long tail effect, is a concept developed by Chris Anderson which recognizes that as a result of falling costs of production, there is today the opportunity to develop wider, individualistic product assortments rather than generic one-size-fits-all approach. (Anderson 2006). Long tailing and the opportunities for a highly individualised approach to range planning have obvious relevance within fashion, facilitated within the e-retail arena by the lack of physical barriers, in the form of a fixed store size, to expand product ranges.

The long tail effect and the opportunity to offer much wider product ranges sourced from a wider supplier base means that a greater number of options can be offered for sale. To be competitive, fashion e-retailers are able to increase the suitable width of their product ranges, and for a merchandiser, this potentially endless range planning process can change the characteristics of a completed range plan.

As an example of this, take the Prentice Day casual wear range plan from Chapter 9 as shown in Table 12.1 .

Table 12.1 Casual wear range plan

Product group	OTB budget	Average selling price	OTB units	Rate of sale	Life cycle	Sell-through rate	Average unit buy	Ideal option plan
Trousers	£19,824	£50	396	5	8	85%	47 units	8 options
Shirts	£12,244	£35	350	5	8	85%	47 units	7 options
T-shirts	£26,237	£16	1,640	8	8	85%	75 units	22 options
Total	£58,305	£24.44	2,386	6	8	85%	56 units	37 options

As long tailing places a greater emphasis on wider product ranges, with a greater proportion of these being low-volume in opportunity, average unit sales per option would naturally be reduced. This reducing unit volume would over time reduce the achieved rates of sale that an e-retailer could expect to achieve within a products life cycle. A potential effect of this is shown in Table 12.2 , where a halving of the rates of sale within the casual wear range plan affects the number of options ranged.

Table 12.2 Casual wear range plan with halved rates of sale

Product group	OTB budget	Average selling price	OTB units	Rate of sale	Life cycle	Sell-through rate	Average unit buy	Ideal option plan
Trousers	£19,824	£50	396	2.5	8	85%	24 units	17 options
Shirts	£12,244	£35	350	2.5	8	85%	24 units	15 options
T-shirts	£26,237	£16	1,640	4	8	85%	38 units	43 options
Total	£58,305	£24.44	2,386	3	8	85%	28 units	75 options

Note: Data calculation – (rate of sale * life cycle)/sell-through rate = average unit buy
Data calculation – OTB units/average unit buy = ideal option plan calculation

By making no other changes to the range plan, average unit buys halve and ideal option plans double. The manipulation as demonstrated in Table 12.3 could come from other sources. A reduced life cycle would also increase ideal option plans, as would a reduction in the sell-through rate presumption. What is relevant to note is the implication of a changed range plan shape within an e-retailing arena, rather than the micro factors that influence it. The positive benefit of increased choice is a widened product offer to the customer and the opportunity for the retailer to move into new ancillary product ranges. These opportunities could, however, come at a cost to the business if the average unit buy/ideal option plan relationship is not well managed. Within fashion in particular, size fragmentation within options or stock unavailability of co-ordinating options (for example, jackets and matching trousers or skirt) is a significant drag on value addition within the retail business model.

A further aspect of product management within the e-retailing distribution channel is the scale of the potential market, which necessitates well-executed KPI budgeting and resultant OTB budgets being central to the creation of balanced range plans. If one accepts that e-retailing affords a retailer a large, more diverse market within which to operate, logically the financial opportunity is bigger, in turn meaning KPI and OTB budgets applied to the range plan could be bigger, too.

Quantifying a definitive impact on OTB budgets is impossible; there are too many variables to take into consideration. However, the significance of the recent growth of e-retailers such as asos and Net-a-Porter, coupled with impressive sales mix contributions from the e-stores of retailers such as John Lewis, implies that there is an opportunity to be exploited. Take John Lewis: its e-store accounts for 25 per cent of gross sales turnover, meaning its 40 bricks and mortar stores account for the remaining 75 per cent between them, giving an average 2 per cent share for each. Reliance of headline figures without knowing the detail within is dangerous; in this example, sales turnover may be generated online but actually executed within store, but an opportunity in some form clearly exists.

Again, to demonstrate how a new incremental opportunity could influence range planning, Table 12.3 further reflects the impact on the range plan if the OTB budget applied to it is 50 per cent larger. With a halved rate of sale presumptions and a larger OTB budget, the ideal option plan mushrooms still further to a potential 111 options, a 200 per cent increase over the 37 options identified in the original range plan.

Table 12.3 Casual wear range plan with increased OTB budget

Product group	OTB budget	Average selling price	OTB units	Rate of sale	Life cycle	Sell-through rate	Average unit buy	Ideal option plan
Trousers	£29,736	£50	595	2.5	8	85%	24 units	24 options
Shirts	£18,366	£35	525	2.5	8	85%	24 units	22 options
T-shirts	£39,356	£16	2460	4	8	85%	38 units	65 options
Total	£87,458	£24.44	3,580	3	8	85%	28 units	111 options

Note: Data calculation – OTB budget/average selling price = OTB units
Data calculation – OTB units/average unit buy = ideal option plan

The presumptions made are of course presumptions, used to demonstrate an academic concept, but the three tables do point to a changed relationship between budgeting and range planning within e-retail. The implied additional opportunity of operating within a global or national market rather than simply a local one places a much greater emphasis on the relationship between the qualitative and quantitative characteristics of a product range, to first, be aware of potential opportunity and second, to place emphasis on inherent changes in the width versus depth dynamic within the business model.

The relevance of wider ideal option plans and shallower unit buys is further supported by a third factor, the increased ease for customers to remotely search and comment upon individual products through social media or blogging. The enabling of consumers to search across wider and wider information points to select products drives demand 'further down into the niches' (Marshall and Consedine 2007). This new emphasis, where potential unit demand becomes increasingly small as products become increasing unique, further changes the mix of range-planning assumptions relevant within e-retailing.

Within the e-retailing industry itself there are various examples of a changed approach to range planning and OTB management. Sally Heath, Head of E-retailing at New Look, comments that 'the business has to be product authoritative' (Heath 2014), because the start point of the customer's journey is different. It may be in store, but it could be through a search engine, and so search engine optimization is key to making sure that a brand's products are ranked highly. This in turn makes presenting product to the world difficult, as, unlike a bricks and mortar store, there is no one single window with which to display the product offer, and so there is an emphasis on mapping out the customer's journey to the end purchase.

This emphasis is important because long tailing within range planning carries risks. For most brands, an unlimited long tail is unachievable because 'totally elastic walls within e-retailing is an illusion' (Heath 2014). Whilst brands like New Look do offer wider ranges online than in their bricks and mortar stores, there is a limit to the number of pages that a customer will be willing to search through to find that perfect outfit. Therefore, whilst e-retailing affords opportunity to re-define the width versus depth discussion within range planning and develop wider product ranges, it too has potential limitations to truly individuality within fashion.

FOCUS POINT 12.1: THE E-RETAILER AND THE CONSUMER

Murphy's Law – in which if it can go wrong, it will – seems particularly apt within B&M. The buyer could misread their market or their customer, resulting in options ranged that are out of synch with the brand and its target customer. The merchandiser too may misread research and pump volume buys into the wrong product group. Whilst at board level, many retail businesses have made moves into a new product area that have backfired spectacularly.

The skill of matching a target customer to a product range is one which naturally has a good dose of subjectivity to it, and where product ranges are narrow, it is easier to score a direct hit and create a winning range. As OTB grows and the potential ideal option plan expands, there comes a time when additional options no longer add something new to the range, and simply are duplications of other options within the range. In a long tailing environment the risks of getting it wrong are amplified, and whilst the total market may be larger, the likelihood of getting the buys wrong is just as real in an e-retailer as a bricks and mortar one.

The inclusion of social media as an integral part of modern-day marketing communications offers a route to range planning safety by first building a relationship with the customer and then simply asking them what they would like to buy. Jack Jia – in his e-commerce *Times* article from 2007 – wrote that latest buying techniques include 'what is called "crowdsourcing," or using the behaviour of the invisible crowd of online shoppers to make product recommendations to one another on behalf of the retailer' (Jia 2007).

Crowdsourcing examples within B&M could include the Modcloth example within this chapter, the Timberland design a boot, or the US T-shirt brand Threadless, which encourages the uploading of designs to their website, with the most popular being put into production. These explicit approaches coupled with more subtle approaches such as analyses of web pages browsed and purchases made, together enable a fashion e-retailer to refine product ranges, create targeted capsule ranges, or target a particular niche within the wider market.

Wider ideal options plans, crowdsourcing and micro analyses all suggests that long tailing within e-retailing will add more and more choice and complexity within product ranges. Not so, says Jack Jia, who writes that long tail is not just about adding more and more products, but actually good product management is more about targeting 'a smaller set of products to the right people at the right time' (Jia 2007).

Activity: Review the crowdsourcing concept and review a number of e-retailers. How many of them employ crowdsourcing techniques? How might they help take risk out of the range-planning process?

E-RETAILING AND STOCK MANAGEMENT

The previous section identified that the potential changes in the width versus depth relationship within an e-retailing environment are driven by changes in the relationship between supply and demand within a trading and cultural context. This changed planning process output implies that the ingredients within the range plan are either different (for example, different OTB values), or significantly changed in their contribution to the final option detail (for example, differing range assumptions). Taking these implications on further, there must, therefore, be a differential in the process of stock management versus a classic model demonstrated in Part Two of this book.

Stock management is highlighted as being core to the merchandiser role, as identified by the Jackson and Shaw definition presented in Chapter 3. The many stock management tools at the disposal of the merchandiser such as the WSSI, KPI budgeting and OTB management reinforce that position. The long tail effect, in identifying changes to the size and shape of product ranges, challenges accepted phasing of stock practices, as well as the logistical processes that manage stock through the value chain. In an ideal world, a merchandiser would be in professional heaven if every new product were delivered on time, sold at a 100 per cent full-price sell-through and there were no customer returns allowed. This utopian dream, while unlikely to ever exist, is relevant to all retail business models but can be particularly difficult to achieve within an e-retailing environment.

To amplify this point, consumers browse Internet sites without having the ability to try on, or easily compare and contrast different options before making a purchase. This inherent weakness within the purchasing process naturally leads to higher levels of returns, as customers could potentially change their minds once they see and feel the physical garment. This weakness has meant that a returns policy has become an integral part of the business model, and is an important contributor to an e-retailer's service proposition. In fact, a returns policy is now so integral, a report in *Retail Week* highlighted, that fashion e-retailers are facing increasing returns rates as a result of increased e-retailing activities, with figures of up to 40 per cent return rates quoted (Retail Week 2013).

Generous returns policies mean that e-retailer stock management models have an added dimension to them, where stock is delivered into the business, is sold, leaves the business, only to potentially re-enter the business if it is returned by the customer. At low levels of returns, the impact on stock management is marginal, but a potential 40 per cent returns rate fundamentally changes the stock dynamic and the resultant management of OTB.

Tables 12.4 and 12.5 reintroduce the Prentice Day WSSI, this time with a returns column added that demonstrates the impact on stocks between return rates of 0 per cent and 40 per cent.

Table 12.4 *Prentice Day casual wear WSSI with a 0 per cent returns rate*

		Week 52		£25,798				
Weeks/ Months	Sales budget	Mark down budget	Closing stock forecast	Closing stock budget	Returns	OTB	Cover forecast	Cover budget
Week 1	£1,014	£0	£30,094	£25,798	£0	£5,310	29.7	25.4
Week 2	£1,167	£0	£28,927	£25,798	£0	£0	24.8	22.1
Week 3	£1,318	£0	£27,609	£25,798	£0	£0	20.9	19.6
Week 4	£1,413	£0	£30,286	£25,798	£0	£4,090	21.4	18.3
January	£4,912	£0				£9,400		

Table 12.5 Prentice Day casual wear WSSI with a 40 per cent returns rate

		Week 52		£25,798					
Weeks/ months	Sales budget	Mark down budget	Closing stock forecast	Closing stock budget	Returns	OTB	Cover forecast	Cover budget
Week 1	£1,014	£0	£30,560	£25,798	£466	£5,310	30.1	25.4
Week 2	£1,167	£0	£29,907	£25,798	£514	£0	25.6	22.1
Week 3	£1,318	£0	£29,169	£25,798	£580	£0	22.1	19.6
Week 4	£1,413	£0	£32,469	£25,798	£623	£4,090	23.0	18.3
January	£4,912	£0			£2,163	£9,400		

Note: Data calculation – (opening stock – sales forecast – markdown forecast + OTB + returns) = closing stock

At a 40 per cent returns rate, the value of product to be put back into stock for the month is £2,163. With no other changes to the WSSI, this has the effect of increasing total stock levels, while average cover by Week 4 has increased by almost two weeks to 23 weeks. Without a mechanism to reduce stock levels, by the end of the season they would be out of control, with pressure to significantly increase the markdown spend to clear the emerging stock problems.

One saviour of this is that stock returns can be resold over the course of the season, but even with this, there are potential logistical issues. The rise of buy online return in store (BORIS) means that there is no single point of entry of returns back into a retail business, and so imbalances in stock levels could arise if one store has an excessive level of returns. Table 12.6 presumes that a multichannel retail business of four stores experiences a 40 per cent returns rate, all of which are returned to Store 1. The effect is to inflate that store's stock position, and in this example it would take an extra four weeks within the season to sell out of the product, which in the fashion world of short product life cycles and fast fashion is not a desirable position to be in.

Table 12.6 Potential impact of BORIS on stock and sales

Stores	Rate of sale	Weeks life cycle	Sell-through rate	Stock required	Sales	Stock remaining	Plus 40% returns	Extra weeks required to sell out
Store 1	16	8	80%	160	160	0	64	4 weeks
Store 2	16	8	80%	160	160	0	0	
Store 3	16	8	80%	160	160	0	0	
E-store	16	8	80%	160	160	0	0	

Data calculation – E-store sales = 160 units
Data calculation – E-store returns to Store 1 = 160 units * 40 per cent = 64 units
Data calculation – 64 units/rate of sale assumption = four weeks

The ability to sell out of any returned stock is limited by the randomness of the process. Imbalances in options and sizes are inevitable, as is the lag between online sale and customer return, which gives the merchandiser little forward visibility of what stock will be returned, or where or when the return will occur. Further to this, once stock has been returned, it is not always resalable and there is always a risk that the product may be damaged, have been worn, or is simply no longer in fashion.

Returned stock requires an efficient reverse logistics supply chain, where activities are put in place to enable product to flow backwards from the customer to a point where it can be made available for either resale or disposal. Despite various impediments, *Retail Week* commented favourably on the assertion by Kurt Salmon that 90 per cent of product returns within the clothing segment of the retail market can be resold, often at full price (Retail Week 2013).

The competitive emphasis placed by e-retailers on easier delivery of product to customers and then, as required, its return is telling. The offering of delivery service convenience, coupled with a returns incentive, can encourage customers to increase their basket sizes beyond buying one or perhaps two items. The effect of an increasing basket size, coupled with an efficient reverse logistics process to enable a high resale rate can grow sales turnover faster than if the incentive were not there. Table 12.7 shows a theoretical impact of increasing basket sizes on sales units and closing stocks, assuming a 40 per cent returns rate and a 90 per cent resale rate, of which 65% is sold at full price and 25% at 50 per cent off.

Table 12.7 Units example on sales and closing stock of encouraging increased basket sizes

Units	No returns	25% volume increase	50% volume increase	100% volume increase
Opening stock	260	325	390	520
Sales per week	10	12.5	15	20
Sales per 26-week season	260	325	390	520
Returns @ 40%	0	130	156	208
Total sales without returns re-sale	260	195	234	312
65% of returns sold at full price	0	84	101	135
25% of returns sold at 50% off	0	33	39	52
10% returns unsold, valued at 50% off	0	13	16	21
Total sales including returns re-sale	260	312	374	499

Unit sales increases do not automatically translate into matching sales turnover and gross trading profit growth, and so Table 12.8 translates the data into a possible financial impact. Using the 25 per cent volume increase column from Tables 12.7 and 12.8 as a guide, the £11,000 gross trading profit is calculated as follows:

- Total selling value of £29,550 comprises
  - Total sales without returns resale = 195 units * £100 selling price = £19,500
  - 65% of returns sold at full price = 84 units * £100 selling price = £8,400
  - 35% of returns sold at 50% off = 33 units *£50 selling price = £1,650

- Total markdown value of £2,300 comprises
  - o 35% of returns sold at 50% off = 33 units * £50 selling price = £1,650
  - o 10% returns unsold, valued at 50% off = 13 units * £50 = £650

- Total gross trading profit of £11,000 comprises
  - o Total selling value − total markdown value − total cost value
  - o £29,550 − £2,300 − £16,250 = £11,000

Table 12.8 shows that, based on the assumptions made, it takes a 50 per cent unit uplift to generate marginal profitability growth of £240 over the no returns figures. Differing intake margin, markdown spends and re-sale rate presumptions would all change the absolute financial numbers generated, but would not change the conclusion that the process of total stock management, as highlighted by Jackson and Shaw, is paramount within an e-retailing business model. Total stock management takes on a more complex persona, particularly within trading activities, and understanding the exact point at which optimum financial success is found requires knowledge of the variables employed and their sensitivity within the mix of influences that comprises a season's final gross trading profit outcome.

Table 12.8 Impact example on gross trading profit of a returns policy

Value	No returns	25% volume increase	50% volume increase	100% volume increase
Selling price	£100	£100	£100	£100
Cost price	£50	£50	£50	£50
Total selling value	£26,000	£29,550	£35,490	£47,320
Total markdown value	£0	£2,300	£2,750	£3,650
Total cost value	£13,000	£16,250	£19,500	£26,000
Total gross trading profit	£13,000	£11,000	£13,240	£17,670
Total closing stock	£0	£650	£800	£1,050

Note: Excluding VAT

This sensitivity means that analysis within an e-retailing environment differs to a bricks and mortar operation. Central to the setting of stock management tools is the budgeted traffic to site presumption, out of which other control mechanisms will fall. Building KPI budgets based on traffic allows them to be assembled as follows:

- traffic to site growth presumption
- of which a conversion to sales presumption can be created
- using conversion history to create an AOV (average order value)
- to create budget presumptions to lead to an OTB budget based on traffic presumption.

FOCUS POINT 12.2: CLEAR RETURNS

'The sale is just the beginning. A shopper isn't truly a customer until they decide to keep what they ordered from you. Returns are a fact of life for retailers, but the e-commerce and multichannel environments are bringing changes in customer behaviour that are pushing up your return rates and straining your existing processes to breaking point' (Clear Returns 2014).

The focus put on returns policies by e-retailers places customer service at the heart of the e-retailing business model. John Lewis, for example, allows customers to return products bought online through its stores or for free by post. It also offers a returns process through Collect+, a distribution network of over 500 shops. Asos too offers a flexible returns policy, but being a pure play e-retailer also offers flexible delivery choices. Most recently, the brand started offering 15-minute delivery windows, with Nick Robertson telling *Retail Week* that 'We want to continue to exceed customer expectations and this is an example of Asos yet again redefining the online retail experience' (Retail Week 2014).

A well-articulated and thought-through delivery and returns policy has enabled e-retailers to improve service standards and also offer a strong USP over bricks and mortar stores. It does of course come at a cost. Returns can be a heavy cost to a retailer. Tangible costs such as post and packing, reprocessing charges and write-offs are easy to value, but the cost of product being out of the supply chain, irregular stock flows and multiple points of re-entry into the business also weigh heavily on retailer overheads.

Quoted returns rates sit between the 25 per cent and 50 per cent levels, meaning that every other product sold could find its way back to the retailer. Where the product can be re-sold then there is the opportunity to manage returned stock back out into the supply chain. Returns become more troublesome when they cannot be re-sold. Stock may be returned damaged, or particular products may have unusually high returns rates due to a mismatch between appearance online and in real life. More worrying still is where product is returned and fashion trend has moved on and it is no longer a desirable purchase, meaning that the stock is virtually worthless to the retailer.

Clear Returns has developed a predictive software tool that identifies reasons for customer returns and, importantly, triggers intelligent responses. Their software highlights the products, processes, suppliers and customers causing costly returns – and generate timely alerts after as few as five returns. Problems become apparent in days and not months, meaning cost-saving actions can be taken fast.

Activity: Review the differing delivery and returns policies of different e-retailers and bricks and mortar stores. Identify which have the easiest policies and assess impacts on stock management.

E-RETAILING AND DROP SHIPPING ACTIVITIES

The Clear Returns focus point that completed the previous section is interesting, as it points to another consequence of returns policies and resulting additional stock management activities; they are overhead-heavy. Whilst overhead costs such as postage, packing and processing are beyond the remit of the merchandiser, they do weigh on the P&L and the final achieved net profit for a season, placing an emphasis on the merchandiser to best manage the business's stock holding. Of direct relevance to the merchandiser is the analysis of the composition of sales, returns and then resale, with their focus being on managing stocks to limit its potential to damage profitability. Data from Clear Returns (2014) point to ways in which this can be achieved, with the following taken from its quarterly review of the e-retailing market in early 2014.

- Average return rate does not change with seasonal peaks although returns volumes do increase in line with dispatch volumes.
- Up to 50 per cent of retailers' returns are caused by just 10 per cent of their products.
- When stock is returned, it can lose between 5 and 10 per cent of its value.
- The dilution in stock value can be minimized by reducing the lead time for return.
- Within the clothing sector, the product categories creating the highest volume of returns are dresses and tops.

To the merchandiser, knowledge such as the above provides much support in creating good, commercial KPI budgets and resulting stock management processes. Data regarding seasonal peaks and stock flow impacts their WSSI planning, knowledge of which products are more likely to be returned contributes to the range-planning process, whilst value dilution knowledge links very clearly to markdown planning. However, no amount of past experience or forward trend guidance can remove the ultimate uncertainty within product management. The risk of getting the range wrong is inherent in all that buyers and merchandisers do, and for an e-retailing merchandiser there are plenty of activities that would add to the risks involved within their role remit.

- The opportunities afforded by long tailing to widen the product range could increase average stock holdings. As the tail lengthens, the demand for each additional option declines, potentially resulting in decreased stock turn, overstocks and excessive debt loads.
- As product ranges fragment into smaller segments, KPI budgeting becomes less accurate due to the micro-planning of small numbers within the product hierarchy.
- The trading of a widened range becomes more difficult due to the higher number of priorities to be handled on a daily or weekly basis.
- Trading is also further complicated by the additional trading decisions created by returns management and stock flow visibility.
- Visibility of a total potential stock position that includes owned, ordered and potential returns is challenging, which impacts effective OTB management.

A better approach to stock management within e-retailing is to limit the business's exposure to the stock KPI, and so delivery of the product range. The route to achieve this chosen by many e-retailers, as well as bricks and mortar businesses, is through being able to generate sales turnover without physically owning some or all of the stock involved. This concept, known as drop shipping, has been embedded into the e-retailing business model and is an order fulfilment supply chain operation where 'a retailer simply forwards customers' orders to the manufacturer or a distributor who fills the orders directly to the customers and is paid a predetermined price by the retailer' (Khouhja and Stylianou 2008: 896). Drop shipping offers the opportunity to offer wider ranges without incurring the costs and risks associated with buying stock in advance (less debt, warehousing costs and risk of range failure). It also facilitates a wider choice of products, in line with long tailing and in the case of short life cycle fashion items, a faster route to market in a time-pressured environment. Drop shipping does carry its share of disadvantages, most notably in the form of fragmented orders from consumers that may increase overhead costs, as well as inefficiencies in order deliveries if the products are delivered from multiple suppliers.

For the merchandiser, charged with efficient stock management, the advantages of drop shipping are numerous. Tables 12.9 and 12.10 present two scenarios using the Prentice Day sales turnover and stock KPI budgets created in Chapter 7. Table 12.9 presumes that all OTB is bought and delivered via the Prentice Day store, while Table 12.10 then presumes that 50 per cent of the product range is instead drop shipped via a new website direct to the customer from the supplier.

Tables 12.9 and 12.10, while simplistic, do imply that drop shipping can be a compelling strategy within stock management. The potential advantages of an increased stock turn are appealing, as is the flexibility afforded of not having to manage the supply chain processes of part or all of a product range. A further opportunity could come in the form of using drop shipping for repeat orders, peripheral options or sizes only, relying on bulk orders for the core of the range. For the business as whole, these planning and trading opportunities would be considered in tandem with the likely disadvantages of moving towards incorporating drop shipping into their models. Issues such as a much wider supplier base to manage, increased order processing costs, margin pressures between retailer and supplier, or the risk of the supplier not delivering could dilute the flexibility afforded by drop shipping.

Drop shipping if is employed offers a flexible route to product management and can facilitate the widening of product ranges and delivery of the cost of stock ownership. Its principle is not

Table 12.9 *Interest costs and stock turn without drop shipping*

Total Prentice Day OTB for season	£128,980
Sales turnover budget	£108,500
Average stock	£55,432
Stock turn	1.96

Note: Data calculation – sales turnover budget/average stock

Table 12.10 *Interest costs and stock turn with 50% drop shipping*

Total Prentice Day OTB for season	£128,980
50% of OTB delivered to store	£64,490
Sales turnover budget	£108,500
Average stock	£27,716
Stock turn	3.91

Note: Data calculation – sales turnover budget/average stock unlike the use of concessions within the bricks and mortar model, where space in a host store is given over to a third-party concession in return for a share of the sales turnover achieved. Like a concession operation, it carries risks and operational challenges, such as greater uncertainty within the supply chain, but the ability to be flexible throughout the fashion season is compelling to the merchandiser.

FOCUS POINT 12.3: NEW RESEARCH APPROACHES

The development of technology has facilitated a surge in capabilities in product analysis, which coupled with the advances within Multi and Omni channel retailing has widened the available measures with which the merchandiser can analyse their business. At the heart of new analysis capability is the big data phenomena, about which the *Harvard Business Review* comments 'because of big data, managers can measure, and hence know, radically more about their businesses, and directly translate that knowledge into improved decision making and performance' (Harvard Business Review 2012).

At the heart of big data is the phenomenal growth in the volume of data available, the speed at which it can be accessed and the sheer variety of analysis that is now possible. A good example of this is provided by EDITD, the world's biggest apparel data warehouse, which states that it is 'a trading, merchandising and buying powerhouse that's as easy to use as an iPad' (EDITD 2014). It provides users with analysis of competitors' offers, price discounting trends, options plans, best sellers and emerging trends. This in itself is significant, but it is made more dynamic as it looks beyond just the merchandiser's own business and assesses competitors', too, giving a real-time snapshot of the market as a whole.

On-demand access to data such as this transforms research capabilities by widening the net of available knowledge, but by itself it could be too big, too daunting to fully assess. Predictive analysis which takes knowledge and uses it to direct business actions, so linking the two together, has been at the forefront of e-retailing approaches to gaining market share and financial success. To better demonstrate this, if one considers the analysis tools of rate of sale, cover or sell-through rate, all are useful to define the shape of KPI budgets or option details. If a business were to offer a POS markdown to entice customers to spend with them, then the results of all the quoted analysis tools would change for the better, but finances would possibly worsen due to the cost of markdown.

With e-retailing, there is a much wider knowledge about the customer, because big data allows an e-retailer to see what the customer is doing and what motivated them to spend. The *Harvard Business Review* develops this point and refers to e-retailers being able to 'track not only what customers bought, but also what else they looked at; how they navigated through the site; how much they were influenced by promotions, reviews, and page layouts; and similarities across individuals and groups' (Harvard Business Review 2012). Detailed knowledge such as this then enables targeted offers based on prediction of past history, which over time have increased in sophistication and results.

> For the merchandiser, research and analysis is now not just about knowing what happened, but predicting what will happen and making sure that it does. Search engine optimization adds to the process by ensuring that a retailer's products are high within search rankings and use the best routes to market to enable the concept-to-carrier bag model to be followed through its end point.
>
> Activity: Research the term *big data* and investigate its use within product management

SUMMARY

The announcement by asos in April 2014 that, whilst its sales had increased by over 30 per cent in the previous six months, its profits had actually fallen by 20 per cent (Guardian 2014) was followed by some debate as to its long-term meaning. Expansion into new territories weighed on profits, outweighing the reported increase in average customer spend and dampening the brand's performance. The risks in e-retailing are very real, and while some brands have thrived to date, constant success over the long term is not guaranteed. Central to the e-retailing business model is the changed meaning of value addition and service, with the ability to offer wide product ranges, flexibility through easy delivery and return processes and customer engagement activities through crowdsourcing.

The impacts of these are keenly felt by the merchandiser through the fundamental rewriting of the criteria that go into the KPI budgeting, range planning and stock management activities of the role. E-retailing affords the opportunity to re-shape product ranges into wider and more extensive ones which are not constrained by physical store size, affording e-retailers the opportunity to be authoritative within their ranges. It also changes the role played by stock within retailing, as volume presumptions change and so too do the OTB budgets that lie behind them.

Most importantly, there is a greater flexibility to plan more loosely and emphasis trading more emphatically. With this comes the need for improved analysis in the form of wider analysis measures such as basket size, returns rates and website viewing habits as close to real time as possible to micro manage stock flow between e-retailer and their customers. The growing trading focus in all retail distribution channels puts inevitable pressures on relationships particularly those between retailer and supplier. Chapter 13 will discuss this and identify how the merchandiser can help to preserve a responsible approach to their own activities when time is precious and trading is volatile.

SELF-DIRECTED STUDY

1. Research the development and growth of Amazon and eBay to understand their business models in relation to long tailing and drop shipping.
2. Compare differing product categories of an e-retailer and a similar local store. Review the options available, price points and sizes available to build up a picture of the differences in product offers between the two.

Further Reading

Anderson, C. (2010) *The Long Tail: How Endless Choice is Creating Unlimited Demand.* London: Random House

Gamans-Poloian, L. (2009) *Multi-Channel Retailing.* New York: Fairchild

Chaffey, D. (2011) *E-business and E-Commerce Management, 5th ed.* Harlow: Pearson

Bibliography

Asos PLC. (2013) *Annual report,* [Internet]. Available from http://www.asosplc.com/~/media/Files/A/ASOS/results-archive/pdf/annual-report-2013.pdf [Accessed 20th January 2014]

Clear returns, [Internet]. Available from http://www.clearreturns.com/ [Accessed 20th January 2014]

Coen, D. (2013) *Primark could have enormous potential online.* Drapers, [Internet]. Available from http://www.drapersonline.com/Journals/2013/09/12/m/q/o/Fashion-Index-September-14-2013.pdf [Accessed 20th January 2014]

EDITD, [Internet]. Available from http://editd.com/[Accessed 20th January 2014]

Gamans-Poloian, L. (2009) *Multi Channel Retailing.* New York: Fairchild

Jia, J. (2007) *The Long Tail of E-Commerce.* E-Commerce Times, [Internet]. Available from http://www.ecommercetimes.com/story/57766.html [Accessed 20th January 2014]

Lewis, J. (2013) *Interim results,* [Internet]. Available from http://www.johnlewispartnership.co.uk/financials/financial-reports/interim-reports.html [Accessed 20th January 2014]

Khouhja, M. and Stylianou, A. (2009) A (QR) inventory model with a drop-shipping option for e-business. *The international journal of management science,* volume 37, number 4, pp. 896–908

Marshall, W. and Consedine, T. 2007. The long tail. *Monthly labour review,* volume 130, number 3 pp. 69–70

McAfee, A. and Brynjolfsson, E. (2012) Big data: The management revolution. *Harvard business review magazine,* [Internet]. Available from http://hbr.org/2012/10/big-data-the-management-revolution/ar [Accessed 20th January 2014]

Mercer, J. (2013) *E commerce- reviewing 2013.* Mintel, [Internet]. Available from http://academic.mintel.com/display/688313/?highlight [Accessed 20th January 2014]

Parry, C. (2013) Asos steps up fulfilment war with 15-minute delivery windows. *Retail Week,* [Internet]. Available from http://www.retail-week.com/multichannel/online-retail/asos-steps-up-fulfilment-war-with-15-minute-delivery-windows/ 5050299.article [Accessed 20th January 2014)

Rankin, J. and Butler, S. (2014) Asos halted by Chinese puzzle as profits fall on cost of expanding. *The Guardian,* [Internet]. Available at http://www.theguardian.com/business/2014/apr/02/asos-profits-fall-expansion-costs [Accessed 6th April 2014]

Sender, T. (2013) Fashion online UK. *Mintel,* [Internet]. Available from http://academic.mintel.com/display/638243/ [Accessed 20th January 2014]

Siegal, J. (2013) Amazon sold 426 items per second during its 'best ever' holiday season. *BCGR*, [Internet]. Available from http://bgr.com/2013/12/26/amazon-holiday-season-sales-2013/ [Accessed 20th January 2014]

Starkey, A. and Turner, E. (2014) IMRG clear returns quarterly fashion returns review. *IRMG*, [Internet]. Available from http://www.imrg.org/index.php?catalog=625 [Accessed 6th April]

Tierney, J. (2012) Neiman Marcus goes global with fifty one. *Multi-channel merchant*, [Internet]. Available from http://multichannelmerchant.com/opsandfulfillment/warehouse/neiman-marcus-goes-global-with-fiftyone-07112012/ [Accessed 20th January 2014]

13 Corporate Social Responsibility

INTENDED LEARNING OUTCOMES

1. A discussion of the corporate social responsibility (CSR) concept and its relevance within fashion business.
2. The application of relevant research to identify the potential impact on responsible operations by B&M teams.
3. A focus on the activities of the merchandiser and how a change in operation could lead to improvements in the buyer–supplier relationship.
4. Examples of how activities within the concept-to-carrier bag process could be applied to the CSR concept.

INTRODUCTION

The fashion trade press headlines in December 2013 were full of a decision by Debenhams to change its trading terms with its suppliers that allowed them to take greater trading discounts. Over the course of that year, another department store John Lewis, design brand Laura Ashley and others such as asos and Mothercare also made changes to trading terms to the fury of their suppliers. This type of activity is not uncommon and is regularly reported; in 2002, Philip Green was reported to have 'slapped a retrospective 1.25 per cent price cut on its clothing suppliers' (just-style.com 2002) and House of Fraser undertook a similar activity in 2006.

A business reviewing its contract terms – if done for perfectly valid business reasons – is a natural part of commerce as trading conditions change and markets adjust to new macroeconomic realities. There is of course an implied responsibility to behave fairly and a legal requirement for transparent dealings, and while the businesses just mentioned were able to make changes and in many cases made commitments with regard to future business, there was a natural questioning of the implications of their decisions.

What makes these examples the more interesting and relevant to this chapter is that in a world of multi-stakeholder, integrated supply chains, at face value it would seem that unilateral actions go against the logic of today's operating methods. This chapter will consider this, and discuss in broad terms how fashion businesses could adapt policies and practices to ensure that there is fairness within their supply chains and, from there, identify the potential impact that this can have on B&M and the role of the merchandiser in particular.

The evidence for an ethical approach within many business sectors is broad, covering operational practices such as supplier management, delivery processes, worker contracts and others. This chapter will incorporate some of these topics into the corporate social responsibility debate and then relate them to the concept-to-carrier bag model and from there to the activities of the merchandising function.

CORPORATE SOCIAL RESPONSIBILITY

Ensuring responsibility within the strategic direction and day-to-day operations of business is not a new concept, as demonstrated by the Marks and Spencer staff welfare programme of the 1930s and the Bill Gates Foundation, which supports healthcare, education and action to overcome poverty. Initiatives like these have tended to be driven by individual beliefs and values, but increasingly there is recognition that businesses are citizens of the world, whose activities have a big impact on us all. Perhaps the most seminal example of this was experienced by Nike, who found to their cost in the 1990s that campaigns made against them were a direct result of failings in their own supply chain. The resulting sweatshop conditions in some of the factories used by their suppliers made them appear to the world as engaging in corporate ethical fickleness (Zadek cited in Crane et al. 2008). Articulating the extent of the potential remit of business responsibility has become an important and increasingly diverse debate, which has over time led to the emergence of the CSR concept to guide its development and methods for its measurement and recording.

CSR to date has been defined in many ways by differing interest groups such as academics, governments, non-government organizations (NGOs) and charities. Crane et al. in their 2008 book *Corporate Social Responsibility* point to the myriad of definitions, quoting UK, Chinese and European authorities, Gap and Christian Aid, all of whom define it differently. One of the more holistic academic definitions that they cite comes from Matten and Moon, who define CSR as being 'a cluster concept which overlaps with such concepts as business ethics, corporate philanthropy, corporate citizenship, sustainability and environment responsibility' (Crane et al 2008: 5).

A second approach to understanding the breadth of responsible trading can be gleaned from the OECD 'Guidelines for Multinational Enterprises' (2011) which are an annex to the OECD 'Declaration on International Investment and Multinational Enterprises'. These guidelines provide principles and standards for responsible business conduct for multinational corporations operating in or from countries which have adhered to the Declaration. The guidelines are described as far-reaching recommendations for responsible business conduct (OECD 2011) that encourage multinational organizations to observe wherever they operate. The Declaration is practical and business operation-focused. It covers topics such as human rights, the environment and consumer interests.

A third position is articulated by the development of many NGOs. A good example of this is the Ethical Trade Initiative (ETI), which is a multi-stakeholder alliance of businesses, trade unions and voluntary organizations which together focus on improving the lives of vulnerable workers around the globe. Their vision is a world in which 'all workers are free from exploitation and discrimination, and work in conditions of freedom, security and equity' (ETI 2014). Their activities centre on working to ensure that all workers have access to fair working hours, health and safety policies and the right of access to free trade unions, rights that many of their ultimate customers, the consumers, would take for granted.

The ETI website is a useful resource for better understanding the concept of CSR, and within its landing page description of why it is needed, neatly helps to inform the remainder of this chapter. The site states that 'doing ethical trade is much harder than it sounds. Modern supply chains are vast, complex and span the globe' (ETI 2014). The merchandiser as one part of the fashion business supply chain is relevant within the debate and so does have a collaborative part to play in the embedding of CSR principles within their strategic and operational role.

CSR policies, where implemented within business, can have a significant positive impact. However, the scale and effectiveness with which CSR has been integrated within the fashion supply chain in particular has been mixed. There are still many instances reported in the press of unethical business practices or a wider lack of insight into the appropriateness of retailer–supplier relationships. The much pub-licized collapse of the Rana Plaza building in Bangladesh that claimed the lives of over 1,000 people is a case in point. Crucially, safety concerns about cracks in the building were ignored by managers, who insisted their workforce continue work-ing, driven by pressures to deliver products as much as by any local issues that they faced. This led the prime minister of Bangladesh to comment that Western consumers should accept higher selling prices for the clothes that they purchased (The Times 2014), implying that the competitive landscape of shortened buying cycles, selling-price pressures and rampant competition requires a more robust and effective counterbalance through applied CSR approaches.

If one then considers the B&M function and its activities within the context of the competitive landscape, a number of clear examples begin to emerge where a buyer or merchandiser could unwittingly act or make decisions that impact the supply chain upon which they rely:

- Time – there is enormous pressure within the fashion supply chain for a supplier to deliver product on time or face a possible financial penalty. This is made more acute where collections need to be delivered together to ensure a co-ordinated look within stores.
- Demand patterns – if demand patterns result in large bulk orders, then often excessive overtime is expected of the factory workers to hit deadlines. Very often, as seen in the Rana Plaza case, factory workers have very few rights to protect themselves with, or are unable to have a voice as they are unaware of the extent of the rights that they do have.
- Production planning – Unstable flows of purchase orders lead to volatility and often short-term contracts within the supplier sector. These unstable, low-pay

approaches to employment can be made worse when production is outsourced to unregulated factories in peak periods of production.

- Delivery management – the delivery of product from supplier to retailer is one that is highly anticipated once the option detail has been completed and the delivery schedule created. Trading decisions to use air as opposed to sea freight to hit WSSI phasing deadlines are often taken.

Buyers and merchandisers of course do not work alone, and are but one part of the supply chain. It is that chain as a whole, and the various bottlenecks within it, rather than ad hoc individual initiatives that can take actions to encourage responsibility within the supply and retail of product. Taking the definition and practical evidence of business operations together, the spirit and character of CSR and its practical application begin to emerge and are summarized by Crane et al. (2008) into six points:

- CSR is voluntary in its application.
- Internalizing or managing externalities by being aware of the impact of operations and actively promoting use of the good and managing the bad.
- Multiple stakeholder orientation needs to be uniform in approach.
- There is an alignment of social and economic responsibilities in business operation.
- It is led by practice and values, and embedded into a business's operation.
- Therefore, CSR goes beyond philanthropy and becomes integral to normal business operation.

At a first review of these characteristics, it would be easy to presume that CSR's adoption would inevitably increase costs; for example, through higher cost prices to fund worker benefit, or slower response times to demand by adopting rigid approaches to production management. This does not need to be the case. A study into CSR within the textile industry concluded that research undertaken between 1972 and 2000 suggested, there was a positive relationship between CSR and financial performance in 68 per cent of cases (Van Yperen 2006). Cost benefits such as economy of scale, better production rates due to improved employee morale and selling benefits of enhanced reputation or demand patterns from customers could be derived from a different perspective on product management.

In taking the discussion of CSR to the fashion buyer and merchandiser roles in the next section, it is evident that the concept is relevant within product management, and that there is a natural bias and greater resonance within this towards the buyer. Fashion buyers in general are the guardians of supplier management, and so many CSR-driven initiatives – either voluntarily or competitively undertaken, or enshrined in any local legislation – will influence their activities first and foremost. However, the merchandiser does have a role to play, and as guardian of the financial and logistical elements within product management, can support CSR credentials through ensuring their activities promote responsible business success.

CASE STUDY 13.1: TIMBERLAND – CSR WITHIN THE BRAND PERSONALITY

'Our mission is to equip people to make a difference in their world. We do this by creating outstanding products and by trying to make a difference in the communities where we live and work' (Timberland 2014, p. 1).

The Timberland Company can trace its history back to the early 20th century, and has evolved into a successful international brand that manufactures and sells clothes and footwear with a distinct outdoors theme. The brand emphasizes its rich heritage, and has developed a very precise personality in its history, with one of the elements of this being its commitment to CSR.

The business prides itself on its commitment not just to its shareholders, but also its employees, third-party stakeholders, customers and the world in which it lives and breathes. Timberland responsibility is a dedicated area of its website (http://responsibility.timberland.com/executive-commitment/), where it lays out the approach to its business operations. The landing page makes a good initial point when – in his welcome – the president of the company states that 'corporate responsibility doesn't need to be an add-on, but instead can be a powerful competitive advantage' (Timberland 2014). This underscores the value of CSR and ethical approaches to manufacturing and selling, and it ties into the ultimate aim of all businesses to profit from their efforts and so create a long-term viable future for themselves.

Financial viability has always been the bottom line of accountancy. However, in recent years, there has been a developing focus on the concept of the triple bottom line, where two more elements are added to the mix: social and environmental concerns. Many fashion businesses have taken this approach on board with notable proponents being Marks and Spencer with its wide-ranging Plan A laying out commitments to ensure it is a responsible member of society.

If one reviews Timberland and its commitments, its own approach to triple bottom reporting shines through. It places a focus on its operational effect on the climate, and actively seeks to reduce emissions. Within its product it uses recycled raw materials and promotes its cradle-to-cradle design approach. Finally, with its people it has codes of conduct for its business operations and actively encourages employees to take part in voluntary work to the benefit of the community.

Activity: Review the annual financial reports of a number of retailers to review a cross-section of approaches to CSR. In particular, review Plan A and assess its scope and successes to date.

RELATING CORPORATE SOCIAL RESPONSIBILITY TO THE CONCEPT-TO-CARRIER BAG MODEL

Relating the ten process activities of the model to the wide breadth of CSR, like much of the product management process, cannot be evidenced in a single one-size-fits-all series of paragraphs (Table 13.1) . Connecting CSR examples to the many fashion retail business models, product concepts and target customer types means that this would be impossible. However, it is possible to use established research to narrow the debate to the significant influences that directly relate to the B&M function, and from there to articulate how the merchandiser could help influence the promotion of CSR within a fashion retail business.

Table 13.1 *The concept-to-carrier bag model*

Concept-to-carrier bag activity	Definition
1. Research	Undertaking and collation of relevant fashion research
2. Concept	Creation of product range concept and design direction
3. Product development	Finalization of concept as a product range
4. Sourcing	Sourcing of suppliers and manufacturers for the range
5. Manufacturing	Manufacture of the product range
6. Shipping	Shipping and delivery of the product range
7. Warehousing	Receipt of the product range, its allocation to store and storage
8. Distribution	Delivering initial store allocations
9. Retail	Display, sale, promotion and stock replenishment
10. Carrier bag	Purchase of the product by a consumer

Research by Galland and Jurewicz (2010) identified six key themes that place pressure on the workings within the retailer–supplier supply chain relationship. These they defined as:

• Unstable buyer–supplier relationships

If faux fur is on-trend, then retailers will buy faux fur. If leather is on-trend, they will buy leather. There is an inherent instability in the buyer–supplier relationship, but as Nike found, unstable relationships are not just borne out of the fickleness of trends, but also from divergent interests. The buyer looks for the best quality product at the most favourable commercial terms and often is given incentives such as bonuses to achieve them. The supplier meanwhile looks for efficiency within their processes with a consistency of approach. The outcry that met the decisions to change trading terms by retailers at the beginning of the chapter is one source of instability, as are imposition of fines for late deliveries regardless of reason, which many B&M teams use as 'margin enhancers' to protect gross trading profit and bonuses.

• Continued downward pressure on cost prices

The £2 Primark T-shirt is perhaps the perfect example of the significant price deflation experienced within the fashion retail industry that has come about as a result of the changes to the demand and supply model over the past 20–30 years. In the four-year period 2003–2007, retail prices within clothing fell by 10 per cent (Felsted 2009), driven by consumer demand, voracious competition and easy supply. While improved economy of scale can absorb some of the effects of price deflation, it cannot necessarily also equitably manage rising raw material costs.

The jump in cotton prices over 2010 and 2011 was met with great concern within the retail industry. Their collective response, while mixed, had a common theme: they aimed to hold selling prices steady, even though their gross margins may be affected (Daily Telegraph 2011). Fashion buyers are tasked to negotiate the best possible intake margins, and with cotton prices almost doubling at one point, and little movement in selling prices, the likelihood of a further squeeze on cost prices was evident.

- Increased quality demands and processes

There are many staging posts in the creation of product that ensure the quality of a garment is not just in line with the expectations of the end consumer but also complies with relevant legal requirements. The development and emphasis placed on brand management mean that quality entails not just the right colour, fabric type or button, but also the right placement of labelling, use of hangers and other pre-retail activities. Each can add time to the process while the additional quality demands will add complexity.

- Shorter lead time pressures between order placing and delivery

The twin emergence of competitive pressures such as high competition levels and technological advancements has enabled lead times to be cut, and increased the reliance on flexibility within the supply chain. Nowhere is this more apparent than within the fast fashion context which can turn product concepts into stock within six weeks or fewer. The consumer has a regular supply of fresh fashion to buy, and the retailer the opportunity to better manage cash flow and commercial risk. For suppliers, this has had a very subtle but powerful impact of changing the direction of the supply chain from pushing product to the customer, to it being pulled by them. In order to be effective, this pulling of product ordering requires postponement strategies such as the use of bulk fabrics, which are coloured or trimmed at the very last minute, which in turn adds complexity and uncertainty to the planning of efficient manufacturing.

- Regular changes to product specification and purchase orders

One of the challenges of product management is the length of time that a concept-to-carrier bag model can comprise. The setting of a creative and financial concept around which product development, budgets, OTB and range planning can pivot has many decision points which can often be used to action changes of mind. New trends may emerge or the macroeconomic environment may throw a curve ball into the planning process. Beyond commercial pressures, there may simply be a consensus that a colour needs to be changed, a trim altered or unit buys reviewed.

It is not possible to anticipate every potential change; however, many companies are taking action to limit the number of changes made to product specifications. Monsoon, in its ethical trading report, stated that 'We recognise that many of our buying decisions and the management of the critical path involving the design, manufacture and delivery of our products can have adverse (albeit unintended) consequences for the application of our Code. For example, last minute design changes can have a dramatic impact on manufacturing lead times causing suppliers to have to work excessive overtime. This in turn can impact productivity, health & safety and quality. Our programme aims to highlight the potential impacts of purchasing decisions on ethical compliance to buyers and to help achieve a "Right First Time" process' (Monsoon 2014).

- Cancellation of indicated or confirmed orders

Buyers and merchandisers are often responsible for multimillion pound product categories that encompass many different product types, and the pressure on these individuals is immense. They are constantly searching not just for good deals but flexibility, too, in their quest to provide a product which is creatively astute but also capable of creating wealth. One source of flexibility is to manage OTB up or down dependent on trading conditions, and where OTB reduces, purchase orders can often be cancelled or indicated orders may be abandoned.

This poses issues for suppliers who operate capital-intensive businesses – from fixed costs such as machinery and plant to variables costs such as long payment terms demanded by retailers. Balancing production in an environment such as this is difficult. The phenomenon of the bullwhip effect, in which ever changing consumer demand means that forward forecasts often deviate from actual production requirements, causing continuous changes to forward purchase orders, is prevalent within the fashion industry.

Reviewing the six themes presented highlights that in a commercial environment, where activities are undertaken not just to express creativity but also to generate wealth, there arise uncertainty, changes of mind and a need to maximize financial return. Imposing an idealistic CSR approach would only constrain a business's ability to compete, and would allow other businesses to take market share. Instead, a more realistic approach of tempering the hard edges of business, and changing of focuses within the concept-to-carrier bag model, should enable a strengthened product management process, and the merchandiser as a stakeholder within that process has much to contribute.

The three sections that follow present routes by which the merchandiser could use the activities within their role to maintain competitive advantage for their business, but also embed CSR into their decision making. These examples are operational as opposed to strategic, reflecting the point that the merchandiser is one role within a complex global supply chain as described by the ETI. Relevant topics such as emissions management within stock transportation, or the efficient use of scare resources such as water in the manufacturing process, are not discussed. This is because, whilst the merchandiser may have an influence or interest in these topics, they do not own the activity, and so cannot within their own concept-to-carrier bag process effect change.

The next three sections will discuss utilize the six themes developed by Galland and Jurewicz, and will narrow them into the following activities of the merchandiser role:

- Product budgeting to improve the buyer–supplier relationship
  o How the KPI budgeting process focus could be influenced by CSR.
- Stock management and the rebalancing of the delivery process
  o How the shape of WSSI phasing could be influenced by CSR.
- Product management and the management of purchase orders
  o How product management could be influenced by CSR.

CASE STUDY 13.2: PEOPLE TREE – ETHICAL TRADING IN FOCUS

People Tree, the British–Japanese trade fashion company, began life as Global Village in Japan in 1991, launching in the UK in 2001. The brand ethos and its designs explore ways in which to balance the wellbeing of its makers with delight for its 25–40-year-old female wearers. People Tree is a design-led company that sees clothing as a vehicle for poverty alleviation and puts its focus on community-centred sustainability through economic stability, skills preservation and low-impact production methods in all that it does. As part of this, the company promotes the use of local skills to create employment, and works closely with 50 fair-trade groups in marginalized communities across 15 countries including Bangladesh to manage the supply chain from growing cotton to weaving and embroidery, to stitching and delivery.

The design process starts with a kick-off meeting between the People Tree teams in the UK and Japan, who work collaboratively to plan fabrics, colour palettes and share inspiration. Designs are inspired by trends, but more fundamentally by the producers they work with, of whom many of these have rich textile histories, use traditional techniques and provide inspiration and an identity for designers to work with. Preparation for a new collection starts up to 18 months ahead of the season, meaning that producers can plan their production, preventing the bottlenecks prevalent in mainstream fashion that can result in unpaid overtime to fulfil orders and insecure employment due to peaks and troughs in the flow of purchase orders. The long lead times create challenges at the distribution end as this means that staggered drops into stores are needed. As Head of Design, Tracy Mulligan says, 'There's always a way to make it work – it's a lot of fun and it's important to have a sense of humour when trying to overcome challenges. There's a lot of laughter in the People Tree office' (Parker 2011).

To enable financial stability within the supplier base, 50 per cent of the order value is paid in advance and the balance is paid on delivery, compared to the three months that it takes many fashion retailers to pay for stock. This helps to facilitate close working relationships between the design and production and the sales and marketing teams which in turn enables existing skills utilization as well as new skills development. The resultant knowledge of the potential customer in terms of aesthetic and quality demands, alongside practice-based skills and working environments that are aligned to People

Tree's values, offers a framework for product development and capacity building. This forms creative possibility rather than constraint, and adds an element of surprise and uniqueness to the collection as it is not produced in the same way as other competitor brands.

This case study is based on the work of Liz Parker and is a summary of a larger case study that can be found in Parker (2011).

Activity: Research artisan cloth and accessories suppliers in developing countries and review how relationships such as those People Tree has with its suppliers can bring economic benefits to small communities.

PRODUCT BUDGETING TO IMPROVE THE BUYER–SUPPLIER RELATIONSHIP

At the heart of the merchandiser role, is the responsibility to create and manage the financial parameters of a product range. This is done through the creation of KPI budgets, which articulate how a product range will create sales turnover and ultimately gross trading profit. Table 13.2, replicated from Chapter 7, is a summary of the calculated KPI budgets for the Prentice Day case study.

Table 13.2 Prentice Day KPI summary

Product category	Menswear		
	Planning year	Previous year	% Variance
Sales budget			
Total sales turnover £	108,500	90,000	20.6%
Markdown budget			
Markdown %	19%	25%	−24.0%
Markdown spend £	20,480	22,250	−7.9%
Intake margin budget			
Intake margin %	62%	62%	0.0%
Gross profit budget			
Gross trading profit %	50.2%	46.7%	7.5%
Gross trading profit £	45,476	35,005	30%
Stock budget			
Opening stock £	55,432	50,000	+11%
Closing stock £	55,432	55,500	−0%
Stock turn	1.96	1.7	15%
VAT: 20%			

One of the key messages that emerges from the research of Galland and Jurewicz is that suppliers are often faced with ever shorter lead times, so making any delays to production a significant problem. Often these delays are beyond their control – weather, customs delays or earthquakes, for example. However, there are occasions when production is delayed due to problems within the supply chain or simply because lead times are too tight. The merchandiser may respond to these by imposing fines on the supplier to cover the lost sales opportunity. Over time, such penalties tend to become a KPI budget within their own right, and as a source of security and potential additional gross trading profit, are chased with at times alarming ferocity.

Table 13.3 is an amended KPI budget summary with an added provision for such supplier funding. It presumes that the sum of late delivery fines equates to 2.3 per cent of turnover, and as supplier funding is seen as a financial benefit, it increases gross trading profit, in this case by £1,293, all at the expense of the supplier.

Table 13.3 Revised KPI summary to include supplier funding

Product category	Menswear	
	Planning year with supplier funding	**Planning year without supplier funding**
Sales budget		
Total sales turnover £	108,500	108,500
Markdown budget		
Markdown %	19%	19%
Markdown spend £	20,480	20,480
Intake margin budget		
Intake margin %	62%	62%
Supplier funding		
Late delivery fines	2,500	0
Gross profit budget		
Gross trading profit %	50.60%	50.2%
Gross trading profit £	46,768	45,476
Stock budget		
Opening stock £	55,432	55,432
Closing stock £	55,432	55,432
Stock turn	1.96	1.96
VAT: 20%		

Calculation

- (£108,500/1.20 VAT) * 62% = £56,057 sales at cost price
- (£2,500/1.20 VAT) * 62% = £1,292 supplier funding at cost price

- (£20480/1.20 VAT) * 62% = £10,581 markdown at cost price
- £56,057 + £1,292 – £10,581 = £45,768 gross profit

The practice of including supplier funding as part of the product budgeting process can also extend beyond the B&M function. The introduction to this chapter discussed cases where fashion businesses have extracted additional margin from their suppliers; however, those first examples do show a way in which supplier funding activities within the B&M context could continue, but in a more inclusive, responsible way.

House of Fraser emphasized in 2006 that it was asking suppliers to accept changed trading terms to fund a brand development plan with the promise of future orders. This collaborative approach can also be applied to B&M, in the form of a retrospective discount also known as an incentive bonus scheme (IBS). This is a financial agreement that encourages a partnership approach between retailer and supplier by setting financial incentives for the retailer to increase its trade with its suppliers over the course of several seasons.

By agreeing to a long-term partnership that is expected to grow each year, as the retail business develops, a supplier can naturally expect orders to rise gradually over time both in terms of unit buy and number of options produced. This type of agreement reduces the uncertainty of forward production and overhead planning for the supplier, and could also produce economy of scale in manufacture. In return for this safety and long-term order placing, the retailer, who may be passing up opportunities to source elsewhere, would be entitled to a retrospective payment from the supplier at the end of a season dependent on the volume of business that had taken place.

To demonstrate this, Table 13.4 takes from Chapter 9 the calculated Prentice Day OTB budget of £128,980 to show how such a scheme could work.

Table 13.4 *Retrospective discount approach to supplier funding*

Open to buy selling value	£128,980	
Open to buy cost value	£66,640	(£128,980/1.2) * 62%
Open to buy growth	10%	
Incremental open to buy	£6,664	(£66,640 * 1.1) = £73,304 – £66,640
Retrospective discount selling value	£2,500	
Retrospective discount cost value	£1,292	(£2,500/1.2) * 62%
Retrospective discount as % of OTB	1.9%	(£1,292/£73,304)

To generate the same £2,500 taken in late delivery fines, the table shows that the retailer would need to grow its OTB by 10 per cent. In reality, where retailers spend OTB calculated in the millions, growth rates required to generate meaningful retrospective discounts would be much lower and so represent a viable option to consider. The table also demonstrates that relationship building and collaboration, if managed with a different approach, can result in financial as well as operational benefits to both retailer and supplier.

STOCK MANAGEMENT AND REBALANCING OF THE DELIVERY PROCESS

The stop-start approach to product ordering, and potentially wild variances in production planning, puts the order management within the CSR focus. Central to stock deliveries is the accurate phasing of OTB to allow regular injections of new product trends, and it supports the management of cash flow. For the merchandiser, this is managed through the creation of the WSSI that phases the total OTB across all the weeks of a financial period. The creation of the WSSI helps inform the range-planning process and allows both retailer and supplier to see required delivery dates in advance of production commencing.

The real world is unfortunately anything but logical, and a number of issues occur that may impact the supplier. First, fashion ranges by their nature are built around colour stories or trend themes, and so – to be cohesive in store – require to be delivered together. This naturally builds peaks and troughs into production planning; a mad rush to get all options of a product range delivered at the same time, followed by potential inactivity until the next range launches. A similar dilemma is faced once the planning season is over and the trading season begins. Many retailers do not release all the available OTB prior to the season beginning, reserving a percentage of the budget value to spend on repeats of best sellers. The problem this presents is that until a product begins to sell, it is impossible to accurately predict, first, how it will sell; and, second, if the rate of sale will be high enough to require a repeat order. Key to resolving these issues are finding ways to overcome a stop-start production process, and employing a forward forecasting tool that is option-specific as opposed to the higher-level WSSI.

Taking the stop-start production process first, it is inevitable that there will be peaks and troughs in production; however, it is possible to smooth out severe pinch points. The development of information technology has greatly expanded the capability of supply chains, which can facilitate the supply of product in response to the pulling of stock by actual demand rather than supply based on pushing product to customers in anticipation of future demand. By linking IT systems, both retailer and supplier can electronically pass information, such as purchase order details, between them. Crucially, they could share stock information, and so transform the production process. By adopting a replenishment approach, in which stock shortages against pre-set targets are identified to the supplier on a continuous basis, deliveries can be made as required, rather than via a best guess forecast.

The merchandiser influences this mode of operation at the point that they decide the delivery phasing of an option on the WSSI. Table 13.5 , taken from Chapter 10, shows the casual wear product range being split into two orders to be delivered in Weeks 1 and 4 of the season.

This phasing was decided by working through planned rates of sale to identify at which point deliveries would be required to maintain the display factor for the store (see Chapter 10). Within a continuous replenishment environment, it would be possible to deliver product at least weekly, meaning that the Week 1 delivery need only amount to enough stock to cover the display factor and the first-week sales. It would then be followed by weekly deliveries in Weeks 2, 3 and 4 that would reflect

Table 13.5 *Phased WSSI*

Weeks/ months	Sales budget	Mark down budget	Closing stock forecast	Closing stock budget	OTB	Cover forecast	Cover budget
		Week 52		£25,798			
Week 1	£1,014	£0	£30,094	£25,798	£5,310	29.7	25.4
Week 2	£1,167	£0	£28,927	£25,798	£0	24.8	22.1
Week 3	£1,318	£0	£27,609	£25,798	£0	20.9	19.6
Week 4	£1,413	£0	£30,286	£25,798	£4,090	21.4	18.3
January	£4,912	£0			£9,400		
Week 5	£1,413	£0	£28,286	£25,798	£0	20.0	18.3
Week 6	£2,028	£0	£26,845	£25,798	£0	13.2	12.7
Week 7	£1,471	£0	£25,798	£25,798	£424	17.5	17.5
Week 8	£1,471	£0	£25,798	£25,798	£1,471	17.5	17.5
February	£6,383	£0			£1,895		

sales and closing stock patterns. Taking this approach to weekly deliveries could change the WSSI to reflect the following OTB phasing plan (Table 13.6):

This approach to trading brings the benefits of further improved cash flow to the retailer, as seen in the reducing covers on the WSSI, in tandem with an improved production flow to the supplier. It does have its limitations as, to be truly effective, suppliers need to be able to produce and ship in shorter lead times and so the retailer

Table 13.6 *Amended WSSI phasing*

Weeks/ Months	Sales Budget	Mark down Budget	Closing stock Forecast	Closing stock Budget	OTB	Cover Forecast	Cover Budget
		Week 52		£25,798			
Week 1	£1,014	£0	£27,304	£25,798	£2,520	26.9	25.4
Week 2	£1,167	£0	£27,397	£25,798	£1,260	23.5	22.1
Week 3	£1,318	£0	£27,339	£25,798	£1,260	20.7	19.6
Week 4	£1,413	£0	£27,186	£25,798	£1,260	19.2	18.3
January	£4,912	£0			£6,300		
Week 5	£1,413	£0	£27,733	£25,798	£1,960	19.6	18.3
Week 6	£2,028	£0	£26,685	£25,798	£980	13.2	12.7
Week 7	£1,471	£0	£26,194	£25,798	£980	17.8	17.5
Week 8	£1,471	£0	£25,798	£25,798	£1,075	17.5	17.5
February	£6,383	£0			£4,995		

could become overly reliant on a local sourcing strategy. There are also questions over the handling of very small order quantities and the efficient management of the purchase order's creation and delivery process. In addition to these questions, another concerns the relevance to fashion or high fashion options which, by their nature, are volatile in their sales potential and limited in their in-season life cycles. Not surprisingly, it is within core basic product that this approach is most effective and relevant, as the switching cost to a customer of buying opening price point easy styles across a number of brands is low to non-existent.

Despite these benefits, there is a potential flaw in a continuous replenishment approach to core basic stock management. It is reliant on accurate initial planning to ensure that the range assumptions that are used to derive unit buys are well thought-through and do not require constant revision. Once in-season, there is also a need for a mechanism to ensure actual trading results are reviewed with any required changes to forward planning actioned and communicated immediately.

PRODUCT MANAGEMENT AND RAISING PURCHASE ORDERS

Following on from better managing the phasing of core basic stock through the WSSI, the question arises of how best to manage the forward forecasting of the many differing options within the range. Galland and Jurewicz found that cancellation of orders was a significant source of problems for suppliers, and whilst there has to be some flexibility for changes of mind and trends, some of these pressures can be alleviated by the merchandisers trading of their core basic range.

The delineation of products into distinct attribute types reflecting different characteristics is a common approach to maintaining a balanced product, as shown in Part Two, where the fashionability attribute was extensively discussed (Table 13.7).

Table 13.7 Examples of fashionability attributes

Fashionability	Definition	Product example
Core basic	Non-trend-led and has wide customer appeal and sales volume	Basic T-shirt
Fashion	Product that interprets current trends for a target customer	T-shirt with trend-led trim
High fashion	Directional trend product ranged often for fashion credibility	Laser-cut T-shirt with slogan

Reviewing the fashionability attribute definitions, it seems natural, as discussed in the previous section, that efforts to better manage purchase orders sit most prominently with core basic product. The characteristics of such products lend themselves to longer life cycles, are regular in their demand patterns and so offer the efficiency of easier matching of unit buys to production planning. This is seen in the fashion industry across countless examples. Galland and Jurewicz cite two cases, the first being Nike, which focuses on forward forecasting around their core or classic styles; and the second is Zara, which puts small quantities of fashion styles into stores and then does not allow re-orders, instead focusing on delivering new fresher styles (Galland and Jurewicz 2010). For Nike, efficient product management of core basics helps to support the demands for its fashion products; while for Zara, forward production uncertainty has been all but eliminated from its supply chain.

The question for the merchandiser therefore is how best to manage the forward forecasting of core products to allow greater accuracy in product planning and delivery. Setting a planned life cycle and rate of sale is one thing, but once in-season, all bets are off and anything could happen. In-season trading is notoriously fast paced and ever changing, and to keep control of required adjustments to forward OTB, the merchandiser has historically run line monitors (also known as line cards) to plan and reforecast all core basic options on a weekly basis.

Line monitors are in effect a mini WSSI, created for each core basic option ranged, with one replicated in Table 13.8 . Recorded in units, it is in effect a rolling document that identifies sales, stocks and any resultant OTB for any option that does not have a defined life cycle and will require being regularly reordered. Table 13.8 reflects a line card for a newly ranged basic white T-shirt and presumes that:

- The rate of sale is 16 units per week.
- The ideal closing stock holding is 20 units.
- Orders have already been placed for Weeks 1–8 in the season
  o Week 1 order of 36 units comprises sixteen units to cover Week 1 sales and a further 20 units to fulfil the ideal closing stock requirement.
- The OTB generated in Weeks 9–26 uses the standard OTB calculation.

Working through the line monitor and reviewing its details tells the merchandiser that:

- The total unit sales opportunity for the season is 416 units.
- There are a further 288 units of potential OTB to be ordered.

Running ongoing core basic products through a line monitor rather than including them within the range-planning process is a far more effective way for the merchandiser to manage the forward forecasting requirements of these product types. As actual sales results are recorded, the forward sales, stocks and OTB assumptions can flex in line with demand, allowing true potential to be identified and bought for. For the supplier, they no longer need to wait for orders for a significant part of the product range to be identified as part of a concept-to-carrier bag process. Line monitors take the pressure off trying to plan, buy and trade all products within a range at the same time, taking further related pressures out of the buyer–supplier relationship.

SOME FINAL THOUGHTS ON CSR AND THE MERCHANDISER

Like much of the merchandiser role, existing awareness of the activities of B&M and its application within the CSR context lie heavily on the buyer and less so on the merchandiser. Beyond that, CSR within business operations, as articulated by

Table 13.8 White basic T-shirt line monitor

Description		White basic T-shirt						
Month	Week	Unit sales	Cumulative unit sales	Unit closing stock	Cover	Commitment	Unit OTB	Cumulative unit OTB
January	1	16	16	20	1.25	36		
	2	16	32	20	1.25	16		
	3	16	48	20	1.25	16		
	4	16	64	20	1.25	16		
February	5	16	80	20	1.25	16		
	6	16	96	20	1.25	16		
	7	16	112	20	1.25	16		
	8	16	128	20	1.25	16		
March	9	16	144	20	1.25	0	16	16
	10	16	160	20	1.25	0	16	32
	11	16	176	20	1.25	0	16	48
	12	16	192	20	1.25	0	16	64
	13	16	208	20	1.25	0	16	80
April	14	16	224	20	1.25	0	16	96
	15	16	240	20	1.25	0	16	112
	16	16	256	20	1.25	0	16	128
	17	16	272	20	1.25	0	16	144
May	18	16	288	20	1.25	0	16	160
	19	16	304	20	1.25	0	16	176
	20	16	320	20	1.25	0	16	192
	21	16	336	20	1.25	0	16	208
June	22	16	352	20	1.25	0	16	224
	23	16	368	20	1.25	0	16	240
	24	16	384	20	1.25	0	16	256
	25	16	400	20	1.25	0	16	272
	26	16	416	20	1.25	0	16	288

Note: Data calculation: Closing stock – unit sales = unit OTB

Crane et al. (2008), is not limited to B&M, but is relevant throughout the value chain. This means that the merchandiser, as one of many stakeholders, can have an influence on the promotion of responsibility within the concept-to-carrier bag process, but cannot singlehandedly impose it. The breadth of CSR goes far beyond that one role, and within the B&M context, it is the creative roles that seem to have a bigger immediate impact on responsibility within the supply chain. But this is not the case: buyers' decisions are taken in tandem with their contacts, and so are at least influenced, and at most directed, in their decision making. The merchandiser as a key – if not the greatest – contact in their decision making can significantly add to the application of a CSR-led product management approach.

Like the buyer, the merchandiser does not have absolute power over the market, supply chain or customer, with many of their planning and trading decisions that could negatively influence the world out of their control. Decisions about shipping strategies, payment terms to suppliers or quality assurance are often out of the remit of B&M, and so this chapter has concentrated only on the merchandiser, and offered potential solutions to how that role could contribute to responsible business. This chapter is not therefore a review of CSR in its broadest sense, but mixes practical evidence of poor business relationships with targeted practical interventions.

On reviewing the contents of this chapter, a sense of the merchandiser being one cog of many in a retailer and supplier value chain strikes a chord. As such, all cogs are reliant upon one another, and at the heart of CSR are responsible relationships that work together. A final thought on this will be given offered to complete all the discussions held in the preceding chapters.

SUMMARY

Schwopping, the Marks and Spencer and Oxfam clothes recycling initiative, adds extra weight to ideas of responsibility and good citizenship. The spirit Of CSR is filtering into the mind-set of the customer, adding to the already heavy expectations placed on B&M teams. It is clear that the move to a fast-paced competitive retail landscape has, in the short term, added to pressures within the supply chain to react as quickly as it can to the ever changing fashions coming off the catwalks. All, however, need not be lost, and a change of perception by B&M, and in the workings of the merchandiser in particular, can restore some of the ground lost in management of the buyer–supplier relationship over recent years.

In looking back over this chapter, there is nothing new or seminal in retrospective discount, WSSI phasing or line monitors; they have been used in some form or another for many years. CSR does, though, re-emphasize their roles within the merchandiser activities, demonstrating an added imperative for their use, with an ancillary thought being the emphasis that CSR places on all relationships within product management. The concept-to-carrier bag process highlighted, and CSR fully embeds, the need for collaboration not just to get the work done, but also to understand the importance and value that each role brings to the creation of a product range. Product is not just about a buyer or designer, and is certainly not about one person being able to practically create a range and also intellectually understand the micro implications of their activities. The notion of relationship management is perhaps the biggest single facilitator of the concept-to-carrier bag and will be the subject of the next, final chapter.

SELF-DIRECTED STUDY

- Review the ethical trading initiative website to review the scope of ethical trading. This can be found at http://www.ethicaltrade.org/
- Review the Investor Relations section for fashion retail businesses' websites to review varying commitments to corporate social responsibility and ethical trading.

Further Reading

Christopher, M. (2011) *Logistics and Supply Chain Management*. Harlow: Prentice Hall

Crane, A., Matten, D. and Spence, L. (2008) *Corporate Social Responsibility*. London: Routledge

Matten, D. and Moon, J. (2004) *Corporate Social Responsibility: Readings and Cases in Global Context*. London: Routledge

Bibliography

Crane, A., Matten, D. and Spence, L. (2008) *Corporate Social Responsibility*. London: Routledge

Daily Telegraph (2011) *Cotton prices – what the retailers say*, [Internet] Available from http://www.telegraph.co.uk/finance/markets/8302160/Cotton-prices-what-the-retailers-say.html [Accessed 20th January 2014]

ETI (2014) *About ETI*, [Internet] Available from http://www.ethicaltrade.org/about-eti [Accessed 20th January 2014]

Felsted, A. (2009) A heftier toll at the till. *Financial Times*, [Internet] Available from: http://www.ft.com/cms/s/0/72320f58-9b0f-11de-a3a1-00144feabdc0.html#axzz2sXSRz3dE [Accessed 20th January 2014]

Galland, A. and Jurewicz, P. (2010) *Best current practices in purchasing: The apparel industry*, [Internet]. Available from: As you sow http://www.asyousow.org/human_rights/purchase.shtml [Accessed 20th January 2014]

Matten, D and Moon, J. (2004) Cited in Crane, A. Matten, D. Spence, L. (2008) *Corporate social responsibility: Readings and cases in global context*. London: Routledge

Monsoon (2010) *Ethical Trading summary report*, [Internet]. Available from http://media.monsoon.co.uk/assets/pdf/monsoon/heritage/Monsoon_Accessorize_ETI_Report_summary290413.pdf [Accessed 20th January 2014]

OECD (2011) *OECD guidelines for multinational enterprises*, OECD Publishing, [Internet]. Available from http://dx.doi.org/10.1787/9789264115415-en [Accessed 20th January 2014]

Pagmamenta, R. (2014) Shoppers told suffering is price of cheap clothes. *The Times*, [Internet] Available from: http://www.thetimes.co.uk/tto/money/consumeraffairs/article3965519.ece [Accessed 20th January 2014]

Parker, E. (2011) *Steps towards Sustainability in Fashion: Snapshot Bangladesh*, edited by Hammond, L., Higginson, H. and Williams, D. London: College of Fashion and Fashioning an Ethical Industry

Timberland (2014) The Timberland Story [Internet] Available from: http://www.timberlandonline.co.uk/on/demandware.store/Sites-tbl-uk-Site/default/Link-Page?cid = about_timberland_our_story [Accessed 20th January 2014]Van Yperen, M. (2006) *Corporate social responsibility in the textile industry – international overview*. IVAM: Amsterdam

Zadek, S. Cited in Crane, A., Matten, D. and Spence, L. (2008) *Corporate social responsibility*. London: Routledge

14 The Merchandiser within the Supply Chain

INTENDED LEARNING OUTCOMES

1. Defining supply chain management within a fashion retailer.
2. Supply chain agility and its relevance to product and the activities of the merchandiser.
3. The global supply chain and the impact on the role of the merchandiser.
4. Summarizing the fashion merchandising role and its place within a fashion retailer.

INTRODUCTION

In laying out the principles and practice of the role of the merchandiser, references have been made numerous times to the influence of supply chain management within the merchandiser decision-making process. Part One emphasized the linkage between the role of the merchandiser and the somewhat conflicting roles of buying and finance by discussing control processes that the merchandiser can bring to product management. Part Two, in describing the activities of the merchandiser, made references to linking quantitative and qualitative characteristics together to create a defined product range. Finally, Part Three to date has discussed the impact of trading, e-retailing and CSR within the merchandising role.

All of the chapters within this final part have related in some way to collaboration, or the relationships between the merchandiser and the other roles within product management. The previous chapter concluded that the merchandiser is just one of many roles that together plan, create and trade a product range. Collaboration can take many forms, but for it to be effective requires not just an alignment of interests, but also processes and communication flows. This chapter will discuss this point using the theme of supply chain management and the merchandiser role within it.

DEFINING SUPPLY CHAIN MANAGEMENT

The breadth of supply chain management is greater than just the heavy goods vehicles that deliver raw materials or finished products from one location to another. It is a broad discipline within any business that touches not just all the roles that are part of a concept-to-carrier bag process, but all roles within a fashion business. Supply chains have been defined many times, but Chapter 1, as an introduction to the subject, used the excellent Christopher definition of supply chain management, summarizing it as being 'the management of upstream and downstream relationships with suppliers and customers in order to deliver superior customer value at less cost to the supply chain as a whole' (Christopher 2011: 3). In reviewing the definition and pulling out its keywords, the discipline can be further explained as follows:

- Management – Management does not mean a singular approach where one role defines a process that others follow, but it is the co-ordination of diverse roles and activities into one process that suits all, including the end consumer.
- Relationships – As Nike found to its cost, where roles do not align around a common aim, then serious issues, in this case the use of sweatshops, can arise. To develop relationships, the processes employed should be fit for all, and the sharing of information commonplace.
- Deliver – Great product ranges need to be delivered on time within the trend life cycle and identified WSSI phasing. Delivery requires the co-ordination of activities that are located apart and possibly in different parts of the world and time zones.
- Superior value – The obvious exampling of this would be the alignment of quality and value for money for the consumer. There is also a quantitative element, via good stock management, on-time deliveries and replenishment to maintain full-size curves during a product's life cycle.
- Less cost – Less cost within the supply chain brings advantages to the consumer in the form of stable or reduced selling prices. For all businesses within the chain, it also means the elimination of inefficiency within the chain, reduced wastage of raw materials and the elimination of buffer stocks of raw materials.

In using the definition, Christopher goes on to refine it, focusing on the word *relationships* within his discussion, acknowledging that to deliver greater levels of superior value, reduced cost and profitability, there may be occasions where 'the narrow self-interest of one party has to be subsumed for the benefit of the chain as a whole' (Christopher 2011: 3). For the merchandiser as for the other interested parties within the chain, for this to occur there needs to be an understanding, first, of the peculiarities of the fashion supply chain, and second, to work flexibly within it to deliver their product range to the target consumer.

THE FASHION SUPPLY CHAIN

Fashion supply chains have been irrevocably changed by the rise of the fast fashion business model, which harnessed free-trade and technology developments to revolutionize the supply of fashion product to meet rising consumer demand. In adopting the fast fashion principle, the fashion supply chain has to all intents and purposes moved towards a rolling range-plan approach, where collections are launched on a regular basis over the course of a season, requiring a constant flow of processes when compared to a legacy model of planning collections within a defined spring/summer or autumn/winter period.

The fast fashion concept has been so well received by the consumer that it is considered ubiquitous within the fashion industry. Its precise shape and form can of course differ from business to business: Zara champions a vertical business model that focuses on in-house control, whereas the Primark model focuses on entry price points on the high street. The commonality between all fast fashion models, however, is speed to market, where in response to up-to-the-minute sales data, rolling range plans create ranges in real time, so postponing many of the planning decision points into the trading activities of the concept-to-carrier bag process.

Using again the Christopher definition, but this time considering it within a fast fashion context, its key words show that:

- Management – Where concept-to-carrier bag planning processes are condensed from months into weeks, overall management is achieved through speed of decision making, agility in coping with ever changing priorities and activities and a constant flow of relevant information to all stakeholders for synchronized decision making.
- Relationships – The constant flow of relevant information in turn requires an emphasis on all roles within the chain talking to each other. Within Zara, for example, designers, market specialists (country managers) and buyers work together to dissect performance and create new prototype products. The market specialists link to the retail stores to bring their voice into the discussions (Leeman 2010).
- Deliver – With rolling-range plans and greater delivery phases come widened option choice and implied overall lower unit buys. The supply chain must be able to co-ordinate more transactions within a compressed period of time. This is further complicated by the mix of options, with core basics requiring a volume supply chain approach, while fashion styles will require a highly responsive supply chain to be able to react to volatile demand patterns.
- Superior value – Different trends will overlap as each is layered onto the product range, risking no clear distinction between one trend finishing and another beginning. A seamless transition of cutting dead one trend, without incurring ongoing markdown and brand dilution, requires constant and detailed micro product analysis and review.
- Less cost – Time is the biggest cost within the fast fashion arena, so, to facilitate reduced lead times, supply chains have to be able to support speed-to-market strategies. The complex mix of product types, fashionabilities and price points requires dual sourcing strategies. These strategies are a mix of long lead-time suppliers to provide regular volume deliveries of core basics, operated parallel to a local short lead-time supplier base for fashion or high fashion options.

Reviewing the summaries above, additional key words emerge that supplement those of the Christopher definition. Words such as *responsive*, *agility* and *communication* emerge suggesting that to relate supply chain management to the role of the fashion merchandiser requires thought as to identifying elements of their activities that lend themselves to agile decision making.

FOCUS POINT 14.1: LUXURY BRANDS AND SUPPLY CHAIN MANAGEMENT

Coco Chanel is attributed as saying that girls should be both classy and fabulous, and so it is not surprising that *supply chain*, *logistics* and *efficiency* are not words normally associated with luxury fashion brands. It is more likely that words like *rarity*, *exclusiveness* and *status* come to mind when thinking of a favourite brand. A pair of Gucci sunglasses makes statements about the self, far more than a generic, mass-market version.

The luxury business model, like its products, can be quite distinct from the rest of the fashion industry. There is evidence that the notions of lean supply chain efficiency and agile quick-response activity are not relevant, with luxury brands occasionally looking for 'voluntary inefficiencies (e.g. manual labour, long waiting lists), pursuing competitive advantage over rarity and brand exclusivity' (Luzzini and Ronchi 2010). However, innovation has always been at the forefront of luxury, and the changed commercial world of improving technological capability and reducing barriers to trade have brought supply chain management firmly into the luxury segment of the market.

Brun and Castelli noted that modern luxury brands have to support multiple supply chain approaches where they offer a broad product mix, encompassing different segments such as ready to wear, bespoke and accessories (Brun and Castelli 2008). This point is an important one to note, as the rise of *masstige*, a term that merges mass and prestige, which is the phenomenon of the ranging of luxury products at attainable price points (think Gucci sunglasses), means that volume supply chain practices must sit alongside those of scarcity and bespoke.

Luxury fashion brands by their nature are fashion leaders and innovators, and so the juggling of prestige and masstige product offers needs thought. For bespoke ranges where past sales and stock analysis is either not available or relevant, there is a requirement for a broad, small-scale sourcing and manufacturing base that requires quality and control mechanisms to work effectively. These mechanisms centre on keeping the concept and product development stages within their concept-to-carrier bag processes firmly within the fashion house (Brun and Castelli 2008). The key, however, is to use the discipline of supply chain management to manage wide relationships, rather than pursuing inappropriate mass market operational efficiency.

By contrast, the masstige elements of a luxury brand product offer require a different approach. Mass-market principles applied within the luxury context can be seen anywhere on the high street, from the licensing of luxury names via brand extensions into beauty, eyewear or accessories, through to the seemingly endless supply of leather goods such as handbags and luggage. With wide distribution, regularity of sale and a strong emphasis of core basic products, the supply chain focus broadens beyond strict product developmental control towards an emphasis further down the concept-to-carrier bag towards shipping, distribution and retail is apparent.

Activity: Visit your local luxury fashion stores. How big is the range of product that could be described as masstige? Where is it located within the store? What parallels in retail execution are there to nearby mid-market brands?

SUPPLY CHAIN AGILITY

The biggest focus of superior value addition and cost reduction within fashion retailing is the fulfilment of customer demand today; not yesterday or tomorrow, but *today*. Regular flows of new exciting fashion ranges instil a scarcity mentality that is matched by the social media phenomenon where trending products and ideas on Instagram or blogs urge consumers on to be 'of the moment' in what they wear. Parallel to this frenetic activity but no less important are the less exciting products, the easy pick-up core basics which act as simple regular purchases season after season. Matching these two differing demand patterns within quantitative planning and stock management is at the heart of the merchandiser role within the greater supply chain of a fashion retailer.

The ranging of different options which have different characteristics and hence different reasons for being ranged allows for a balanced product range to be constructed by the buyer. Table 14.1 replicates from Chapter 2 the different characteristics split by the fashionability attribute.

Table 14.1 Examples of fashionability attributes

Fashionability	Definition	Product example
Core basic	Non-trend-led and has wide customer appeal and sales volume	Basic T-shirt
Fashion	Product that interprets current trends for a target customer	T-shirt with trend led trim
High fashion	Directional trend product ranged often for fashion credibility	Laser cut T-shirt with slogan

The product attribute definitions above demonstrate that a single supply chain approach to stock management is not effective within a fashion retail business. Core basic options by their nature are part of an incredibly competitive market, due to the wide availability of this type of product, easy designs with little need for seasonal change, with keen selling prices that are often the key deciding factor within a purchasing decision. This fashionability type requires a focus on tight cost management or a 'lean supply chain' to ensure tight stock control processes to eliminate any fat from the supply chain, regular and easily identifiable demand flows to predict volume demand, and standardization within product design to reduce the cost of manufacture.

Fashion and high fashion options by contrast face demand volatility and increasingly short lead times between trends emerging and being picked up by the mainstream consciousness before quickly falling out of it. By their nature, they also carry higher levels of risk, reliant on the buyer being able to accurately identify and interpret trends on behalf of their target consumer. Rather than focusing simply on lean supply chains, these products require agility and responsiveness within their processes. Hines discusses this point by linking responsiveness and agility together. 'Suppliers need to be responsive to variable customer demand by being agile enough to deal with shifts in volume while keeping inventories to a minimum' (Hines 2004: 282). Within this agile supply chain environment, the emphasis is therefore on the 'dominant buying behaviours of customers 'dominant buying behaviours of customers is demanding quick response' (Gattorna 2010: 228), placing agility as the central success criterion for on-demand trend products. Zara is of course the paragon of this, able as it is to launch collections every two weeks and also replenish stores bi-weekly.

To amplify the differences between agile and lean supply chains, Table 14.2 replicates the completed Prentice Day option detail from Chapter 9. The core basic options reflect characteristics that lend themselves to a lean supply chain; basic T-shirts in colours that will be in regular demand. Their presumed rates of sale are high and based on consistent product performance identified during the research into the previous season's product range. By contrast, the Polo shirts have colours which could appeal to a more limited customer demographic and volume buys are lower, limiting the ability to achieve economy of scale and so lower cost prices.

Fashion supply chains therefore require a hybrid approach to their construction, the shape of which is driven by the mix of differing products within the range. Linking this hybrid approach to the activities of the merchandiser within the concept-to-carrier bag models identifies the differences in approaches needed for different fashionabilities.

- Research – There is a greater emphasis placed on accurate attribute analysis to delineate products by fashionability to fully understand how each performs:
  - Core basics – Analysis should not be constrained by seasons, but should be undertaken beyond predetermined season ends to become predictive of the future, so gaining as much visibility of demand down to size level as is possible.
  - Fashion – Research should look for demand patterns within season, looking for extreme performance and overall volatility within the options to assess how the customer reacts to differing trends or colours.
  - High fashion – Research beyond rate of sale and sell-through rate is often not beneficial. High fashion by its nature will have an extreme performance and past history is often not indicative of the future.

Table 14.2 The completed option detail for casual wear T-shirts

Option	Description	Colour	Fashionability	Cost price	Selling price	Weeks life cycle	Rate of sale	Sell-through rate	Unit buy	Buy cost value	Buy selling value
1	Basic T-shirt	White	Core basic	£4.00	£15.00	8	12	80%	120	£480.00	£1,800.00
2	Basic T-shirt	Black	Core basic	£4.00	£15.00	8	12	80%	120	£480.00	£1,800.00
3	Basic T-shirt	Navy	Core basic	£4.00	£15.00	8	12	80%	120	£480.00	£1,800.00
4	Polo T-shirt	Blue	Fashion style	£7.70	£25.00	8	8	80%	80	£616.00	£2,000.00
5	Polo T-shirt	Red	Fashion style	£7.70	£25.00	8	8	80%	80	£616.00	£2,000.00
							12	80%	520	£2,672.00	£9,400.00

- Concept – The KPI budgeting process requires a further layer of detail. Budgets for product groups should be further broken down between core basics and fashion:
  - Core basic – KPI budgets decisions are likely to follow the previous year size and shape. Ultimately, stock turn should be high to reflect regular and controlled intake phasing and OTB management.
  - Fashion – Sales turnover planning will use the sales planning pyramid approach to build new emerging trends in, and dying trends out of, the sales turnover budget to build early notice of the likely pressures on the supply chain.
  - High fashion – Beyond planning an overall budget shape, the nature of the product, its uncertainty and lack of reliable history, limits the value of deep budgeting thought within the process.
- Product development – The splitting of KPI budgets by fashionability ring fences OTB for each type which can give early visibility of the likely size and shape of each to support the supply chain team within their planning:
  - Core basic – These can be managed through a line monitor process that uses long-term forecasting to identify weekly delivery requirements. Little or no OTB will be spent in advance of the season beginning as a result.
  - Fashion – Rolling-ranges plans delay ranges being finalized until in-season. Therefore, only the initial phases as identified through the WSSI will be bought and manufactured in time for the beginning of the season.
  - High fashion – the limited size and shape of the offer will mean that its costs of production will be higher and so selling prices will reflect that. Managing the supplier to manufacture small and difficult range will require high levels of communication and decision making between B&M and the supplier.
- Sourcing and manufacturing – To eliminate fat within a lean supply chain, and ensure responsiveness within an agile one, involves different focuses at this point:
  - Core basic – The merchandiser must place a deeper focus on size curve analysis to ensure optimal stock management of core basics to maintain demand momentum.
  - Fashion – Tight turnaround requires a high level of administration to ensure purchase orders, trims, hangers, labels and packing are ready and waiting. The emphasis with the supplier is on optimal production planning and good information flows from the retailer.
  - High fashion – With smaller unit buy quantities and eclectic trend influences, high fashion options are likely to be low-cost to source. Their place within the product range and the risk of a poor financial return means that added value fabrications and trims sourcing, rather than usual sourcing strategies, may be needed.
- Shipping, warehousing and distribution – Allocation plans for all product types should be completed in advance of shipment to allow suppliers to pack goods by allocation to facilitate cross-docking through the Distribution Centre (DC) and delivery to store within one day:
  - Core basics – Daily sales and stock data can be fed to the supplier via online B2B links. If volumes are high, daily deliveries based on actual sales can

be facilitated through the supply chain, using continuous replenishment operations.
- Fashion – Allocations will in most cases include a residue balance for replenishment. This will need storage, and replenishment allocations created by the merchandiser for a warehouse or distribution centre to process.
- High fashion – Often, due to small unit buys, allocations will use up all the stock bought in one go. This reflects the limited demand and low-range planning assumptions of the product.
- Retail – Responsive trading requires regular review of sales and stocks to enable immediate responses to trading:
  - Core basics – Within core basics, line monitors should be updated daily or weekly to re-balance forward orders and identify changes in long-term KPI and OTB budgets.
  - Fashion – Detailed trading analysis to identify success and failure in the range needs to be undertaken early to capture sales data to influence the size and shape of waiting ranges. Wide counsel with retail operations and the supplier are needed to fine-tune products in development.
  - High fashion – Analysis often focuses on loss prevention, rather than identifying repeat buys. Branch consolidation or stock rotation activities take precedence with this product type.
- Carrier bag – The ongoing cycle begins again and each time more lessons are learnt and better fulfilment of customer demand is expected, adding further pressures within the supply chain operation.

In reviewing the above points there are subtle but important differences in planning and trading different product types, with a resultant knock-on effect to supply chain design and management. All products require appropriate lean and agile approaches to their management, but the depth and appropriateness will vary. There is therefore a need for both, or a 'leagile' approach within fashion product management. Leagile supply chains support different product types and range-planning approaches from the Pareto principle through to the more recent emergence of the long tail effect. They do, as seen, set differing success criteria, and the merchandiser within the supply chain contributes to their effective implementation.

FOCUS POINT 14.2: THE PLETHORA OF SUPPLY CHAIN APPROACHES

Supply chain management is full of abbreviations and exotic terminology, which for a discipline that many find dry, is quite refreshing. This focus point presents a whistle-stop tour of the most prolific. To set the scene for the differing approaches, there is first the little matter of the distinction between push and pull supply chains to discuss.

Historically supply chains have pushed products from supplier to the end consumer. This approach has its origins in a trading environment where supply chain capabilities were limited, but it also was built around using known historic demand patterns to supply consumers. The obvious in-built inefficiency of such approaches is that demand is unlikely to be linear and reacting to changes in demand is slow, meaning that push supply chains, if applied to the wrong product type, can develop bullwhip characteristics and the risk of obsolete stocks within the supply chain.

Pull supply chains by contrast are those where the consumer pulls product through the supply chain. The chain in effect reacts to consumer demand and maintains a very small stock to keep goods flowing, adjusting production to demand patterns as they emerge. A pull supply chain is, in effect, an agile one, while a push supply chain emphasizes as lean an operation as possible.

Push and pull supply chain strategies can then be further refined using the following supply chain approaches:

Materials requirement planning (MRP) – a push supply chain approach whose focus is to order materials against a projected demand. It relies upon timely decision making within the supply chain to best match supply to demand. Within a fashion retail context, the merchandiser could apply the principles of MRP within their planning and trading of core basics.

Just in time (JIT) – a pull system, similar to MRP in that it aims to match demand and supply, but does so at the very latest moment possible, with as accurate sale and stock data as possible. To work, JIT requires a high degree of integration between retailer and supplier, flexible trading activities and short lead-time product. For the merchandiser, it emphasizes their trading activities and good relationships with suppliers.

Quick response (QR) – QR further emphasizes integration of retailer and supplier and manages time within the concept-to-carrier bag process to reduce lead times as much as possible. Quick response is the supply chain model around which the fast fashion concept was created; Zara is famous for not just short lead times, but its quick response to emerging trends and demand management. As QR is focused on lead time reduction, if this can be achieved, its relevance can be for all products in the range, and so alters the entire concept-to-carrier bag process and timings.

Continuous replenishment (CR) – This is an ultra-responsive supply chain where sales data is passed electronically from retailer to supplier automatically to replenish stocks as needed. As orders are created in real time as demand requires, the trading dynamic changes and the notion of creating orders and purchase orders as part of the trading supply chain disappears. It is therefore ultra lean, as it eliminates the need for high stock levels and can significantly increase stock turn presumptions within the KPI budgeting process.

Activity: Research each of the supply chain approaches and identify their relevance to different product types, fashionabilities and business models.

GLOBALIZATION AND THE SUPPLY CHAIN

The reduction in trade barriers is most often discussed in terms of its impact on agreements such as the Multi-Fibre Agreement and quota systems. There has also been movement at the consumer end of the supply chain, with fashion retailers operating as global players, opening stores, franchises and concessions in foreign markets. The effect of these twin influences has been to widen opportunity, but also to increase the risks of trading. The opportunities for chasing the lowest-cost producer to facilitate price deflation have led to quantitative benefits but sometimes at the cost of originality, while retailing in new unproven markets has brought sales turnover growth but not always profits, as asos are finding in China and Uniqlo found in its first disastrous foray into the UK market.

The term *China price* came into focus as a result of that country's ability to supply low-cost consumer goods in large quantities as a result of the emergence of its manufacturing industry and the vast numbers of people moving from rural areas to cities in search of employment. More recently, as the Chinese economy has matured, newer production sources have emerged such as Vietnam, Indonesia and Cambodia (Karlsen 2009), leading to new sources of cost-effective production.

A second aspect to global sourcing is the development dual sourcing where low-cost producers are mixed with short lead-time producers. The principle that lies behind this approach is the same as the leagile discussion in the previous section. Lean suppliers that provide price-competitive bulk orders are mixed with agile, time-focused suppliers that can produce and deliver product with short lead times to support rolling range plans. This dual approach is being increasingly felt in the UK, with the first signs of a re-emergence of British manufacturing within the fashion industry. Asos sources short lead-time product from manufacturers in North London, while brands such as Marks and Spencer are promoting the Best of British within their product ranges.

At the other end of the supply chain, retailers are extending their footprints through retail expansion into overseas markets. Business models such as Gap, Forever 21 and Zara have all grown out of their home markets and entered the international arena to take advantage of liberal trade agreements, but also to further develop volume opportunities to support their competitive positions. The development of e-retail has further allowed brands to become global, as has the development of the franchising concept, with Debenhams, for example, using this route to expansion for a number of years. Finally, brands such as House of Fraser (HoF) have been acquired by overseas investors, in this case by Sanpower of China, who plan to open fifty HoF stores in China as well as stores in Russia (Daily Telegraph 2014).

Not surprisingly, the merchandiser role is impacted twice by the effects of globalization. Dual sourcing strategies require a keen focus on the intake margin KPI budget, and where there is a lot of variation in sources of supply it is easy to lose control of the intake margin budget. To overcome this potential risk, rolling margins are used to keep track of the true value of stock that has been delivered over the course of a season. Table 14.3 details four deliveries over a three-week period, with Week 1 comprising a long-lead-time high-margin delivery and a short-lead-time low-margin delivery. The following three weeks solely comprise short lead-time deliveries of up-to-the-minute fashion trend product types. As each delivery is made, and more stock delivered comprises the low-margin products, the rolling margin declines, reflecting the reducing influence of the high-margin delivery within total stocks.

Table 14.3 Rolling margin

Product type	Delivery	Cost value	Selling value	Intake margin	Rolling margin
Long lead time	Week 1	£17,499	£70,000	70%	70%
Short lead time	Week 1	£4,166	£10,000	50%	67%
Short lead time	Week 2	£4,166	£10,000	50%	66%
Short lead time	Week 3	£4,166	£10,000	50%	64%

Rolling margin therefore is an effective tool to assess the impact of differing sources of product on overall profitability, and can act as a warning sign should the budgeted intake margins risk not being delivered by the end of the season.

The second impact centres on the planning of retail sales opportunities within a global store estate. Managing opportunity across a wide geographic area has its challenges. Cultures are different; attitudes to fashion vary, as will the impact of nature, where different seasons will present issues in creating ranges for both northern and southern hemispheres at the same time. Creating the right shape within which to plan and trade is therefore of great importance.

This shaping can take many forms and is relevant throughout the concept-to-carrier bag process. Examples of this are:

- Product hierarchy planning – Product hierarchies similar to the accessories, casual wear and formal wear approach of Prentice Day require additional layering.
- Hierarchies that separate different markets or regions enable each to be planned individually, rather than as a generic whole.
- Research and analysis – There is a much broader research approach required to match market to analysis. Regional differences in size, skin colour and wealth will all influence individual trading results.
- Budgeting and OTB – The mix of budget ingredients changes from region to region and so separate budgets and OTB need to be built through the deeper hierarchy to identify realistic gross trading profits and stock turns.
- Trading – While juggling more markets is complex, the ability to flex stock between markets is invaluable. Wholesale brands can shift slow-moving stock around the world, so avoiding the need for excessive markdowns to clear within one season, as, for example, when one winter season ends in one hemisphere and the same season is just beginning in the other.

The effect of globalization on the merchandiser is two-pronged and offers much to enable them to develop their businesses. To do this – as seen in the other sections within this chapter – as one role within a supply chain, the merchandiser has to be agile and responsive to change and uncertainty. They are, though, supported in this, as are all the other roles and activities within the fashion concept-to-carrier bag process, by good and effective supply chain management.

FOCUS POINT 14.3: GLOCAL FASHION

Theodore Levitt's 'The Globalization of Markets' asserted that globalization had delivered uniform products and services, as businesses moved away from individuality of product offer to ones that were standardized, functional and low-priced. Consumers buoyed by increasing product awareness and mobility were undergoing a convergence of tastes, and future success lay in viewing the global market as one (Levitt 1983). Within fashion, it is easy to see evidence of this general theory: fashion brands that operate in a number of different territories, all having the same logo, product ranges and service standards. Similarly, with the adoption of social media such as Facebook, Instagram and Twitter, brands are able to communicate globally and in doing so project a consistent personality to all markets.

In terms of supply chain management, mass customization brought significant capacity gains, but over time there has been evidence of a disconnect between customer and product as the world economy has developed and newer competitors have emerged offering new and exciting products and services. Moves today towards a glocal strategy where businesses use their global experience and power, but then tailor their products or services to suit local markets, are becoming widespread. There are numerous examples of tailored product ranges, or the influence of differing markets within a total product range. Chanel's 2012 Bombay-Paris collection or the Hermes saris are examples in the luxury market of the mixing of influences and cultures. Glocal influences are not limited to luxury brands. Fast-fashion global brand H&M 'had to change its product range in the United States, given the fact that the US male customers were less fashion conscious then their European counterparts' (Dumitrescu and Vineran 2009).

Glocal strategies are natural answers to the paradox of matching the opposing characteristics of fashion and business. Fashion at its heart is individual, and while there will always be a tribal mentality in the way consumers buy-in to trends and are loyal to particular brands, there is always room for innovation, new ideas and fresh ways to do business. Glocal product ranges are one way of constantly striving to be different within the self-imposed perimeter fence of the definition of fashion. After all, range planning by demographic or customer profile as discussed within Chapter 9 is evidence of fashion businesses evidence of fashion businesses striving to be relevant in all their markets within their range-planning processes.

Activity: Research glocalization strategies with reference not just to product management but also to marketing and communications methods.

CHAPTER AND PART THREE SUMMARY

Words such as *responsive*, *lean* and *relationships* that characterize supply chain management also neatly summarize the role of the fashion merchandiser. As one role within an increasingly diverse fashion retail supply chain, the merchandiser provides important links to connect many of the dots within the chain. Those connections are increasingly important as product management is no longer limited to buyers, designers and suppliers; a whole army of roles now contributes to the process.

Marketing, information technology, international relations and retail operations all influence product management in ways that have never been seen before, meaning that B&M is fully integrated into the wider supply chain. This is increasingly vital to support omni-channel retailing, where all distribution channels and their supporting teams are organized to offer a seamless experience to the customer, allowing them to use all or some of the various channels available to them whenever and however they wish. This naturally means that B&M activities are now broader than creating and retailing a good product range; they are about trading and developing ideas on the go, often with little or no thinking time to assess what is being done.

To expect a single role, the buyer, to be able to create ranges for global markets or different distribution channels within a dynamic market is one thing, but then to expect them to be able to fully research, make decisions and understand the implications of their actions for a broad measure of variables is unrealistic. The value of the merchandiser today is that they are able to balance a wide range of partisan positions within a business and contribute to holistic decision making. This places the merchandiser deeply within the context of supply chain management as defined by Christopher, bringing further activities within the supply chain into the thinking process of product management.

Finally, pulling all the various strands together into a summary for all chapters, there is an overall feeling of change within fashion retailing. The merchandiser of today is very different to the one of 30 years ago, but more interestingly the role in just five years' time will be very different to that of now. The processes laid out in Part Two are evolving to accommodate new distribution channels and cultural forces. Speed to market and in-season planning and trading are changing the organization of the concept-to-carrier bag model, and the touch points within it. Many roles concerning social media, analytics and digital are joining the product management team, so, to stay relevant, B&M is evolving and adapting to a new world order within which the fashion merchandiser can thrive.

SELF-DIRECTED STUDY

1. Investigate the history and development of lean and agile supply chains and the changed focus from pushing product to customer to models where the supply chain reacts to product pull factors.
2. Research the demand chain concept and the redefinition of value and supply chains.

Further Reading

Christopher, M. (2011) *Logistics and supply chain management 4th ed.* Harlow: Pearson

Gattorna, J. (2010) *Dynamic supply chains: delivering value through people 2nd ed.* Harlow: Pearson

Hines, T. (2004) *Supply chain strategies.* Oxford: Elsevier

Bibliography

Brun, A. and Castelli, C. (2008). Supply chain strategy in the fashion industry: developing a portfolio model depending on product, retail channel and brand, *International journal of production economics*, volume 116, number 2, pp. 169–181

Christopher, M. (2011) *Logistics and Supply Chain Management 4th ed.* Harlow: Pearson

Dumitrescu, L. and Vinerean, S. (2009). *The Glocal Strategy of Global Brands.* Romania: University of Sibiu.

Gattorna, J. (2010) *Dynamic Supply Chains: Delivering Value Through People 2nd ed.* Harlow: Pearson

Harrison, N. (2014) House of Fraser confirms £480m acquisition by China's Sanpower Group. *Daily Telegraph*, [Internet]. Available from http://www.retail-week.com/sectors/department-stores/house-of-fraser-confirms-480m-acquisition-by-chinas-sanpower-group/5059311.article [Accessed 10th May 2014]

Hines, T. (2004) *Supply Chain Strategies.* Oxford: Elsevier

Karlsen, K. (2009) *The New China Price: The Future of Sustainable Supply Chain Management in China.* University of the Arts. London: University of the Arts

Leeman, J. (2010) *Supply Chain Management: Fast, Flexible Supply Chains in Manufacturing and Retailing.* Books on demand

Levitt, T. (1983) *The Globalization of Markets.* Boston: Harvard Business Review

Luzzini, D. and Ronchi, S. (2010). Purchasing management in the luxury industry: organization and practices. *Operations management research*, volume 3, number 1/2, pp. 7–21

Glossary

4PS   See Marketing mix.

% MIX   The value or importance of a series of variables within a common measure.

% VARIANCE   The extent to which a variable differs to a comparable variable. For example, sales of shirts this year compared to sales of shirts last year.

ALLOCATION PLAN   A calculated plan that dictates the number of units per size of each option that will be allocated to each store that is to be ranged.

ATTRIBUTE   A characteristic or trait that sets one or more objects apart from another attribute type; for example, different fashionabilities.

AVERAGE LINE BUY   The number of units bought of an option. An average line buy is the average number of units bought across a range of options.

AVERAGE SELLING PRICE   The calculated average of the selling prices of all options within a product range; for example, the average selling price of two shirts priced £5 and £10 is £7.50.

B2B/B2C   Business to business (B2B) refers to trading between two separate businesses. B2C refers to businesses trading with consumers.

BALANCE SHEET   A ledger that summarizes the value of a business by quantifying its assets and liabilities and identifying its resulting value as a going concern.

BASKET SIZE   A measurement of the number of products sold within one transaction.

BUY ONLINE, RETURN IN STORE (BORIS)   The activities of customers who buy product from an online store and return it to a bricks and mortar store.

BRAND PERSONALITY   The combined set of attributes or characteristics that together identify to consumers consistent personality traits and values within a business's products, marketing communications and supply chain operation.

BRANDED BUYING   The buying of products from a wholesale brand where buyers select predesigned and manufactured options to range within their stores.

BRICKS AND MORTAR (B&M) STORE   A physical store on a high street.

BUDGET   An estimate of the expected value of an income or expenditure item for a specified period of time (see also KPI).

BUSINESS MODEL   A business model comprises defined processes, organizational structure, product types and trading strategies that together create value by being consistent and applicable throughout all aspects of the business's operation.

BUYING BUDGET   See open to buy (OTB).

BUYING SEASON   A specified period of time during which a retailer sources and purchases options to range in their business.

CASH FLOW   The movement of cash into a business in the form of sales and out in the form of expenses over a specified period of time

CLOSING STOCK   The calculated value of all stock that a business owns at the end of a specified period of time. It is usually recorded as a cash figure at selling price value.

COMMITMENT   The total sum value of all outstanding purchase orders for products that have been ordered but not yet delivered.

CONCEPT-TO-CARRIER BAG MODEL   A theoretical linear process map that identifies the sequential steps that a retail business may take to translate product research into a product range which is subsequently bought by a target customer.

CONSUMERISM   The culture of consumers buying more products than they need to cover individual basic need in order to reflect status and growing wealth.

CONTINUOUS REPLENISHMENT   A supply chain process whereby a product supplier replenishes a retailer's stock by receiving daily information electronically of sales and stock movements and supplies product to replenish back to pre-agreed stock levels.

CORE BASIC   An option that is not influenced by fashion trends and is demanded consistently across a number of seasons.

CORPORATE SOCIAL RESPONSIBILITY (CSR)   The voluntary adoption by a business of practices that are designed to support society, people and the environment in its strategic and day-to-day operation.

COST PRICE   The negotiated and agreed price paid by a business to its suppliers for products that it will buy.

CROWDSOURCING   An activity where an organisation uses a large mass of individuals to gain information and ideas that can be used by itself for future opportunities

DELIVERY SCHEDULE   A ledger that plots over a number of weeks anticipated delivery dates of new product into a retail business. It is usually created for the length of a season and is continuously updated with changes to delivery dates and size of order. It is created to show orders by size (units, cost and selling value) and the date on which the order is due to be delivered

DISPLAY FACTOR   The total number of units of an option or a number of options needed to fill a fixture or a number of fixtures.

DISTRIBUTION CHANNEL   A single channel by which a product moves from

supplier to retailer and on to the end customer. Distribution channels vary in type, and for the customer include physical stores, online stores and catalogues. See also Multi-channel retailing and Omni-channel retailing.

DROP SHIPPING   An order-fulfilment supply chain process in which retailers pass customer orders directly to a manufacturer or wholesaler who will deliver product directly to the customer.

ELECTRONIC DATA INTERCHANGE (EDI)   An early system of two computers talking to each other to share information between two businesses and to enable the transmission of data.

E-RETAILER   An online retailer that conducts its business through a website and delivers customer purchases either from their own warehouse or direct from the manufacturer.

FASHION STYLE   A product type or option that interprets current trends for an identified target customer.

FASHIONABILITY   A subjective measure of the level to which an option conforms to current fashion trends. For example, a trend-led option has a high fashionability while a core basic option has low fashionability.

FAST FASHION   A business model in which shortened lead times within the supply chain enable ranges to be offered for sale faster than in traditional business models.

FORECAST   A revision of a previous decision that relates to the re-forecasting of KPI budgets for a season to change them to better reflect current trading conditions and resulting financial expectation.

GLOCALIZATION   A business term that refers to the adaptation of a product or service that is specific or altered in some way to be traded within an individual locality or culture.

GROSS DOMESTIC PRODUCT (GDP)   The market value of the production of goods and services within a specified period of time.

GROSS TRADING PROFIT   The financial benefit accrued by a business through its trading activities for a specified period of time.

HIGH FASHION   The first or most relevant options in a new trend or style.

INTAKE MARGIN %   The difference in value between the cost of buying an option from a supplier and the selling price offered to a retail customer. This is expressed as a percentage.

JUST IN TIME (JIT)   A supply chain method of operation in which product is manufactured at the point that it is needed rather than based on future demand.

KEY PERFORMANCE INDICATOR (KPI)   Performance metrics that measure the success of an individual or range of items. KPIs are applicable in any situation where measuring success is required; for example, financial budgets.

LEAN, AGILE AND LEAGILE   Supply chain systems where the designed supply chain reflects the characteristics of the products being supplied. Lean supply chains place an emphasis on supplying product with minimal cost, while agile supply chains emphasize flexibility. A leagile supply chain is a combination of the two focuses into one.

LIFE CYCLE   The length of time measured in weeks that an option has been available to buy by customers.

LIKE FOR LIKE (LFL)   An identical comparison between two similar or identical variables to enable an undistorted measurement of the performance of the variables.

LINEAR FOOTAGE   An arm on a fixture or a space available for on a table for displaying stock. Each arm or pile carries a specified size presumption that enables the linear footage of a display area to be calculated.

LONG TAIL EFFECT   An approach to product management in which a retailer offers a very wide number of products, but in very shallow quantities.

MANUFACTURING REQUIREMENT PLANNING   A supply chain approach that pushes product to consumers using pre-identified demand patterns.

MARK UP   To apply an apply an increase to a given cost price to derive a selling price.

MARK DOWN SPEND   To reduce selling prices. Markdown values are expressed in cash and are the difference between the original price and the new reduced price. There are two types of markdown: point of sale (POS) where product is discounted when sold only; and clearance, where product is discounted regardless of whether it has been sold or not.

MARKDOWN SPEND % TO SALES   The value of markdown spend expressed as a percentage of sales value. For example, where markdown values are £10 and sales values are £100, the markdown % to sales is 10%.

MARKETING MIX   A theoretical model used by business that mixes various elements of a business's proposition to assess the balance between them and to identify gaps within the proposition. Historically referred to as the 4Ps, the model has extended to become the 7Ps.

MINIMUM CREDIBLE OFFER (MCO)   The minimum numbers of units that must be on display in a shop to make the product offer look credible to the customer.

MULTICHANNEL DISTRIBUTION   A process of offering products for sale to a customer in more than one way; for example, simultaneously offering a product range through a mix of physical stores, online and catalogues.

MULTI-FIBRE AGREEMENT   A trade agreement that imposed quotas and tariffs on commercial trade between developing and developed nations between 1974 and 2004.

OMNI CHANNEL   A recent development of multi-channel retailing where a retailer co-ordinates all of its various distribution channels to offer a seamless transaction to its customer. All channels offer the same range of products and services, and facilitate the customer to engage with more than one channel when making a purchase (for example, click and collect).

OPEN TO BUY (OTB)   The amount of budget available at any given point within a financial period to purchase stock with. OTB is expressed at selling value and derived from KPI budgets. Released OTB is a proportion of the budget that can be spent by the buyer.

OPENING STOCK   The value of stock in a business at the beginning of a specified period of time. Usually recorded as a cash figure at selling-price value.

OPTION   A style/colour. A jumper is a style and red jumper is an option. If the jumper is available in red, white and blue then the one style has three colour options.

OUT OF STOCK (OOS)   The difference between planned and actual stock levels. The OOS is expressed as a percentage and the higher it is the more out of stock a business is to its planned level.

OWN-LABEL BUYING   A range of options designed by a retailer to be sold under their own branding or sub-branding.

PERCENTAGE MIX   See % mix.

PHASING   The breaking-down of a variable into smaller amounts which add up to the whole. For example, when phasing sales, the total budget will be broken down across all the weeks of the season.

PREVIOUS YEAR   A season or financial period that has finished and is comparable to the season or financial period that is being planned or currently in operation.

PRODUCT CATEGORY   A collection of product groups that all appeal to a specific customer demographic or product end use; for example, menswear or casual wear.

PRODUCT GROUP   A grouping-together of similar products that can be planned in the same way; for example, trousers, shirts.

PRODUCT PLANNING   See Range planning.

PROFIT AND LOSS ACCOUNT (P&L)   The profit and loss account of a business that records all trading income and expenses for a defined financial period.

PROMOTIONAL CALENDAR   A calendar of dates during which a business actions a promotion to influence business performance (for example, a mid-season sale), or a date where an outside influence had an impact on business performance (for example, The Olympics).

PURCHASE ORDER (PO)   Between two companies, a legally binding agreement to trade that states the products to be bought and all negotiated terms of trade.

QUICK RESPONSE   Quick-response manufacturing is a process whereby emphasis is placed on the reduction of the time taken to manufacture a product. This enables the manufacturer to respond to market demand faster and reduces waste in the manufacturing process.

RANGE PLANNING   The process undertaken to identify options to be ranged in a future product range. A completed range plan will blend a mix of options to be balanced across product type, colour, selling price, attribute and depth of unit buy.

RATE OF SALE   Rate of sale measures the average number of units sold of an option per week per store during its life cycle.

REPLENISHMENT   The resupply of stock to shops as a result of stock being sold to customers.

RESUPPLY TIME   The length of time measured in weeks that a supplier takes to deliver a repeat order.

SALES DENSITY   A measure of performance that identifies the value of sales achieved from available store selling space. It is expressed in currency, and the higher the sales density the more effective the use of available space.

SALES TURNOVER   The cash value paid by a customer to a retailer for a product or service.

SEASON   A defined period of time in which product ranges are sold; for example, a spring/summer season or an autumn/winter season.

SELLING PRICE   The price at which a retailer offers product for sale to consumers.

SELL-THROUGH RATE %   Sell-through rate measures the amount sold of an option by expressing sales units as a percentage of the units bought.

SIZE CURVE (ALSO CALLED A SIZE RATIO)   A size curve measures the quantifiable value that each size offered of an option represents.

SQUARE FOOTAGE A measurement of the floor space available in a physical store that can be used as retail selling space. This space can also be measured in square meters.

STOCK/INVENTORY The products available to be sold to customers at any given time, measured in units and value.

STOCK TURN A ratio measuring the rate at which stock is converted into sales over a given time period. Generally the higher the stock turn the better the business performs.

STYLE A product such as a jumper or dress (see also Option).

SUPPLY CHAIN MANAGEMENT A system of resources that working together plan and manage the process of designing, sourcing, manufacturing and delivering a product.

SWOT An analysis tool that identifies the (internal) Strengths and Weaknesses and (external) Opportunities and Threats that influence a business or individual.

UNIT BUY QUANTITIES The number of units bought in total of an option within a product range.

VALUE ADDED TAX (VAT) A consumption tax levied by governments on goods and services at the point of sale.

VALUE CHAIN A model developed by Michael Porter that organizes the activities of a business into primary or support. The co-ordination of these activities will enable the delivery of optimal product at a reduced cost, so leading to an improved margin for the business.

WEEKLY SALES, STOCK INTAKE REPORT (WSSI) A document that breaks seasonal KPI budgets into weekly budgets and is used to calculate OTB budgets by week.

WEEKS COVER The number of weeks in which an option would sell out at current unit-sales-per-week levels.

Index

Note: bold page numbers indicate figures and tables.